E-Praise 4 Gifting

✝

*A Collection of Christian
Devotional E-Mail*

*Edited by
Al Allaway*

Title: *E-Praise 4 Gifting* © 2008 by Al & Del Allaway

Contents: No copyright: All parts of this book MAY be reproduced, etc., except articles credited to a specific author, and those MAY be reproduced as long as name credit is given to the author or company listed.

First printing, September, 2007
Second printing, January, 2008
Third printing, September, 2012

ISBN 978-0-6151-6362-8
www.allawaybooks.com
www.lulu.com/content/1143832
Printed in the United States of America

Collected and Edited by Al Allaway
A Collection of e-Praise Foreword to Volume 4

Some very good e-mail buddies over the years have shared many emotional and charismatic stories and devotions by tickling the "forward" key on their computer. And I'm certainly glad that I was privileged to be in their address book, to receive, read, forward and store the wonderful stories of praise and faith; faith in such a loving and awesome God as He that we serve...

Sometimes, these e-mail missals contained humor, but not the "typical jokes" that flood the ether waves of the world-wide web. There is no possible way for me to give authorship credit to some of these stories or devotions. Authors are credited, where known. I pray that no violation of copyright will occur. Some of these stories have circulated and re-circulated through Internet servers so many times that "public domain" must be assumed.

Warning!

Rick Warren's book, *The Purpose Driven Life*, is all about finding the answer to that age-old question, "WHAT ON EARTH AM I HERE FOR?" Churches all across the nation are using the book as a guide to **The 40-days of Purpose** campaign.

I want to offer you a warning about the following "Inspirational stories", quoted from page 20 of Rick's book where he says: "God is not just the starting point of your life; he is the *source* of it. To discover your purpose in life you must turn to God's Word, not the world's wisdom. You must build your life on eternal truths, **not** pop psychology, success-motivation, or inspirational stories."

In Ephesians 1:11, one Bible translation puts it like this: ***"It's in Christ that we find out who we are and what we are living for. Long before we first heard of Christ and got our hopes up, he had his eye on us, had designs on us for glorious living, part of the overall purpose he is working out in everything and everyone."***

So, enjoy these "Inspirational Stories", but don't make a "religion" out of them. Base your faith on Christ, instead.

TABLE OF CONTENTS

Foreword to Volume Four....Page iii

Rick Warren; Caution....iv

Introduction....x

Abstain....1   Ann Margret....3

As the Deer....4   Attitude....6

Baby Erik and the Old Man....7   The Baptist Dog....9

Be Still and Know That I Am God....10

Be Still With God....11   Bible and Bullies....13

Bible Sale....13   The Big Wheel....15

Biker's Road of Life....18   The Bill of Non-Rights....19

The Birdies....21   A Birthday Celebration....25

Bless My Computer Too...26   Bless the Children...27

Blessings....29   Blue Ribbon Makes a Difference....31

The Boat....33   Breakfast at McDonald's....34

Breast Cancer Awareness 36

The Bricklayer's Report....38

Carrot, Egg or Cup of Coffee?....39

Center of the Bible....41   Change Your Ways....42

Children!....44   The Choice....45

Christian One-Liners....47   A Christmas Story....48

Christmas – Teach the Children....52

Clutch This Tree....54   Coat Hanger Angel....54

A Columbine Thesis....55
Computer Gender....56
Counting the Pecans...57
The Creation of Pets...58
Cut Your Taxes in Half...60
"D" in Devil...60
Daddy's Empty Chair...61
The Daffodil Principle...63
Darrell Scott's Testimony...65
A Daughter's Love...68
A Debt of Marbles...71
Do You Believe in Easter?...73
Do You Love Jesus?...77
Dr. Seuss: Computers...77
Drug Problem...78
Eagles in a Storm...79
Empty Bird Cage...80
Excuse Me... 82
Failure...82
Fair's Fair Football...83
The Filling Station...85
A Fire of Desire...90
Fire Walking...91
First Grader's Insight...92
For a Glass of Milk...93
From the Heart of God...94
Giver God...95
God Brings You to It...96
God Lives Under the Bed...96
God's Diet...98
God's Grace...99
Good Deeds Pay..100
Good Morning!..101
Graham Interview..102
Grandmas and Grandkids..103
Grandpa's Hands..105
The Greatest Golfer in the World...106
A Grizzled Atheist..107
He Is ...108.
Heaven, Please..110
Highway 109...111
History Forgotten..114
The Holiday..116
Homeless Visitor..117
The Hospital Window..121
The Hug..123
I Asked God ...124

Ice Cream for the Soul..124

'Jesus' Is Watching You..125   Fourth of July Poem..126

Kansas Senate Prayer...127   Keepers...127

Kids Letters to God...128   The Letter...130

Letter from Heaven...132

A Letter from Yakima County Jail...134

The Little Green Snake..135   Long-Stemmed..Thorns 137

Look At Me!...141   Lord's Prayer...142

Love Defined ...146   The Majority Rules...148

Manger Story...149   Mary Had a Little Lamb...151

The Mayonnaise Jar and Coffee..152   Mikey..153

Mom Is an Angel..155   Montana Easter..156

More Than Enough..159   Morning Talk with God..160

My Perfect Squelch..161   My Spiritual Attorney..161

My Sunshine...163   Neat Prayer...165

The "New" Bible..167   New School Prayer..169

Night Watch..170   The Old Man and His Dog171

The Old Telephone...175   One-Liners...178

Only a Mother ...179   Penicillin...181

Pennies From Heaven..182   Perspective..184

Phoenix Fire Department Littlest Firefighter...185

The Pink Dress...187   The Portal...189

Positive Choices...190   Profit, My Way...192

Puppies For Sale..192   The Question..194

Remember the Duck..194   The Right to Sneeze..195
The Right Words..196   Run Through the Rain..197
Sandstorms..199   School Shootings!..200
Scripture Kitty..202   Seven Wonders..204
The Silversmith..205   Slow Dance..206
Slow Down, Now!..208   The Small Tree..210
The Soldier at Valley Forge..210   Somebody Said…211
Son of the Master..213   Speed the Brick..215
Start Over Page..216   Stevie..217
The Story of Carl..220   Suburban Lawns..224
Teddy's Teacher..226   The U in JesUs..227
There Are Angels Among Us …228
Things God Won't Ask..230   Three Trees..230
Timing to Share..232   Timmy..234
Tommy's True Theology…235
Tonsils Needing Ice Cream…239
Too Much Change…240   The Torn Quilt…240
Touché..242   Twas' the Night Jesus Came..242
Twinkle, Twinkle Little Star..243   Two Pots..244
Unfolding a Rose..245   Use This Day Wisely..246
Visiting Day..247   Warm-up for Mother's Day..248
Watch This!..250   The Weathered Old Barn..251
Went To a Party, Mum..252   What is Heaven Like …253
What's Great About Hugs?..257

When You Thought I Wasn't Looking..258

When I Whine…259   Who's Your Daddy?...260

Why God Created Eve…262   Windows?...262

Winfrey Interviews Graham…264

Winter Morning Guest..266   Words over Coffee..268

Worth Your Time…270   Wrinkles…272

Wrong Number; Caller ID…272

WWJD Is For Photographers Too…273

Yellow Roses, Three..278   The Yellow Shirt..281

You'll Find Jesus There…283

INDEX OF CONTRIBUTORS…285

Introduction to Volume Four

Four years ago, when I printed the first copies of "A Collection of E-Praise" (see the Foreword) we had no idea of the demand that would be created for such a collection. There were fifty-two stories copied and bound by Office Max into an eighty-page booklet. My out of pocket cost was about $3 per booklet. The few we sold netted a $2 "profit" which was fast eaten up by the hundreds we gave away free to nursing homes and individuals.

The second volume was somewhat larger at 144 pages and was bound in a more professional way, at much more cost. There were some great stories of faith and praise, which many folks enjoyed. Too much demand however, soon resulted in another "Sorry, Out of Print" notice.

"Volume Three" was a few Xerox pages shared with close friends when financial constraints caused us to assume the "ministry" was over. But God held more surprises... Bookstores in Nevada and Arizona started demanding more copies of *"E-Praise Two"*. This Volume Four is my answer. It contains all the stories and poems from previous editions, plus a whole lot more.

Enjoy! God will bless you, I know!

Al Allaway, Yakima Washington,
1st Edition, Volume 4: **February 2006**
2nd Printing: **January 2008**
3rd Printing: **September, 2012**

Abstain

I was holding a notice from my 13-year-old son's school announcing a meeting to preview the new course in sexuality. Parents could examine the curriculum and take part in an actual lesson presented exactly as it would be given to the students.

When I arrived at the school, I was surprised to discover only about a dozen parents there. As we waited for the presentation, I thumbed through page after page of instructions in the prevention of pregnancy or disease. I found abstinence mentioned only in passing. When the teacher arrived with the school nurse, she asked if there were any questions. I asked why abstinence did not play a noticeable part in the educational material. What happened next was shocking. There was a great deal of laughter, and someone suggested that if I thought abstinence had any merit, I should go back to burying my head in the sand. The teacher and the nurse said nothing as I drowned in a sea of embarrassment. My mind had gone blank, and I could think of nothing to say. The teacher explained to me that the job of the school was to teach "facts," and the home was responsible for moral training.

I sat in silence for the next 20 minutes as the sexuality course was explained. The other parents seemed to give their unqualified support to the materials. At the break time, the teacher announced that there were donuts in the back of the room and requested that everyone put on a nametag and mingle with each other. Everyone moved to the back of the room. As I watched them affixing their nametags and shaking hands, I sat deep in thought. I was ashamed that I had not been able to convince them to include a serious discussion of abstinence in the educational materials.

I uttered a silent prayer for guidance. My thoughts were interrupted by the teacher's hand on my shoulder.

"Won't you join the others, Mr. Layton?" The nurse smiled sweetly at me. "The donuts are good."

"Thank you, no," I replied.

"Well, then, how about a name tag? I'm sure the others would like to meet you."

"Somehow I doubt that," I replied.

"Won't you please join them?" she coaxed.

Then I heard a still, small voice whisper, "Don't go." The message in my head was unmistakable: "Don't go!" "I'll just wait here," I said. When the class was called back to order, the teacher looked around the long table and thanked everyone for putting on nametags.

She ignored me.

Then she said, "Now we're going to give you the same lesson we'll be giving your children. Everyone please peel off your name tags and look at the back of the tag." I watched in silence as the tags came off. "Now then, I drew a tiny flower on the back of one of the tags. Who has it, please?" the teacher asked.

The gentleman across from me held it up. "Here it is!"

"All right," she said. "The flower represents disease. Do you recall with whom you shook hands?" He pointed to a couple of people. "Very good," she replied. "The handshake in this case represents intimacy. So the two people you had contact with now have the disease." There was laughter and joking among the parents. The teacher continued, "And whom did the two of you shake hands with?"

The point was well taken, and she explained how this lesson would show students how quickly disease is spread. She concluded by saying, "Since we all shook hands, we all have the disease."

It was then that I heard the still, small voice again. "Speak now," it said, "but be humble." I wryly noted the latter admonition, then rose from my chair. I apologized for any upset I might have caused earlier, congratulated the teacher on an excellent lesson that would impress the youth, and concluded by saying I had only one small point I wished to make.

"Not all of us were infected with the disease," I said. "One of us... abstained."

---*Author Unknown*

Ann Margret

Richard, (my husband), never really talked much about his 1966 time in Viet Nam other than he had been shot by a sniper. However, he had a rather grainy, 8 x 10 black and white photo he had taken at a USO show of Ann Margret with Bob Hope in the background that was one of his treasures.

A few years ago, Ann Margret was doing a book signing at a local bookstore. Richard wanted to see if he could get her to sign the treasured photo so he arrived at the bookstore at 12 o'clock for the 7:30 signing.

When I got there after work, the line went all the way around the bookstore, circled the parking lot and disappeared behind a parking garage. Before her appearance, bookstore employees announced that she would sign only her book and no memorabilia would be permitted.

Richard was disappointed, but wanted to show her the photo and let her know how much those shows meant to lonely GI's so far from home. Ann Margret came out looking as beautiful as ever and, as second in line, it was soon Richard's turn. He presented the book for her signature and then took out the photo. When he did, there were many shouts from the employees that she would not sign it.

Richard said, "I understand. I just wanted her to see it."

She took one look at the photo, tears welled up in her eyes and she said, "This is one of my gentlemen from Viet Nam and I most certainly will sign his photo. I know what these men did for their country and I always have time for 'my gentlemen.'"

With that, she pulled Richard across the table and planted a big kiss on him. She then made quite a to-do about the bravery of the young men she met over the years, how much she admired them, and how much she appreciated them There weren't too many dry eyes among those close enough to hear. She then posed for pictures and acted as if he were the only one there.

Later at dinner, Richard was very quiet. When I asked if he'd like to talk about it, my big strong husband broke down in tears. "That's the first time anyone ever thanked me for my time in the Army," he said.

That night was a turning point for him. He walked a little straighter and, for the first time in years, was proud to have been a Vet. I'll never forget Ann Margret for her graciousness and how much that small act of kindness meant to my husband.

I now make it a point to say "Thank you" to every person I come across who served in our Armed Forces. Freedom does not come cheap and I am grateful for all those who have served their country.

If you'd like to pass on this story, feel free to do so. Perhaps it will help others to become aware of how important it is to acknowledge the contribution our service people make.

As The Deer...

It was one of the hottest days of the dry season. We had not seen rain in almost a month. The crops were dying. Cows had stopped giving milk. The creeks and streams were long gone back into the earth. It was a dry season that would bankrupt seven farmers before it was through. Every day, my husband and his brothers would go about the arduous process of trying to get water to the fields. Lately this process had involved taking a truck to the local water rendering plant and filling it up with water. But severe rationing had cut everyone off. If we hadn't learned the true lesson of sharing and witnessed the only miracle I had seen, with my own eyes, who knows what would have happened.

I was in the kitchen making lunch for my husband and his brothers when I saw my six-year old son, Billy, walking toward the woods. He wasn't walking with the usual carefree abandon of a youth but with a serious purpose. I could only see his back. He was obviously walking with a great effort...trying to be as still as possible. Minutes after he disappeared into the woods, he came running out again, toward the house. I went back to making sandwiches, thinking that whatever task he had been doing was completed.

Moments later, however, he was once again walking in that slow purposeful stride toward the woods. This activity went on for an hour: walk carefully to the woods, run back to the house. Finally I couldn't take it any longer and I crept out of the house and followed him on his journey. He was cupping both hands in front of him as he walked; being very careful not to spill the water he held in them...maybe two or three tablespoons were held in his tiny hands. I sneaked close as he went into the woods. Branches and thorns slapped his little face but he did not try to avoid them. He had a much higher purpose. Spying on him, I saw a most amazing sight.

Several large deer loomed in front of him. Billy walked right up to them. I almost screamed for him to get away. A huge buck with elaborate antlers was dangerously close. But the buck did not threaten him...he didn't even move as Billy knelt down. And I saw a tiny fawn laying on the ground, obviously suffering from dehydration and heat exhaustion, lift its head with great effort to lap up the water cupped in my beautiful boy's hand. When the water was gone, Billy jumped up to run back to the house and I hid behind a tree.

I followed him back to the house; to a spigot that we had shut off the water to. Billy opened it all the way up and a small trickle began to creep out. He knelt there, letting the drip slowly fill up his makeshift "cup," as the sun beat down on his little back.

And it came clear to me. The trouble he had gotten into for playing with the hose the week before. The lecture he had received about the importance of not wasting water. The reason he didn't ask me to help him. It took almost twenty minutes for the drops to fill his hands. When he stood up and began the trek back, I was there in front of him. His little eyes just filled with tears. "I'm not wasting," was all he said.

As he began his walk, I joined him...with a small pot of water from the kitchen. I let him tend to the fawn. I stayed away. It was his job. I stood on the edge of the woods watching the most beautiful heart I have ever known working so hard to save another life. As the tears that rolled down my face began to hit the ground, they were suddenly joined by other drops...and more drops ..and more. I looked up at the sky. It was as if God, himself, was weeping with pride.

Some will say that this was all just a coincidence; miracles don't really exist. All I can say is that the rain that came that day saved our farm... I don't know if anyone will read this...but I had to send it out. To honor the memory of my beautiful Billy, who was taken from me much too soon.... But not before showing me the true face of God, in a little sunburned body. *Author Unknown (Reprint from Vol. I)*

Attitude

The 92-year-old, petite, well-poised and proud lady, who is fully dressed each morning by eight o'clock, with her hair fashionably coifed and makeup perfectly applied, even though she is legally blind, moved to a nursing home today.

Her husband of 70 years recently passed away, making the move necessary. After many hours of waiting patiently in the lobby of the nursing home, she smiled sweetly when told her room was ready. As she maneuvered her walker to the elevator, I provided a visual description of her tiny room, including the eyelet sheets that had been hung on her window.

"I love it," she stated with the enthusiasm of an eight-year-old having just been presented with a new puppy.

"Mrs. Jones, you haven't seen the room . just wait."

"That doesn't have anything to do with it," she replied. "Happiness is something you decide on ahead of time. Whether I like my room or not doesn't depend on how the furniture is arranged...it's how I arrange my mind. I've already decided to love it .. "It's a decision I make every morning when I wake up. I have a choice; I can spend the day in bed recounting the difficulty I have with the parts of my body that no longer work, or get out of bed and be thankful for the ones that do. Each day is a gift, and as long as my eyes open... I'll focus on the new day and all the happy memories I've stored away .....just for this time in my life. Old age is like a bank account ..... you withdraw from what you've put in .. So, my advice to you would be to deposit a lot of happiness in the bank account of memories . Thank you for your part in filling my Memory bank. I am still depositing."

Remember the five simple rules to be happy:
1. Free your heart from hatred.
2. Free your mind from worries.
3. Live simply.
4. Give more.
5. Expect less.

Baby Erik and the Old Man

We were the only family with children in the restaurant. I sat Erik in a high chair and noticed everyone was quietly eating and talking. Suddenly, Erik squealed with glee and said, "Hi." He pounded his fat baby hands on the highchair tray. His eyes were wide with excitement and his mouth was bared in a toothless grin. He wriggled and giggled with merriment. I looked around and saw the source of his merriment. It was a man with a tattered rag of a coat; dirty, greasy and worn. His pants were baggy with a zipper at half-mast and his toes poked out of would-be shoes. His shirt was dirty and his hair was uncombed and unwashed. His whiskers were too short to be called a beard and his nose was so varicose it looked like a road map..

We were too far from him to smell, but I was sure he smelled. His hands waved and flapped on loose wrists. "Hi there, baby; hi there, big boy. I see ya, buster," the man said to Erik.

My husband and I exchanged looks, "What do we do?" Erik continued to laugh and answer, "Hi, hi." Everyone in the restaurant noticed and looked at us and then at the man. The old geezer was creating a nuisance with my beautiful baby..

Our meal came and the man began shouting from across the room, "Do ya know patty cake? Do you know peek-a-boo? Hey, look, he knows peek-a-boo." Nobody thought the old man was cute. He was obviously drunk.. My husband and I were embarrassed. We ate in silence; all except for Erik, who was running through his repertoire for the admiring skid-row bum, who in turn, reciprocated with his cute comments..

We finally got through the meal and headed for the door. My husband went to pay the check and told me to meet him in the parking lot. The old man sat poised between me and the door. "Lord, just let me out of here before he speaks to me or Erik," I prayed.

As I drew closer to the man, I turned my back trying to sidestep him and avoid any air he might be breathing. As I did, Erik leaned over my arm, reaching with both arms in a baby's "pick-me-up" position. Before I could stop him, Erik had propelled himself from my arms to the man's. Suddenly a very old smelly man and a very young baby consummated their love relationship. Erik in an act of total trust, love, and submission laid his tiny head upon the man's ragged shoulder..

The man's eyes closed, and I saw tears hover beneath his lashes. His aged hands full of grime, pain, and hard labor-gently, so gently, cradled my baby's bottom and stroked his back..

No two beings have ever loved so deeply for so short a time. I stood awestruck. The old man rocked and cradled Erik in his arms for a moment, and then his eyes opened and set squarely on mine. He said in a firm commanding voice, "You take care of this baby." Somehow I managed, "I will," from a throat that contained a stone. He pried Erik from his chest-unwillingly, longingly, as though he were in pain. I received my baby, and the man said, "God bless you, ma'am, you've given me my Christmas gift."

I said nothing more than a muttered thanks. With Erik in my arms, I ran for the car. My husband was wondering why I was crying and holding Erik so tightly, and why I was saying, "My God, my God, forgive me." I had just witnessed Christ's love shown through the innocence of a tiny child who saw no sin, who made no judgment; a child who saw a soul, and a mother who saw a suit of clothes. I was a Christian who was blind, holding a child who was not. I felt it was God asking.... "Are you willing to share your son for a moment?"... when He shared His for all eternity.. The ragged old man, unwittingly, had reminded me, **"To enter the Kingdom of God, we must become as little children."**

The Baptist Dog

A Baptist couple felt it important to own an equally Baptist pet, so they went shopping. At a kennel specializing in Baptist dogs, they found one they liked a lot.

When they asked the dog to fetch the Bible, he did so in a flash. When they asked him to look up Psalm 23, he complied equally fast, using his paws with incredible dexterity. Impressed, they purchased the animal and went home.

That night, they had friends over. They were so proud of their new Baptist dog and his skills that they called the dog and showed off a little. The friends were impressed and asked whether the dog could do any of the usual dog tricks as well.

This stopped the couple cold, as they hadn't even thought of normal dog tricks. "Well," they said, "Let's try it out." Once more they called the dog in and they clearly pronounced the command, "Heel!"

Quick as a wink, the dog jumped up, put his paw on the man's forehead, closed his eyes in concentration, and bowed his head. It was then that the couple realized they'd been deceived and defrauded.

Obviously, the dog was *Pentecostal!*

Be Still, and Know That I Am GOD

[Ps.46:10]
God, what do you mean to be still and know you are God?
My child, what I mean is:
Though the earth be removed,
Though the waters thereof roar and be troubled,
Though the mountains shake with swelling, [Ps.46:2-3]
Though the wind blow, Though the storm rage;
IN OTHER WORDS:
Though your bills are due,
Though they give you a hard time on your job,
Though your husband won't act right,
Though your wife won't act right,
Though your children are disobedient,
Though there's sickness in your body,
Though your enemies get on your NERVES;
Stop your WORRIES!
Stop your COMPLAINING!
Stop your DOUBTING!
Stop your FROWNING!
Cease your fears, and dry up those tears!
For I'm right there to **comfort** you,
I'm right there to **guide** you,
I'm right there to **hold you** up,

21

I'm right there to **heal** you,
I'm right there to **deliver** you.

So cast your cares upon me for I careth for you. My child this is what I mean by being still and knowing I AM GOD. FOR I AM GOD ALL BY MYSELF!!! Written by the great I AM! *Please pass this on to others, you don't know who may be in need of these words. In the matchless name of Jesus.*

Be Still With God

By Nancy B. Gibbs

All day long I had been very busy; picking up trash, cleaning bathrooms and scrubbing floors. My grown children were coming home for the weekend. I went grocery shopping and prepared for a barbecue supper, complete with ribs and chicken. I wanted everything to be perfect.

Suddenly, it dawned on me that I was dog-tired. I simply couldn't work as long as I could when I was younger. "I've got to rest for a minute," I told my husband, Roy, as I collapsed into my favorite rocking chair. Music was playing, my dog and cat were chasing each other and the phone rang.

A scripture from Psalm 46 popped into my mind. "Be still, and know that I am God." I realized that I hadn't spent much time in prayer that day. Was I too busy to even utter a simple word of thanks to God? Suddenly, the thought of my beautiful patio came to mind. I can be quiet out there, I thought. I longed for a few minutes alone with God.

Roy and I had invested a great deal of time and work in the patio that spring. The flowers and hanging baskets were breathtaking. It was definitely a heavenly place of rest and tranquility. If I can't be still with God in that environment, I can't be still with Him anywhere, I thought. While Roy was talking on the telephone, I slipped out the backdoor and sat down on my favorite patio chair. I closed my eyes and began to pray, counting my many blessings.

A bird flew by me, chirping and singing. It interrupted my thoughts. It landed on the bird feeder and began eating dinner as I watched. After a few minutes it flew away, singing another song.

I closed my eyes again. A gust of wind blew, which caused my wind chimes to dance. They made a joyful sound, but again I lost my concentration on God. I squirmed and wiggled in my chair. I looked up toward the blue sky and saw the clouds moving slowly toward the horizon. The wind died down. My wind chimes finally became quiet. Again, I bowed in prayer. "Honk, honk," I heard. I almost jumped out of my skin. A neighbor was driving down the street. He waved at me and smiled. I waved back, happy that he cared. I quickly tried once again to settle down, repeating the familiar verse in my mind. Be still and know that I am God.

"I'm trying God. I really am," I whispered. "But you've got to help me here." The backdoor opened. My husband walked outside. "I love you," he said. "I was wondering where you were." I chuckled, as he came over and kissed me, then turned around and went back inside.

"Where's the quiet time?" I asked God. My heart fluttered. There was no pain, only a beat that interrupted me yet again. This is impossible, I thought. There's no time to be still and to know that God is with me. There's too much going on in the world and entirely too much activity all around me.

Then it suddenly dawned on me. God was speaking to me the entire time I was attempting to be still. I remembered the music playing as I'd begun my quiet time. He sent a sparrow to lighten my life with song. He sent a gentle breeze. He sent a neighbor to let me know that I had a friend. He sent my sweetheart to offer sincere sentiments of love. He caused my heart to flutter to remind me of life. While I was trying to count my blessings, God was busy multiplying them.

I laughed to realize that the "interruptions" of my quiet time with God were special blessings He'd sent to show me He was with me the entire time.

Bible and Bullies

To the editor *(Yakima Herald-Republic)* -- Bullies are finally getting the recognition they deserve. Legislators, law enforcement people and school administrators are finally beginning to recognize the big bad bully. It is just possibly that the "bully mentality" has had something to do with creating the twisted minds that now get back by attacking their schools.

I tried to tell my principal 55 years ago, but nobody would listen.

The answer is simple: "Do unto others as you would have others do unto you." The only reason this simple answer will no longer work is because the Bible and the things it teaches are no longer allowed in schools. Think about it.

AL ALLAWAY *Yakima*

Bible Sale

A Minister concluded that his church was getting into serious financial troubles. Coincidentally, while checking the church storeroom, he discovered several cartons of new bibles that had never been opened and distributed. So at his Sunday sermon, he asked for three volunteers who would be willing to sell the bibles door-to-door for $10 each to raise the desperately needed money for the church

Peter, Paul and Louie all raised their hands to volunteer for the task. The reverend knew that Peter and Paul earned their living as salesmen and were likely capable of selling some bibles but he had serious doubts about Louie. Louie was just a little farmer, who had always tended to keep to himself because he was embarrassed by his speech; he stuttered very badly. But, not wanting to discourage poor Louis, the reverend decided to let him try anyway.

He sent the three of them away with the back seat of their cars stacked with bibles and asked them to meet with him and report the results of their door-to-door selling efforts the following Sunday, which they did. Anxious to find out how successful they were, the reverend immediately asked Peter,

"Well, Pete, how did you make out selling our bibles last week?"

Proudly handing the reverend an envelope, Peter replied, "Father, using my sales prowess, I was able to sell 20 bibles, and here's the $200 dollars I collected on behalf of the church."

"Fine job, Pete!" The reverend said, vigorously shaking his hand "You are indeed a fine salesman and the church is indebted to you."

Turning to Paul, he asked "And Paul, how many bibles did you manage to sell for the church last week?" Paul, smiling and sticking out his chest, confidently replied, "Reverend, I am a professional salesman and was happy to give the church the benefit of my sales expertise. Last week I sold 28 bibles on behalf of the church, and here's $280 dollars I collected.

The reverend responded, "That's absolutely splendid, Paul. You are a professional salesman and the church is also indebted to you."

Apprehensively, the reverend turned to little Louie and said, "And Lou, did you manage to sell any bibles last week?" Louie silently offered the reverend a large envelope. The reverend opened it and counted the contents. "What is this?" he exclaimed. "Louie, there's $3,200 dollars in here! Are you suggesting that you sold 320 bibles for the church, door to door, in just one week?

Louie just nodded.

"That's impossible!" both Peter and Paul said in unison. "We are professional salesmen, yet you claim to have sold 10 times as many bibles as we could."

"Yes, this does seem unlikely," the reverend agreed. "I think you'd better explain how you managed to accomplish this, Louie."

Louie shrugged. "I-I-I- re-re-really do-do-don't kn-kn-know f-ff-for sh-sh-sh-sure," he stammered.

Impatiently, Peter interrupted. "For crying out loud, Louie, just tell us what you said to them when they answered the door!" "A-a-a-all I-I-I s-s-said wa-wa-was," Louis replied, "W-w-w-wwould y-y-y-you l-l-l-l-l-like t-t-to b-b-b-buy th-th-th-this b-b-b-bbible f-f-for t-t-ten b-b-b-bucks ---o-o-o-or--- wo-wo-would yo-you jj-j-just l-like m-m-me t-t-to st-st-stand h-h-here and r-r-r-r-r-read it tto y-y-you?"

The Big Wheel

An early Christmas Story.

(If you've never seen this, it will thrill your heart; if you have seen it, delete it if you can. I couldn't. It's beautiful and the prayer at the end is something we all need to do for the benefit of each other.)

In September 1960, I woke up one morning with six hungry babies and just 75 cents in my pocket. Their father was gone. The boys ranged from three months to seven years; their sister was two. Their Dad had never been much more than a presence they feared. Whenever they heard his tires crunch on the gravel driveway they would scramble to hide under their beds. He did manage to leave $15 a week to buy groceries.

Now that he had decided to leave, there would be no more beatings, but no food either. If there was a welfare system in effect in southern Indiana at that time, I certainly knew nothing about it. I scrubbed the kids until they looked brand new and then put on mybest homemade dress. I loaded them into the rusty old 51 Chevy and drove off to find a job.

The seven of us went to every factory, store and restaurant in our small town. No luck. The kids stayed crammed into the car and tried to be quiet while I tried to convince whomever would listen that I was willing to learn or do anything. I had to have a job. Still no luck.

The last place we went to, just a few miles out of town, was an old Root Beer Barrel drive-in that had been converted to a truck stop. It was called the Big Wheel.

An old lady named Granny owned the place and she peeked out of the window from time to time at all those kids. She needed someone on the graveyard shift, 11 at night until seven in the morning. She paid 65 cents an hour and I could start that night. I raced home and called the teenager down the street that baby-sat for people. I bargained with her to come and sleep on my sofa for a dollar a night. She could arrive with her pajamas on and the kids would already be asleep. This seemed like a good arrangement to her, so we made a deal.

That night when the little ones and I knelt to say our prayers we all thanked God for finding Mommy a job. And so I started at the Big Wheel. When I got home in the mornings I woke the baby-sitter up and sent her home with one dollar of my tip money--fully half of what I averaged every night.

As the weeks went by, heating bills added a strain to my meager wage. The tires on the old Chevy had the consistency of penny balloons and began to leak. I had to fill them with air on the way to work and again every morning before I could go home.

One bleak fall morning, I dragged myself to the car to go home and found four tires in the back seat. New tires! There was no note, no nothing, just those beautiful brand new tires. Had angels taken up residence in Indiana? I wondered. I made a deal with the local service station. In exchange for his mounting the new tires, I would clean up his office. I remember it took me a lot longer to scrub his floor than it did for him to do the tires.

I was now working six nights instead of five and it still wasn't enough. Christmas was coming and I knew there would be no money for toys for the kids. I found a can of red paint and started repairing and painting some old toys. Then I hid them in the basement so there would be something for Santa to deliver on Christmas morning. Clothes were a worry too. I was sewing patches on top of patches on the boys pants and soon they would be too far gone to repair.

On Christmas Eve the usual customers were drinking coffee in the Big Wheel. These were the truckers, Les, Frank, and Jim, and a state trooper named Joe. A few musicians were hanging around after a gig at the Legion and were dropping nickels in the pinball machine. The regulars all just sat around and talked through the wee hours of the morning and then left to get home before the sun came up.

When it was time for me to go home at seven o'clock on Christmas morning I hurried to the car. I was hoping the kids wouldn't wake up before I managed to get home and get the presents from the basement and place them under the tree. (We had cut down a small cedar tree by the side of the road down by the dump) It was still dark and I couldn't see much, but there appeared to be some dark shadows in the car - or was that just a trick of the night? Something certainly looked different, but it was hard to tell what.

When I reached the car I peered warily into one of the side windows. Then my jaw dropped in amazement. My old battered Chevy was filled full to the top with boxes of all shapes and sizes. I quickly opened the driver's side door, scrambled inside and kneeled in the front facing the back seat. Reaching back, I pulled off the lid of the top box. Inside was whole case of little blue jeans, sizes 2-10! I looked inside another box: It was full of shirts to go with the jeans. Then I peeked inside some of the other boxes: There was candy and nuts and bananas and bags of groceries. There was an enormous ham for baking, and canned vegetables and potatoes. There was pudding and Jell-O and cookies, pie filling and flour. There was a whole bag of laundry supplies and cleaning items. And there were five toy trucks and one beautiful little doll.

As I drove back through empty streets as the sun slowly rose on most amazing Christmas Day of my life, I was sobbing with gratitude. And I will never forget the joy on the faces of my little ones that precious morning. Yes, there were angels in Indiana that long-ago December. And they all hung out at the Big Wheel truck stop.

THE POWER OF PRAYER

When you receive this, say a prayer. This prayer will do. That's all you have to do. There is nothing attached. This is powerful. Prayer is one of the best free gifts we receive. There is no cost but a lot of rewards. Let's continue praying for one another.

Father, please bless my friends reading this right now. Lord, show them a new revelation of Your love and power. Holy Spirit, may You minister to their spirit right now. Amen.

Biker's Road of Life

At first, I saw God as my observer, my judge, keeping track of the things I did wrong, so as to know whether I merited heaven or hell when I die. He was out there sort of like a president. I recognized His picture when I saw it, but I really didn't know Him. But later on when I met Christ, it seemed as though life were rather like a bike ride, but it was a tandem bike, and I noticed that Christ was in the back helping me pedal. I don't know just when it was that He suggested we change places, but life has not been the same since.

When I had control, I knew the way. It was rather boring, but predictable; it was the shortest distance between two points. But when He took the lead, He knew delightful long cuts, up mountains, and through rocky places at breakneck speeds. It was all I could do to hang on!

Even though it looked like madness, He said, "Pedal!" I worried and was anxious and asked, "Where are you taking me?" He laughed and didn't answer, and I started to learn to trust. I forgot my boring life and entered into the adventure, and when I'd say, "I'm scared," He'd lean back and touch my hand. I gained love, peace, acceptance and joy; gifts to take on my journey, My Lord's and mine. And we were off again.

He said, "Give the gifts away. They're extra baggage, too much weight." So I did, to the people we met, and I found that in giving I received, and still our burden was light.

I did not trust Him, at first, in control of my life. I thought He'd wreck it; but he knows bike secrets, knows how to make it bend to take sharp corners, knows how to jump to clear high rocks, knows how to fly to enjoy the view and the cool breeze on my face with my delightful constant companion, Jesus Christ.

And when I'm sure I just can't do it anymore, He just smiles and says..."Pedal."

The Bill of Non-Rights

The following has been attributed to State Representative Mitchell Kaye from GA. This guy should run for President

"We the sensible people of the United States, in an attempt to help everyone get along, restore some semblance of justice, avoid more riots, keep our nation safe, promote positive behavior, and secure the blessings of debt free liberty to ourselves and our great great-great-grandchildren, hereby try one more time to ordain and establish some common sense guidelines for the terminally whiny, guilt ridden, delusional, and other liberal bed-wetters. We hold these truths to be self evident: that a whole lot of people are confused by the Bill of Rights and are so dim they require a Bill of NON-Rights."

ARTICLE I: You do not have the right to a new car, big screen TV, or any other form of wealth. More power to you if you can legally acquire them, but no one is guaranteeing anything.

ARTICLE II: You do not have the right to never be offended. This country is based on freedom, and that means freedom for everyone -- not just you! You may leave the room, turn the channel, express a different opinion, etc.; but the world is full of idiots, and probably always will be.

ARTICLE III: You do not have the right to be free from harm. If you stick a screwdriver in your eye, learn to be more careful; do not expect the tool manufacturer to make you and all your relatives independently wealthy.

ARTICLE IV: You do not have the right to free food and housing. Americans are the most charitable people to be found, and will gladly help anyone in need, but we are quickly growing weary of subsidizing generation after generation of professional couch potatoes who achieve nothing more than the creation of another generation of professional couch potatoes.

ARTICLE V: You do not have the right to free health care.. That would be nice, but from the looks of public housing, we're just not interested in public health care.

ARTICLE VI: You do not have the right to physically harm other people. If you kidnap, rape, intentionally maim, or kill someone, don't be surprised if the rest of us want to see you fry in the electric chair.

ARTICLE VII: You do not have the right to the possessions of others. If you rob, cheat, or coerce away the goods or services of other citizens, don't be surprised if the rest of us get together and lock you away in a place where you still won't have the right to a big screen color TV or a life of leisure.

ARTICLE VIII: You do not have the right to a job. All of us sure want you to have a job, and will gladly help you along in hard times, but we expect you to take advantage of the opportunities of education and vocational training aid before you to make yourself useful.

ARTICLE IX: You do not have the right to happiness. Being an American means that you have the right to PURSUE happiness, which by the way, is a lot easier if you are unencumbered by an over abundance of idiotic laws created by those of you who were confused by the Bill of Rights

ARTICLE X: This is an English speaking country. We don't care where you are from, English is our language. Learn it or go back to wherever you came from. (lastly....)

ARTICLE XI: You do not have the right to change our country's history or heritage. This country was founded on the belief in one true God. And yet, you are given the freedom to believe in any religion, any faith, or no faith at all; with no fear of persecution. The phrase IN GOD WE TRUST is part of our heritage and history, and if you are uncomfortable with it, TOUGH!!!! If you agree, share this with a friend. No, you don't *have* to, and nothing tragic will befall you if you don't

The Birdies

On July 22nd I was en route to Washington, DC for a business trip. It was all so very ordinary, until landing in Denver for a plane change. As I collected my belongings from the overhead bin, an announcement was made for Mr. Lloyd Glenn to see the Customer Service Representative immediately. I thought nothing of it until I reached the door to leave the plane, and I heard a gentleman asking every male if they were Mr. Glenn. At this point I knew something was wrong and my heart sunk.

When I got off the plane a solemn-faced young man came toward me and said, "Mr. Glenn, there is an emergency at your home. I do not know what the emergency is, or who is involved, but I will take you to the phone so you can call the hospital." My heart was now pounding, but the will to be calm took over. Woodenly, I followed this stranger to the distant telephone where I called the number he gave me for the Mission Hospital. My call was put through to the trauma center where I learned that my three year- old son had been trapped underneath the automatic garage door for several minutes, and that when my wife had found him he was dead.

A neighbor, a doctor had performed CPR, and the paramedics had continued the treatment as Brian was transported to the hospital. By the time of my call, Brian was revived and they believed he would live, but they did not know how much damage had been done to his brain, nor to his heart.

They explained that the door had completely closed on his little sternum right over his heart. He had been severely crushed. After speaking with the medical staff, my wife sounded worried but not hysterical, and I took comfort in her calmness.

The return flight seemed to last forever, but finally I arrived at the hospital six hours after the garage door had come down. When I walked into the intensive care unit, nothing could have prepared me to see my little son laying so still on a great big bed with tubes and monitors everywhere. He was on a respirator. I glanced at my wife who stood and tried to give me a reassuring smile. It all seemed like a terrible dream. I was filled-in with the details and given a guarded prognosis. Brian was going to live, and the preliminary tests indicated that his heart was OK, two miracles in and of themselves.

But only time would tell if his brain received any damage. Throughout the seemingly endless hours, my wife was calm. She felt that Brian would eventually be all right. I hung on to her words and faith like a lifeline. All that night and the next day Brian remained unconscious. It seemed like forever since I had left for my business trip the day before. Finally at two o'clock that afternoon, our son regained consciousness and sat up uttering the most beautiful words I have ever heard spoken. He said, "Daddy hold me" and he reached for me with his little arms.

[TEAR BREAK...smile]

By the next day he was pronounced as having no neurological or physical deficits, and the story of his miraculous survival spread throughout the hospital. You cannot imagine when we took Brian home, we felt a unique reverence for the life and love of our Heavenly Father that comes to those who brush death so closely.

In the days that followed there was a special spirit about our home. Our two older children were much closer to their little brother. My wife and I were much closer to each other, and all of us were very close as a whole family. Life took on a less stressful pace. Perspective seemed to be more focused, and balance much easier to gain and maintain. We felt deeply blessed. Our gratitude was truly profound. The story is not over (smile)!

Almost a month later to the day of the accident, Brian awoke from his afternoon nap and said, "Sit down Mommy. I have something to tell you." At this time in his life, Brian usually spoke in small phrases, so to say a large sentence surprised my wife. She sat down with him on his bed, and he began his sacred and remarkable story.

"Do you remember when I got stuck under the garage door? Well, it was so heavy and it hurt really bad. I called to you, but you couldn't hear me I started to cry, but then it hurt too bad. And then the 'birdies' came."

"The birdies?" my wife asked puzzled.

"Yes," he replied. "The birdies made a whooshing sound and flew into the garage. They took care of me."

"They did?"

"Yes," he said. "One of the birdies came and got you. She came to tell you I got stuck under the door." A sweet reverent feeling filled the room. The spirit was so strong and yet lighter than air. My wife realized that a three-year-old had no concept of death and spirits, so he was referring to the beings who came to him from beyond as "birdies" because they were up in the air like birds that fly.

"What did the birdies look like?" she asked.

Brian answered, "They were so beautiful. They were dressed in white, all white. Some of them had green and white. But some of them had on just white."

"Did they say anything?"

"Yes," he answered. "They said the baby would be all right."

"The baby?" my wife asked confused.

Brian answered. "The baby laying on the garage floor." He went on, You came out and opened the garage door and ran to the baby. You told the baby to stay and not leave." My wife nearly collapsed upon hearing this, for she had indeed gone and knelt beside Brian's body and seeing his crushed chest whispered, "Don't leave us Brian, please stay if you can."

As she listened to Brian telling her the words she had spoken, she realized that the spirit had left his body and was looking down from above on this little lifeless form.

"Then what happened?" she asked.

"We went on a trip." he said, "Far, far away." He grew agitated trying to say the things he didn't seem to have the words for. My wife tried to calm and comfort him, and let him know it would be okay.. He struggled with wanting to tell something that obviously was very important to him, but finding the words was difficult. "We flew so fast up in the air. They're so pretty Mommy," he added. "And there are lots and lots of birdies."

My wife was stunned. Into her mind the sweet comforting spirit enveloped her more soundly, but with an urgency she had never before known. Brian went on to tell her that the "birdies" had told him that he had to come back and tell everyone about the "birdies." He said they brought him back to the house and that a big fire truck and an ambulance were there. A man was bringing the baby out on a white bed and he tried to tell the man that the baby would be okay, but the man couldn't hear him. He said the birdies told him he had to go with the ambulance, but they would be near him. He said they were so pretty and so peaceful, and he didn't want to come back.

Then the bright light came. He said that the light was so bright and so warm, and he loved the bright light so much. Someone was in the bright light and put their arms around him, and told him, "I love you but you have to go back. You have to play baseball, and tell everyone about the birdies." Then the person in the bright light kissed him and waved bye-bye. Then whoosh, the big sound came and they went into the clouds.

The story went on for an hour. He taught us that "birdies" were always with us, but we don't see them because we look with our eyes and we don't hear them because we listen with our ears. But they are always there, you can only see them in here (he put his hand over his heart).

Brian continued, stating, "I have a plan, Mommy. You have a plan. Daddy has a plan. Everyone has a plan. We must all live our plan and keep our promises. The birdies help us to do that cause they love us so much."

In the weeks that followed, he often came to us and told all or part of it, again and again. Always the story remained the same. It never ceased to amaze us how he could tell such detail and speak beyond his ability when he talked about his birdies. Needless to say, we have not been the same ever since that day, and I pray we never will be.

You are cordially invited to
A Birthday Celebration

GUEST OF HONOR: Jesus Christ
DATE: Everyday. Traditionally December 25, but He's always around, sothe date is flexible.
TIME: Whenever you're ready. (Please don't be too late, though; or you'll miss out on all the fun).
PLACE: In your heart… He'll meet you there (You'll hear Him knock).
ATTIRE: Come as you are; grubbies are okay. He'll be washing our clothes anyway. He said something about white robe & crown for everyone who stays until the last.
TICKETS: Admission is free. He's paid for everyone. He says we would not be able to afford it. (It's cost Him everything he had).
REFRESHMENTS: New wine, bread, and a far-out drink He calls "Living Water", followed by a supper that promises to be out of this world!!
GIFT SUGGESTIONS: Your heart. He's one of those folks who already has everything. (He's very generous in return, though. Just wait 'til you see what He has for you).
ENTERTAINMENT: Joy, Peace, Truth, Light, Life, Love, Real Happiness, Communion with God, Forgiveness, Miracles, Healing, Power, Eternity in Paradise, and much more! (All rated "G" so bring your family and friends).
RSVP: Very Important! He must know ahead so He can reserve a spot for you at the table. Also, He's keeping a list of His friends for

future reference (He calls it the "Lamb's Book of Life"). Party being given by His kids (us). Hope to see you there. ***"Let us rejoice and be glad and give him glory!"*** (Rev. 19:7-9)

Bless My Computer too

Dear Lord:
Every single evening
As I'm lying here in bed
This tiny little prayer
Keeps running through my head.
God bless all my family
Wherever they may be,
Keep them warm and safe from harm
For they're so close to me.
And God, there is one more thing
I wish that you would do.
Hope you don't mind me asking,
Bless my computer too.
Now I know that it's not normal
To bless a mother board,
But listen just a second
While I explain to you 'My Lord.'
You see, that little metal box
Holds more than odds & ends
Inside those small compartments
Rest so many of my FRIENDS.
I know so much about them
By the kindness that they give
And this little scrap of metal
Takes me in to where they live.
By faith is how I know them
Much the same as you
We share in what life brings us
And from that our friendship grew.

Please, take an extra minute
From your duties up above
To bless those in my address book
That's filled with so much love!
Wherever else this prayer may reach
To each and every friend,
Bless each e-mail Inbox
And the person who hits Send.
When you update your heavenly list
On your own CD-ROM
Remember each who've said this prayer
Sent up to God.com. Amen.

Bless the Children

A four-year-old boy who's next door neighbor was an elderly man who had recently lost his wife. Upon seeing the man cry, the little boy went into the old gentleman's yard, climbed onto his lap, and just sat there. When his mother asked him what he had said to the neighbor, the little boy said, "Nothing. I just helped him cry."

..oOo..

Teacher Debbie Moon's first graders were discussing a picture of a family. One little boy in the picture had a different color hair than the other family members. One child suggested that he was adopted. A little girl said, "I know all about, adoptions because I was adopted." "What does it mean to be adopted?" asked another child. "It means," said the girl, "that you grew in your mommy's heart instead of her tummy."

..oOo..

A four-year-old was at the pediatrician for a check up. As the doctor looked into her ears he asked, "Do you think I'll find Big Bird in here?" The little girl stayed silent. Next, the doctor took a tongue depressor and looked down her throat. He asked, "Do you think I'll find the Cookie Monster down there?" Again, the little girl was silent. Then the doctor put a stethoscope to her chest. As he listened to her heart beat, he asked, "Do you think I'll hear Barney in there?" "Oh, no!" the little girl replied. "God is in my heart. Barney is on my underpants."

..oOo..

Whenever I'm disappointed with my spot in life, I stop and think about little Jamie Scott. Jamie was trying out for a part in a school play. His mother told me that he'd set his heart on being in it, though she feared he would not be chosen. On the day the parts were awarded, I went with her to collect him after school. Jamie rushed up to her, eyes shining with pride and excitement. "Guess what, Mom?" he shouted, and then said those words that will remain a lesson to me: "I've been chosen to clap and cheer."

..oOo..

An eye witness account from New York City: On a cold day in December, a little boy about 10 years old was standing before a shoe store on the roadway, barefooted, peering through the window, and shivering with cold. A lady approached the boy and said, "My little fellow, why are you looking so earnestly in that window?"

"I was asking God to give me a pair of shoes," was the boy's reply.

The lady took him by the hand and went into the store and asked the clerk to get half a dozen pairs of socks for the boy. She then asked if the clerk could give her a basin of water and a towel. He quickly brought them to her.

She took the little fellow to the back part of the store and, removing her gloves, knelt down, washed his little feet, and dried them with a towel. By this time the clerk had returned with the socks.

Placing a pair upon the boy's feet, she purchased him a pair of shoes. She tied up the remaining pairs of socks and gave them to him. She patted him on the head and said, "No doubt, my little fellow, you feel more comfortable now?" As she turned to go, the astonished lad caught her by the hand, and looking up in her face, with tears in his eyes, answered the question with these words: "Are you God's wife?"

..oOo..

Jesus told us, *"Suffer the little children to come unto me, and forbid them not: for of such is the kingdom of God. Verily I say unto you, Whosoever shall not receive the kingdom of God as a little child shall in no wise enter therein."* (Luke 18:16-17 KJB)

Blessings

I dreamt that I went to Heaven and an angel was showing me around. We walked side-by-side inside a large workroom, filled with angels.

My angel stopped in front of the first section and said, "This is the Receiving Section. Here all petitions to God said in prayer are received." I looked around this area and it was terribly busy with so many angels sorting out petitions written on voluminous paper sheets and scraps from people all over the world. Then, we moved on down a long corridor until we reached another section.

The angel said to me, "This is the Packaging and Delivery Section. Here, the graces and blessings the people asked for are processed and delivered to the living persons who asked for them." I noticed again how busy it was there. There were many angels working hard at that station, since so many blessings had bee requested and were being packaged for delivery to earth.

Finally, at the furthest end of the long corridor we stopped at the door of a very small station. To my great surprise, only one angel was seated there, idly doing nothing. "This is the Acknowledgment Section," my angel friend quietly admitted to me. He seemed embarrassed.

"How is it that? There is no work going on here?" I asked.

"So sad," the angel sighed. "After people receive the blessings that they asked for, very few send back acknowledgments."

"How does one acknowledge God's blessings?" I asked.

"Simple," the angel answered. "Just say, 'Thank you, Lord.'"

So, if you have food in the refrigerator, clothes on your back, a roof overhead and a place to sleep, you are richer than 75% of this world. If you have money in the bank, in your wallet, and spare change in a dish, you are among the top 8% of the worlds wealthy. If you get this on your computer or read it in a book, you are part of the 1% in the world who has that opportunity. Also, if you woke up this morning with more health than illness, you are more blessed than the many that will not even survive this day.

If you have never experienced the fear in battle, the loneliness of imprisonment, the agony of torture, or the pangs of starvation, you are ahead of 700 million people in the world. If you can attend a church meeting without fear of reprisal, harassment, arrest, torture or death, three billion people envy you. And if you live in America, you are doubly blessed.

If you can hold your head up and smile, you are not the norm, but are unique to all those in doubt and despair.

Finally, if you can read this message, you just received a double blessing in that someone was thinking of you as very special and you are more blessed than over two billion people in the world who cannot read at all.

Have a good day, count your blessings, and if you want, remind everyone else how blessed we all are.

ATTN: Acknowledgment Department: Thank you Lord, for giving me the ability to share this message and for the media to reach so many wonderful people.

Blue Ribbon Makes A Difference

A teacher in New York decided to honor each of her Seniors in high school by telling them the difference they each made. She called each student to the front of the class, one at a time. First she told each of them how they had made a difference to her and the class.

Then she presented each of them with a blue ribbon imprinted with gold letters, which read, *"Who I Am Makes a Difference."* Afterwards the teacher decided to do a class project to see what kind of impact recognition would have on a community. She gave each of the students three more ribbons and instructed them to go out and spread this acknowledgment ceremony. Then they were to follow up on the results, see who honored whom and report back to the class in about a week

One of the boys in the class went to a junior executive in a nearby company and honored him for helping him with his career planning. He gave him a blue ribbon and put it on his shirt. Then he gave him two extra ribbons and said, "We're doing a class project on recognition, and we'd like you to go out, find somebody to honor, give them a blue ribbon, then give them the extra blue ribbon so they can acknowledge a third person to keep this acknowledgment ceremony going. Then please report back to me and tell me what happened.

Later that day the junior executive went in to see his boss, Who had been noted, by the way, as being kind of a grouchy fellow. He sat his boss down and he told him that he deeply admired him for being a creative genius. The boss seemed very surprised. The junior executive asked him if he would accept the gift of the blue ribbon and would he give him permission to put it on him. His surprised boss said, "Well, sure."

The junior executive took the blue ribbon and placed it right on his boss's jacket above his heart. As he gave him the last extra ribbon, he said, "Would you do me a favor? Would you take this extra one and pass it on by honoring somebody else. The young boy who first gave me the ribbons is doing a project in school and we want to keep this recognition ceremony going and find out how it affects people."

That night the boss came home to his 14-year-old son and sat him down. He said, "The most incredible thing happened to me today. I was in my office and one of the junior executives came in and told me he admired me and gave me a blue ribbon for being a creative genius. Imagine. He thinks I'm a creative genius. Then he put this blue ribbon that says "Who I Am Makes a Difference" on my jacket above my heart. He gave me an extra ribbon and asked me to find somebody else to honor.

As I was driving home tonight, I started thinking about who I would honor with this ribbon and I thought about you. I want to honor you. My days are really hectic and when I come home I don't pay a lot of attention to you. Sometimes I scream at you for not getting good enough grades in school and for your bedroom being a mess, but somehow tonight, I just wanted to sit here and, well, just let you know that you do make a difference to me. Besides your mother, you are the most important person in my life. You're a great kid and I love you!"

The startled boy started to sob and sob, and he wouldn't stop crying. His whole body shook. He looked up at his father and said through his tears, "Dad, earlier tonight I sat in my room and wrote a letter to you and Mom explaining why I had killed myself and asking you to forgive me. I was going to commit suicide tonight after you were asleep. I just didn't think that you cared at all. The letter is upstairs. I don't think I need it after all."

His father walked upstairs and found a heartfelt letter full of anguish and pain. The envelope was addressed, "Mom and Dad."

The boss went back to work a changed man. He was no longer a grouch but made sure to let all his employees know that they made a difference.

The junior executive helped several other young people with career planning and never forgot to let them know that they made a difference in his life... one being the boss's son.

And the young boy and his classmates learned a valuable lesson. Who you are DOES make a difference

Remember that I just gave you a blue ribbon.

The best vitamin for making friends.... B1

Just as there is no beginning or ending to a circle..... there is no beginning or ending to GOD's LOVE.

The Boat

"Oh God, thy sea is so great, and my boat is so small." That's a quote that sat on a plaque on President Kennedy's desk. It was in the movie "13 Days."

I don't know whether that quote actually sat on his desk or whether it was just added for dramatic effect, but I understand it. I understood how he felt.

President Kennedy had just undergone the Cuban Missile Crisis and picked up the plaque and looked at it as the movie ended. He had just finished dealing with a sea of problems. Worlds colliding, governments leaders quarreling, generals trying to prove who was right and the public opinion of a nation.

His close friends questioning his judgment, his father's shadow looming over him, his wife, his allies, and yea, even his enemies made a good night's sleep elusive.

A sea of things for the president. That's one reason why I've never wished to be president. I have enough to deal with handling my own little world much less a nation.

If I were anointed to be president, I could handle it as easy as I handle my toughest job, for you will never have more put on you than you can bear.

Yes, it's a big sea, and yes, your boat may be small in comparison. But it's big enough to keep you afloat and get you to dry land. And big or small, you are the captain, president of your ship.

"Oh God, thy sea is so great, and my boat is so small."

Breakfast at McDonald's

This is a good story and is true, please read it all the way through until the end!

I am a mother of three (ages 14, 12, 3) and have recently completed my college degree. The last class I had to take was *Sociology*. The teacher was absolutely inspiring with the qualities that I wish every human being had been graced with.

Her last project of the term was called "Smile." The class was asked to go out and smile at three people and document their reactions.

I am a very friendly person and always smile at everyone and say hello anyway, so, I thought this would be a piece of cake, literally.

Soon after we were assigned the project, my husband, youngest son, and I went out to McDonald's one crisp March morning. It was just our way of sharing special playtime with our son. We were standing in line, waiting to be served, when all of a sudden everyone around us began to back away, and then even my husband did. I did not move an inch... an overwhelming feeling of panic welled up inside of me as I turned to see why they had moved.

As I turned around I smelled a horrible "dirty body" smell, and there standing behind me were two poor homeless men. As I looked down at the short gentleman, close to me, he was "smiling". His beautiful sky blue eyes were full of God's Light as he searched for acceptance.

He said, "Good day" as he counted the few coins he had been clutching. The second man fumbled with his hands as he stood behind his friend. I realized the second man was mentally challenged and the blue-eyed gentleman was his salvation.

I held my tears as I stood there with them. The young lady at the counter asked him what they wanted. He said, "Coffee is all Miss" because that was all they could afford. (If they wanted to sit in the restaurant and warm up, they had to buy something. He just wanted to be warm). Then I really felt it. The compulsion was so great I almost reached out and embraced the little man with the blue eyes.

That is when I noticed all eyes in the restaurant were set on me, judging my every action. I smiled and asked the young lady behind the counter to give me two more breakfast meals on a separate tray. I then walked around the corner to the table that the men had chosen as a resting spot. I put the tray on the table and laid my hand on the blue-eyed gentleman's cold hand. He looked up at me, with tears in his eyes, and said, "Thank you."

I leaned over, began to pat his hand and said, "I did not do this for you. God is here working through me to give you hope." I started to cry as I walked away to join my husband and son.

When I sat down my husband smiled at me and said, "That is why God gave you to me, Honey, to give me hope." We held hands for a moment and at that time, we knew that only because of the Grace that we had been given were we able to give.

We are not church goers, but we are believers. That day showed me the pure Light of God's sweet love.

I returned to college, on the last evening of class, with this story in hand. I turned in "my project" and the instructor read it. Then she looked up at me and said, "Can I share this?"

I slowly nodded as she got the attention of the class. She began to read and that is when I knew that we as human beings and being part of God share this need to heal people and to be healed.

In my own way I had touched the people at McDonald's, my husband, son, instructor, and every soul that shared the classroom on the last night I spent as a college student.

I graduated with one of the biggest lessons I would ever learn: UNCONDITIONAL ACCEPTANCE !.

Much love and compassion is sent to each and every person who may read this and learn how to LOVE PEOPLE AND USE THINGS - NOT LOVE THINGS AND USE PEOPLE. If you think this story has touched you in any way, please send this to everyone you know.

There is an Angel sent to watch over you. In order for her to work, you must pass this on to the people you want watched over. An Angel wrote: "Many people will walk in and out of your life, but only true friends will leave footprints in your heart. To handle yourself, use your head. To handle others, use your heart."

God gives every bird it's food, but He does not throw it into its nest. A choice can take a second to make and sometimes a lifetime to live *by Kathy Currier*

Breast Cancer Awareness

A handsome, middle-aged man walked quietly into the cafe and sat down. Before he ordered, he couldn't help but notice a group of younger men at the table next to him. It was obvious they were making fun of something about him and it wasn't until he remembered he was wearing a small pink ribbon on the lapel of his suit that he became aware of what the joke was all about.

The man brushed off the reaction as ignorance, but the smirks began to get to him. He looked one of the rude men square in the eye, placed his hand beneath the ribbon and asked, quizzically, "This?" With that the men all began to laugh out loud.

The man he addressed said, as he fought back laughter, "Hey, sorry man but we were just commenting on how pretty your pink ribbon looks against your blue jacket!"

The middle aged man calmly motioned for the joker to comeover to his table, and invited him to sit down. As uncomfortable as he was, the guy obliged, not really sure why. In a soft voice, the middle aged man said, "I wear this ribbon to bring awareness about breast cancer. I wear it in my mother's honor."

"Oh, sorry dude. She died of breast cancer?"

"No, she didn't. She's alive and well. But her breasts nourished me as an infant, and were a soft resting place for my head when I was scared or lonely as a little boy. I'm very grateful for my mother's breasts, and her health..."

"Umm," the stranger replied, "Yeah."

"And I wear this ribbon to honor my wife", the middle aged man went on.

"And she's okay, too?", the other guy asked.

"Oh, yes. She's fine. Her breasts have been a great source of loving pleasure for both of us, and with them she nurtured and nourished our beautiful daughter 23 years ago. I am grateful for my wife's breasts, and for her health."

"Uh huh. And I guess you wear it to honor your daughter, also?"

"No. It's too late to honor my daughter by wearing it now. My daughter died of breast cancer one month ago. She thought she was too young to have breast cancer, so when she accidentally noticed a small lump, she ignored it. She thought that since it wasn't painful, it must not be anything to worry about

Shaken and ashamed, the now sober stranger said, "Oh, man, I'm so sorry mister."

"So, in my daughter's memory, too, I proudly wear this little ribbon, which allows me the opportunity to enlighten others. Now, go home and talk to your wife and your daughters, your mother and your friends. "And here" the middle-aged man reached in his pocket and handed the other man a little pink ribbon.

The guy looked at it, slowly raised his head and asked, "Can ya help me put it on?"

Every month should be breast cancer awareness month. Do regular breast self-exams and have annual mammograms if you are a woman over the age of 40. And encourage those women you love to do the same.

The Bricklayer's Report

This is an accident report, which was printed in the newsletter of the British equivalent of the Worker's Compensation Board. This is the bricklayer's report, a true story. Had the guy died, he'd have walked away with a Darwin Award for sure.

Dear Sir;

I am writing in response to your request for additional information in Block 3 of the accident report form. I put "Poor Planning" as the cause of my accident. You asked for a fuller explanation and I trust the following details will be sufficient.

I am a bricklayer by trade. On the day of the accident, I was working alone on the roof of a new six-story building. When I completed my work, I found I had some bricks left over which, when weighed later were found to be slightly in excess of 500lbs. Rather than carry the bricks down by hand, I decided to lower them in a barrel by using a pulley, which was attached to the side of the building at the sixth floor.

Securing the rope at ground level, I went up to the roof, swung the barrel out and loaded the bricks into it. Then I went down and untied the rope, holding it tightly to ensure a slow descent of the bricks. You will note in block-11 of the accident report form that my weight is 135 lbs.

Due to my surprise at being jerked off the ground so suddenly, I lost my presence of mind and forgot to let go of the rope. Needless to say, I proceeded at a rapid rate up the side of the building. In the vicinity of the third floor, I met the barrel, which was now proceeding downward at an equally impressive speed. This explains the fractured skull, minor abrasions and the broken collarbone, as listed in Section 3 of the accident report form.

Slowed only slightly, I continued my rapid ascent, not stopping until the fingers of my right hand were two knuckles deep into the pulley.

Fortunately by the time I had regained my presence of mind and was able to hold tightly to the rope, in spite of the excruciating pain I was now beginning to experience. At approximately the same time, however, the barrel of bricks hit the ground and the bottom fell out of the barrel.

Now devoid of the weight of the bricks, that barrel weighed approximately 50 lbs. I refer you again to my weight. As you might imagine, I began a rapid descent down the side of the building. In the vicinity of the third floor, I met the barrel coming up. This accounts for the two fractured ankles broken tooth and severe lacerations of my legs and lower body.

Here my luck began to change slightly. The encounter with the barrel seemed to slow me enough to lessen my injuries when I fell into the pile of bricks and fortunately only three vertebrae were cracked. I am sorry to report, however, as I lay there on the pile of bricks, in pain, unable to move, I again lost my composure and presence of mind and let go of the rope and I lay there watching the empty barrel begin its journey back onto me. This explains the two broken legs.

Yours truly, *"Gomer Fudd"*

Carrot, Egg, or Cup of Coffee?

A young woman went to her mother and told her about her life and how things were so hard for her. She did not know how she was going to make it and wanted to give up. She was tired of fighting and struggling. It seemed as one problem was solved, a new one arose.

Her mother took her to the kitchen. She filled three pots with water and placed each on a high fire. Soon the pots came to boil. In the first she placed carrots, in the second she placed eggs, and in the last she placed ground coffee beans. She let them sit and boil, without saying a word In about twenty minutes she turned off the burners. She fished the carrots out and placed them in a bowl. She pulled the eggs out and placed them in a bowl. Then she ladled the coffee out and placed it in a bowl. Turning to her daughter, she asked, "Tell me, what do you see?"

"Carrots, eggs, and coffee," she replied.

Her mother brought her closer and asked her to feel the carrots. She did and noted that they were soft. The mother then asked the daughter to take an egg and break it. After pulling off the shell, she observed the hard boiled egg. Finally, the mother asked the daughter to sip the coffee. The daughter smiled as she tasted its rich aroma.

The daughter then asked, "What does it mean, mother?"

Her mother explained that each of these objects had faced the same adversity, boiling water. Each reacted differently. The carrot went in strong, hard, and unrelenting. However, after being subjected to the boiling water, it softened and became weak. The egg had been fragile. Its thin outer shell had protected its liquid interior, but after sitting through the boiling water, its inside became hardened. The ground coffee beans were unique, however. After they were in the boiling water, they had changed the water. "Which are you?" she asked her daughter. "When adversity knocks on your door, how do you respond? Are you a carrot, an egg or a coffee bean?"

Think of this: Which am I? Am I the carrot that seems strong, but with pain and adversity do I wilt and become soft and lose my strength? Am I the egg that starts with a malleable heart, but changes with the heat? Did I have a fluid spirit, but after a death, a breakup, a financial hardship or some other trial, have I become hardened and stiff? Does my shell look the same, but on the inside am I bitter and tough with a stiff spirit and hardened heart? Or am I like the coffee bean? The bean actually changes the hot water, the very circumstance that brings the pain. When the water gets hot, it releases the fragrance and flavor.

If you are like the bean, when things are at their worst, you get better and change the situation around you. When the hour is the darkest and trials are their greatest, do you elevate yourself to another level? How do you handle adversity? Are you a carrot, an egg or a coffee bean?

May you have enough happiness to make you sweet, enough trials to make you strong, enough sorrow to keep you human and enough hope to make you happy. The happiest of people don't necessarily have the best of everything; they just make the most of everything that comes along their way. The brightest future will always be based on a forgotten past; you can't go forward in life until you let go of your past failures and heartaches. When you were born, you were crying and everyone around you was smiling. Live your life so at the end, you're the one who is smiling and everyone around you is crying.

Center of the Bible

What is the shortest chapter in the Bible?
(Answer - Psalms 117)
What is the longest chapter in the Bible?
(Answer - Psalms 119)
Which chapter is in the center of the Bible?
(Answer - Psalms 118)
Facts: There are 594 chapters before Psalms118 and there are 594 chapters after Psalms 118. Add these numbers up and you get 1188.
What is the center verse in the Bible?
(Answer - Psalms 118:8)
Does this verse say something significant about God's perfect will for our lives?
The next time someone says they would like to find God's perfect will for their lives and that they want to be in the center of His will, just send them to the center of His Word!
Psalms 118:8 (NKJV) *"It is better to trust in the LORD than to put confidence in man."*
Now isn't that odd how this worked out
(Or was God in the center of it)?

Change Your Ways

Memo from GOD... Effective immediately, please be aware that there are changes YOU need to make in YOUR life. These changes need to be completed in order that I may fulfill My promises to you to grant you peace, joy and happiness in this life. I apologize for any inconvenience, but after all that I am doing, this seems very little to ask of you. I know, I already gave you the 10 Commandments. Keep them. But follow these guidelines, also.

1. QUIT WORRYING Life has dealt you a blow and all you do is sit and worry. Have you forgotten that I am here to take all your burdens and carry them for you? Or do you just enjoy fretting overevery little thing that comes your way?

2. PUT IT ON THE LIST Something needs done or taken care of. Put it on the list. No, not YOUR list. Put it on MY to-do-list. Let ME be the one to take care of the problem. I can't help you until you turn it over to Me. And although My to-do-list is long, I am after all... God. I can take care of anything you put into My hands. In fact, if the truth were ever really known, I take care of a lot of things for you that you never even realize.

3. TRUST ME Once you've given your burdens to Me, quit trying to take them back. Trust in Me. Have the faith that I will take care of all your needs, your problems and your trials. Problems with the kids? Put them on My list. Problem with finances? Put it on My list. Problems with your emotional roller coaster? For My sake, put it on My list. I want to help you. All you have to do is ask.

4. LEAVE IT ALONE Don't wake up one morning and say, "Well, I'm feeling much stronger now, I think I can handle it from here." Why do you think you are feeling stronger now? It's simple. You gave Me your burdens and I'm taking care of them. I also renew your strength and cover you in my peace. Don't you know that if I give you these problems back, you will be right back where you started? Leave them with Me and forget about them. Just let Me do my job.

5. TALK TO ME I want you to forget a lot of things. Forget what was making you crazy. Forget the worry and the fretting because you know I'm in control. But there's one thing I pray you never forget. Please, don't forget to talk to Me - OFTEN! I love YOU! I want to hear your voice. I want you to include Me in on the things going on in your life. I want to hear you talk about your friends and family. Prayer is simply you having a conversation with Me. I want to be your dearest friend.

6. HAVE FAITH I see a lot of things from up here that you can't see from where you are. Have faith in Me that I know what I'm doing. Trust Me; you wouldn't want the view from My eyes. I will continue to care for you, watch over you, and meet your needs. You only have to trust Me. Although I have a much bigger task than you, it seems as if you have so much trouble just doing your simple part. How hard can trust be?

7. SHARE You were taught to share when you were only two years old. When did you forget? That rule still applies. Share with those who are less fortunate than you. Share your joy with those who need encouragement. Share your laughter with those who haven't heard any in such a long time. Share your tears with those who have forgotten how to cry. Share your faith with those who have none.

8. BE PATIENT I managed to fix it so in just one lifetime you could have so many diverse experiences. You grow from a child to an adult, have children, change jobs many times, learn many trades, travel to so many places, meet thousands of people, and experience so much. How can you be so impatient then when it takes Me a little longer than you expect to handle something on My to-do-list? Trust in My timing, for My timing is perfect. Just because I created the entire universe in only six days, everyone thinks I should always rush, rush, rush.

9. BE KIND Be kind to others, for I love them just as much as I love you. They may not dress like you, or talk like you, or live the same way you do, but I still love you all. Please try to get along, for My sake. I created each of you different in some way. It would be too boring if you were all identical. Please, know I love each of your differences.

10. LOVE YOURSELF As much as I love you, how can you not love yourself? You were created by me for one reason only – to be loved, and to love in return. I am a God of Love. Love Me. Love your neighbors. But also love yourself. It makes My heart ache when I see you so angry with yourself when things go wrong. You are very precious to me. Don't ever forget that! *With all My heart I love YOU!* **~God ~**

Children!

To those of us who have children in our lives, whether they are our own, grandchildren, nieces and nephews, or students... here is something to make you laugh. Whenever your children are out of control, you can take comfort from the thought that even God's omnipotence did not extend to His own children.

After creating heaven and earth, God created Adam and Eve. And the first thing he said was, "Don't."

"Don't what?" Adam replied.

"Don't eat the forbidden fruit," God said.

"Forbidden fruit? We have forbidden fruit? Hey Eve... we have forbidden fruit!"

"No way!"   "Yes, way!"

"Do NOT eat the fruit!" said God.   "Why?"

"Because I am your Father and I said so!" God replied, (wondering why he hadn't stopped creation after making the elephants).

A few minutes later, God saw his children having an apple break and was he ticked!

"Didn't I tell you not to eat the fruit?" God, as our first parent, asked?

"Uh huh," Adam replied.

"Then why did you?" said the Father.

"I don't know," said Eve.

"She started it!" Adam said.   "Did not!"

"Did too!"   "DID NOT!"

Having had it with the two of them, God's punishment was that Adam and Eve should have children of their own.

Thus, the pattern was set and it has never changed! But there is reassurance in this story. If you have persistently and lovingly tried to give children wisdom and they haven't taken it, don't be hard on yourself. If God had trouble raising children, what made you think it would be a piece of cake for you?

Advice for the next six days: •If you have a lot of tension and you get a headache, do what it says on the aspirin bottle: "Take two aspirin" and "Keep away from children." •You spend the first 2 years of their life teaching them to walk! and talk. Then you spend the next 16 telling them to sit down and shut-up. •Grandchildren are God's reward for not killing your children. •Cleaning your house while your kids are still growing is like cleaning the driveway before it has stopped snowing. •We child proofed our home 3 years ago and they're still getting in! •Be nice to your kids. They'll choose your nursing home.

The Choice

After a few of the usual Sunday evening hymns, the church's pastor once again slowly stood up, walked over to the pulpit, and gave a very brief introduction of his childhood friend. With that, an elderly man stepped up to the pulpit to speak,

"A father, his son, and a friend of his son were sailing off the Pacific Coast," he began, "When a fast approaching storm blocked any attempt to get back to shore. The waves were so high, that even though the father was an experienced sailor, he could not keep the boat upright, and the three were swept into the ocean."

The old man hesitated for a moment, making eye contact with two teenagers who were, for the first time since the service began, looking somewhat interested in his story. He continued, "Grabbing a rescue line, the father had to make the most excruciating decision of his life...to which boy he would throw the other end of the line. He only had seconds to make the decision. The father knew that his son was a Christian, and he also knew that his son's friend was not. The agony of his decision could not be matched by the torrent of waves. As the father yelled out, 'I love you, son!' he threw the line to his son's friend. By the time he pulled the friend back to the capsized boat, his son had disappeared beyond the raging swells into the black of night. His body was never recovered.

By this time, the two teenagers were sitting straighter in the pew, waiting for the next words to come out of the old man's mouth. "The father," he continued, "Knew his son would step into eternity with Jesus, and he could not bear the thought of his son's friend stepping into an eternity without Jesus. Therefore, he sacrificed his son*. (How great is the love of God that He should do the same for us)*.

With that, the old man turned and sat back down in his chair as silence filled the room. Within minutes after the service ended, the two teenagers were at the old man's side. "That was a nice story," politely started one of the boys, "But I don't think it was very realistic for a father to give up his son's life in hopes that the other boy would become a Christian." "Well, you've got a point there," the old man replied, glancing down at his worn Bible. A big smile broadened his narrow face, and he once again looked up at the boys and said, "It sure isn't very realistic, is it? But I'm standing here today to tell you that THAT story gives me a glimpse of what it must have been like for God to give up His Son for me. You see....I was the son's friend who got rescued."

"I have called you friends, for everything that I have learned from my Father I have made known to you.." - John 15:15

Christian One-Liners

- Many folks want to serve God, but only as advisors.
- The good Lord didn't create anything without a purpose, but mosquitoes and sand gnats come close.
- When you get to your wit's end, you'll find God lives there.
- People are funny, they want the front of the bus, the middle of the road, and the back of the church.
- Quit griping about your church; if it was perfect you couldn't belong.
- If the church wants a better preacher, it only needs to pray for the one it has.
- God Himself does not propose to judge a man until he is dead. So why should you?
- Some minds are like concrete, thoroughly mixed up and permanently set.
- A lot of church members who are singing "Standing on the Promises" are just sitting on the premises.
- Be ye fishers of men. You catch them - He'll clean them.
- Don't wait for 6 strong men to take you to church.
- Forbidden fruits create many jams.
- God doesn't call the qualified, He qualifies the called.
- God loves everyone, but probably prefers "fruits of the spirit" over "religious nuts!"
- God promises a safe landing, not a calm passage.
- The Will of God will never take you to where the Grace of God will not protect you.

"Dear Father: Bless the person reading this in whatever it is that You know they need."

A Christmas Story

Pa never had much compassion for the lazy or those who squandered their means and then never had enough for the necessities. But for those who were genuinely in need, his heart was as big as all outdoors. It was from him that I learned the greatest joy in life comes from giving, not from receiving.

It was Christmas Eve 1881. I was fifteen years old and feeling like the world had caved in on me because there just hadn't been enough money to buy me the rifle that I'd wanted so bad that year for Christmas.

We did the chores early that night for some reason. I just figured Pa wanted a little extra time so we could read in the Bible. So after supper was over I took my boots off and stretched out in front of the fireplace and waited for Pa to get down the old Bible. I was still feeling sorry for myself and, to be honest, I wasn't in much of a mood to read scriptures.

But Pa didn't get the Bible, instead he bundled up and went outside. I couldn't figure it out because we had already done all the chores. I didn't worry about it long though, I was too busy wallowing in self-pity.

Soon Pa came back in. It was a cold clear night out and there was ice in his beard. "Come on, Matt," he said. "Bundle up good, it's cold out tonight." I was really upset then. Not only wasn't I getting the rifle for Christmas, now Pa was dragging me out in the cold, and for no earthly reason that I could see.

We'd already done all the chores, and I couldn't think of anything else that needed doing, especially not on a night like this. But I knew Pa was not very patient at one dragging one's feet when he'd told them to do something, so I got up and put my boots back on and got my cap, coat, and mittens. Ma gave me a mysterious smile as I opened the door to leave the house.

Something was up, but I didn't know what. Outside, I became even more dismayed. There in front of the house was the work team, already hitched to the big sled. Whatever it was we were wood-pile this morning. I got the children a little candy too. It just wouldn't be Christmas without a little candy."

We rode the two miles to Widow Jensen's pretty much in silence. I tried to think through what Pa was doing. We didn't have much by worldly standards. Of course, we did have a big woodpile, though most of what was left now was still in the form of logs that I would have to saw into blocks and split before we could use it. We also had meat and flour, so we could spare that, but I knew we didn't have any money, so why was Pa buying them shoes and candy? Really, why was he doing any of this?

Widow Jensen had closer neighbors than us. It shouldn't have been our concern We came in from the blind side of the Jensen house and unloaded the wood as quietly as possible, then we took the meat and flour and shoes to the door.

We knocked. The door opened a crack and a timid voice said, "Who is it?"

"Lucas Miles, Ma'am, and my son, Matt. Could we come in for a bit?"

Widow Jensen opened the door and let us in. She had a blanket wrapped around her shoulders. The children were wrapped in another and were sitting in front of the fireplace by a very small fire that hardly gave off any heat at all.

Widow Jensen fumbled with a match and finally lit the lamp. "We brought you a few things, Ma'am," Pa said and set down the sack of flour. I put the meat on the table. Then Pa handed her the sack that had the shoes in it. She opened it hesitantly and took the shoes out on e pair at a time. There was a pair for her and one for each of the children---sturdy shoes, the best, shoes that would last.

I watched her carefully. She bit her lower lip to keep it from trembling and then tears filled her eyes and started running down her cheeks. She looked up at Pa like she wanted to say something, but it wouldn't come out.

"We brought a load of wood too, Ma'am," Pa said, then he turned to me and said, "Matt, go bring enough in to last for awhile. Let's get that fire up to size and heat this place up."

I wasn't the same person when I went back out to bring in the wood. I had a big lump in my throat and, much as I hate to admit it, there were tears in my eyes too.

In my mind I kept seeing those three kids huddled around the fireplace and their mother standing there with tears running down her cheeks and so much gratitude in her heart that she couldn't speak. My heart swelled within me and a joy filled my soul that I'd never known before. I had given at Christmas many times before, but never when it had made so much difference.

I could see we were literally saving the lives of these people. I soon had the fire blazing and everyone's spirits soared. The kids started giggling when Pa handed them each a piece of candy and Widow Jensen looked on with a smile that probably hadn't crossed her face for a long time. She finally turned to us. "God bless you," she said. "I know the Lord himself has sent you. The children and I have been praying that he would send one of his angels to spare us."

In spite of myself, the lump returned to my throat and the tears welled up in my eyes again. I'd never thought of Pa in those exact terms before, but after Widow Jensen mentioned it I could see that it was probably true. I was sure that a better man than Pa had never walked the earth. I started remembering all the times he had gone out of his way for Ma and me, and many others. The list seemed endless as I thought on it.

Pa insisted that everyone try on the shoes before we left. I was amazed when they all fit and I wondered how he had known what sizes to get.

Then I guessed that if he was on an errand for the Lord that the Lord would make sure he got the right sizes.

Tears were running down Widow Jensen's face again when we stood up to leave. Pa took each of the kids in his big arms and gave them a hug.

They clung to him and didn't want us to go. I could see that they missed their pa, and I was glad that I still had mine.

At the door Pa turned to Widow Jensen and said, "The Missus wanted me to invite you and the children over for Christmas dinner tomorrow. The turkey will be more than the three of us can eat, and a man can get cantankerous if he has to eat turkey for too many meals. We'll be by to get you about eleven. It'll be nice to have some little ones around again. Matt, here, hasn't been little for quite a spell." I was the youngest. My two older brothers and two older sisters were all married and had moved away. Widow Jensen nodded and said, "Thank you, Brother Miles. I don't have to say, '"May the Lord bless you,' I know for certain that He will."

Out on the sled I felt a warmth that came from deep within and I didn't even notice the cold. When we had gone a ways, Pa turned to me and said, "Matt, I want you to know something. Your ma and me have been tucking a little money away here and there all year so we could buy that rifle for you, but we didn't have quite enough. Then yesterday a man who owed me a little money from years back came by to make things square. Your ma and me were real excited, thinking that now we could get you that rifle, and I started into town this morning to do just that. But on the way I saw little Jakey out scratching in the sawdust of the woodpile with his feet wrapped in those gunny sacks and I knew what I had to do. So, Son, I spent the money for shoes and a little candy for those children. I hope you understand."

I understood, and my eyes became wet with tears again. I understood very well, and I was so glad Pa had done it. Just then the rifle seemed very low on my list of priorities. Pa had given me a lot more. He had given me the look on Widow Jensen's face and the radiant smiles of her three children.

For the rest of my life, whenever I saw any of the Jensens, or split a block of wood, I remembered, and remembering brought back that same joy I felt riding home beside Pa that night. Pa had given me much more than a rifle that night, he had given me the best Christmas of my life. Count your blessings everyday, slowly and thoughtfully.

■ *Author Unknown*

Christmas – Teach the Children

Just a week before Christmas I had a visitor. I just finished the household chores for the night and was preparing to go to bed, when I heard a noise in the front of the house. I opened the door to the front room and, to my surprise, Santa himself stepped out from behind the Christmas tree. He placed a finger over his mouth so I would not cry out.

"What are you doing?" I started to ask. The words choked up in my throat, as I saw he had tears in his eyes. His usual jolly manor was gone. Gone was the eager boisterous soul we all know. He then answered me with a simple statement, "TEACH THE CHILDREN"

I was puzzled; what did he mean? He anticipated my question, and with one quick movement brought forth a miniature toy bag from behind the tree.

As I stood there bewildered, Santa said, "Teach the children! Teach them the meaning of Christmas. The meaning that children now-a-day's have forgotten!"

Santa then reached in his bag and pulled out a FIR TREE and placed it before the mantle. "Teach the children that the pure green color of the stately fir tree remains green all year around, depicting the everlasting hope of mankind. All the needles point heavenward, making it a symbol of man's thoughts toward heaven."

He again reached into his bag and pulled out a brilliant STAR. "Teach the children that the star was the heavenly sign of promises long ago. God promised a savior for the world, and the star was the sign of the fulfillment of that promise."

He then reached in his bag and pulled out a CANDLE. "Teach the children that the candle symbolizes that Christ is the light of the world, and when we see this great light we are reminded of He who displaced the darkness."

Once again he reached into his bag and removed a WREATH and placed it on the tree. "Teach the children that the wreath symbolizes the eternal nature of love. Real love never ceases. Love is one continuous round of affection."

He then pulled out from his bag an ornament of HIMSELF. "Teach the children that I, Santa Clause symbolize the generosity and good will we feel during the month of December."

He reached in again and pulled out a HOLLY LEAF. "Teach the children that the holly plant represents immortality. It represents the Crown of Thorns worn by our Savior. The red holly berries represent the blood shed by Him."

Next he pulled out a GIFT from the bag and said, "Teach the children that God so loved the world that He gave His only begotten Son..." "Thanks be to God for His unspeakable gift. Teach the children that the Wise Men bowed before the Holy Babe and presented Him with gold, frankincense, and myrrh. We should always give gifts in the same spirit as the Wise Men."

Santa reached in his bag and pulled out a CANDY CANE and hung it on the tree. "Teach the children that the candy cane represents the shepherds crook. The crook on the shepherds staff helps to bring back strayed sheep to the flock. The candy cane is the symbol that we are our brothers keeper."

He reached in again and pulled out an ANGEL. "Teach the children that it was the Angels that heralded in the glorious news of the Savior's birth. The angels sang Glory to God in the Highest, on earth peace, and good will toward men."

Suddenly I heard a soft twinkling sound, from his bag he pulled out a bell. "Teach the children that the lost sheep are found by the sound of the bell, it should bring man to the fold. The bell symbolizes guidance and return."

Santa looked back at the tree and was pleased. He looked back at me and I saw that the twinkle was back in his eyes. He said, "Teach the children the true meaning of Christmas, and to not put me in the center, for I am but a humble servant of the One That Is, and I bow down and worship Him, our Lord, our God."

Clutch This Tree
By Patricia Clark

I am but dust.
In me You chose
to breathe Your life,
Give me cause to dance,
Make each cell alive
So I could notice life.
I am so wowed!
Now Your intent is to
Sweep me from the floor,
Direct my daily path.
So You'll make me whole:
Repair from ravages of sin.
My part is to take it in,
Clutch tight this tree of life.
Choice choice is for me
Every moment of the day.
Will I follow my Lord
In the path of peace?
You unfold free access
Bought for me with the
Priceless blood of Christ.

Coat Hanger Angel

A woman was at work when she received a phone call that her young daughter was very sick with a fever. She left her work and stopped by the pharmacy to get some medication for her daughter. When returning to her car she found that she had locked her keys inside. She was in a hurry to get home to her sick daughter and didn't know what to do. She called her home and told the baby sitter what had happened and that she did not know what to do. The baby sitter told her that her daughter was getting worse.

She said, "You might find a coat hanger and use that to open the door." The woman looked around and found an old rusty coat hanger that had been thrown down on the ground possibly by someone else who at some time or other had locked their keys in their car. Then she looked at the hanger and said, "I don't know how to use this." So she asked God to send her some help.

Within five minutes an old rusty car pulled up, with a dirty, greasy, bearded man who was wearing an old biker skull rag. She thought, "Great, God. This is what you sent to help me?" But, she was desperate, so she was also very thankful. The man got out of his car and asked her if he could help. She said "Yes, my daughter is sick. I stopped to get her some medication and I locked my keys in my car. I must get home to her. Please, can you use this hanger to unlock my car?"

He said, "SURE". He walked over to the car, and in less than one minute the car was opened. She hugged the man and through her tears she said, "THANK YOU SO MUCH...you are a very nice man."

The man replied, "Lady, I am not a nice man. I just got out of prison today. I was in prison for car theft and have only been out for about an hour." The woman hugged the man again and with sobbing tears cried out loud . . **"THANK YOU, GOD, FOR SENDING ME A PROFESSIONAL!"** God has a plan.

A Columbine Thesis

We think our younger generation never notices anything, but in truth, they notice more than we as adults do, and they notice and understand more than what we want to admit they do.

A Columbine student wrote this very compelling thesis:

The paradox of our time in history is that we have taller buildings, but shorter tempers; wider freeways, but narrower viewpoints; we spend more, but have less; we buy more, but enjoy it less. We have bigger houses, but smaller families; more conveniences, but less time; we have more degrees, but less sense; more knowledge, but less judgment; more experts, but more problems; more medicine, but less wellness. We have multiplied our possessions, but reduced our values. We talk too much, love too seldom, and hate too often. We've learned how to make a living, but not a life; we've added years to life, but not life to years.

We've been all the way to the moon and back, but have trouble crossing the street to meet the new neighbor. We've conquered outer space, but not inner space; we've cleaned up the air, but polluted the soul; we've split the atom, but not prejudice. We have higher incomes, but lower morals; we've become long on quantity, but short on quality. These are the times of tall men and short character; steep profits and shallow relationships. These are the times of world peace, but domestic warfare; more leisure, but less fun; more kinds of food, but less nutrition. These are the days of two incomes, but more divorce; of fancier houses, but broken homes.

It is time when there is much in the show window and nothing in the stockroom; a time when technology can bring this letter to you, and a time when you can choose either to make a difference...or just hit delete.

Computer Gender

A language instructor was explaining to her class that, in French, nouns, unlike their English counterparts, are grammatically designated as masculine or feminine. "House," in French, is feminine-*"la Maison."* "Pencil," in French, is masculine-*"le crayon."*

One puzzled student asked, "...What gender is computer?..." The teacher did not know, and the word wasn't in her French dictionary. So for fun she split the class into two groups appropriately enough, by gender, and asked them to decide whether "computer" should be a masculine or feminine noun. Both groups were required to give four reasons for their recommendation.

The men's group decided that computers should definitely be of the feminine gender *("la computer"),* because:

1. No one but their creator understands their internal logic;

2. The native language they use to communicate with other computers is incomprehensible to everyone else;

3. Even the smallest mistakes are stored in long-term memory for possible later retrieval; and

4. As soon as you make a commitment to one, you find yourself spending half your pay check on accessories for it.

The women's group, however, concluded that computers should be masculine *("le computer"),* because:

1. In order to get their attention, you have to turn them on;

2. They have a lot of data but they are still clueless;

3. They are supposed to help you solve problems, but half the time they ARE the problem; and

4. As soon as you commit to one, you realize that if you'd waited a little longer, you could have gotten a better model.

(THE WOMEN WON!)

Counting the Pecans

On the outskirts of town, there was a big old pecan tree by the cemetery fence. One day two boys filled up a bucketful of nuts and sat down by the tree, out of sight, and began dividing the nuts. "One for you, one for me. One for you, one for me," said one boy. Several were dropped and rolled down toward the fence. Another boy came riding along the road on his bicycle.

As he passed, he thought he heard voices from inside the cemetery. He slowed down to investigate. Sure enough, he heard, "One for you, one for me. One for you, one for me."

He just knew what it was. "Oh my," he shuddered, "it's Satan and the Lord dividing the souls at the cemetery. He jumped back on his bike and rode off. Just around the bend he met an old man with a cane, hobbling along. "Come here quick," said the boy, "you won't believe what I heard. Satan and the Lord are down at the cemetery dividing up the souls."

The man said, "Beat it, kid, can't you see it's hard for me to walk." When the boy insisted, though, the man hobbled to the cemetery.

Standing by the fence they heard, "One for you, one for me. One for you, one for me."

The old man whispered, "Boy, you've been tellin' the truth. Let's see if we can see the devil himself." Shaking with fear, they peered through the fence, yet were still unable to see anything. The old man and the boy gripped the wrought iron bars of the fence tighter and tighter as they tried to get a glimpse of Satan.

At last they heard, "One for you, one for me. And one last one for you. That's all, now let's go get those nuts down by the fence, and we'll be done."

They say the old guy made it back to town 5 minutes before the boy!

The Creation of Pets

A newly discovered chapter in the Book of Genesis has provided the answer to "Where do pets come from?"

Adam and Eve said, "Lord, when we were in the garden, you walked with us every day. Now we do not see you any more. We are lonesome here, and it is difficult for us to remember how much you love us."

And God said, "No problem! I will create a companion for you that will be with you forever and who will be a reflection of my love for you, so that you will love me even when you cannot see me. Regardless of how selfish or childish or unlovable you may be, this new companion will accept you as you are and will love you as I do, in spite of yourselves."

And God created a new animal to be a companion for Adam and Eve.

And it was a good animal. And God was pleased.

And the new animal was pleased to be with Adam and Eve and he wagged his tail. And Adam said, "Lord, I have already named all the animals in the Kingdom and I cannot think of a name for this new animal."

And God said, "No problem. Because I have created this new animal to be a *reflection* of my love for you, his name will be a *reflection* of my own name, and you will call him DOG."

And Dog lived with Adam and Eve and was a companion to them and loved them. And they were comforted.

And God was pleased. And Dog was content. After a while, it came to pass that an angel came to the Lord and said, "Lord, Adam and Eve have become filled with pride. They strut and preen like peacocks and they believe they are worthy of adoration. Dog has indeed taught them that they are loved, but perhaps too well."

And God said, "No problem! I will create for them a companion who will be with them forever and who will see them as they are. The companion will remind them of their limitations, so they will know that they are not always worthy of adoration."

And God created CAT to be a companion to Adam and Eve. And Cat would not obey them. And when Adam and Eve gazed into Cat's eyes, they were reminded that they were not the supreme beings. And Adam and Eve learned humility. And they were greatly improved.

And God was pleased. And Dog was happy.

And Cat didn't give a rip one way or the other.

Cut Your Taxes In Half

I used to complain about my taxes. That is before my accountant gave me a surefire way to cut them in half. Perhaps you can use the same method if you choose.

As usual, at tax time I grumbled about the high amount of money that I paid each year in taxes. I wasn't concerned about what my tax dollars paid for. I was only concerned that state, federal, social security and other deductions took a huge chunk of my money. So like the vast majority of us, I complained.

So I sat in the chair as the accountant crunched through the numbers. Grumbling and complaining, I sat.

"I've got a way to instantly cut your taxes in half," he said.

My ears perked up. I was at full attention. In half! Did he realize how much money that would save me? Had I missed a deduction. Did he have a surefire tax shelter? Was there a legal loophole that I was eligible for? "How?" I excitedly asked.

"Simple, just cut your salary in half," the accountant answered.

That was over ten years ago, but it taught me a lesson that I will never forget. We complain when we are running short and we complain when we are blessed with much. The key is, there is always something to complain about and there is always something to be thankful for.

You choose. Thank goodness I have a high tax bill.

"D" in Devil

It was advertised that the devil was going to put his tools up for sale. On the date of the sale, the tools were placed for public inspection; each tool being marked with its sale price. They were a treacherous lot of implements...Hatred, Envy, Jealousy, Deceit, Lying, Pride, and so on.

Laid apart from the rest was a harmless looking tool, well worn and priced very high.

"What is the name of this tool?" asked one of the purchasers, pointing to it.

That is Discouragement", replied the devil.

"Why have you priced it so high?"

"Because it is more useful to me than the others. I can pry open and get inside a man's heart with that when I cannot get near him with my other tools. Once I get inside, I can make him do what I choose. It is badly worn because I use it on almost everyone, since very few people know that it belongs to me."

My friend, don't let Satan discourage you in anyway. You are God's child and have the victory already won. All you have to do is keep your faith on the King of Kings and Lord of Lords, Jesus Christ. The devil will not have a chance to discourage you, even with his best tools.

Daddy's Empty Chair

A man's daughter had asked the local pastor to come and pray with her father. When the pastor arrived, he found the man lying in bed with his head propped up on two pillows. An empty chair sat beside his bed.

The pastor assumed that the old fellow had been informed of his visit. "I guess you were expecting me," he said.

"No, who are you?" said the father.

The pastor told him his name and then remarked, "I saw the empty chair and I figured you knew I was going to show up."

"Oh yeah, the chair," said the bedridden man. "Would you mind closing the door?"

Puzzled, the pastor shut the door.

"I have never told anyone this, not even my daughter," said the man. "But all of my life I have never known how to pray. At church I used to hear the minister talk about prayer, but it went right over my head. I abandoned any attempt at prayer," the old man continued, "until one day four years ago, my best friend said to me, "Johnny, prayer is just a simple matter of having a conversation with Jesus. Here is what I suggest. Sit down in a chair; place an empty chair in front of you, and in faith see Jesus on the chair. It's not spooky because he promised; 'I will be with you always'. Then just speak to him in the same way you're doing with me right now."

"So, I tried it and I've liked it so much that I do it a couple of hours every day. I'm careful though. If my daughter saw me talking to an empty chair, she'd either have a nervous breakdown or send me off to the funny farm."

The man of God was deeply moved by the story and encouraged the old man to continue on the journey. Then he prayed with him, anointed him with oil, and returned to the church.

Two nights later the daughter called to tell the pastor that her daddy had died that afternoon.

"Did he die in peace?" he asked.

"Yes, right before I left the house about two o'clock, he called me over to his bedside, told me he loved me and kissed me on the cheek. When I got back from the store an hour later, I found him dead. But there was something strange about his death. Apparently, just before Daddy died, he leaned over and rested his head on the chair beside the bed. What do you make of that?"

The pastor wiped a tear from his eye and said, "I wish we could all go like that."

Prayer is one of the best free gifts we receive.
I asked God for water, He gave me an ocean.
I asked God for a flower, He gave me a garden.
I asked God for a friend, He gave me all of YOU

The Daffodil Principle.

Several times my daughter had telephoned to say, "Mother, you must come see the daffodils before they are over." I wanted to go, but it was a two-hour drive from Laguna to Lake Arrowhead.

"I will come next Tuesday," I promised, a little reluctantly, on her third call. Next Tuesday dawned cold and rainy. Still, I had promised, and so I drove there. When I finally walked into Carolyn's house and hugged and greeted my grandchildren, I said, "Forget the daffodils, Carolyn! The road is invisible in the clouds and fog, and there is nothing in the world except you and these children that I want to see bad enough to drive another inch!"

My daughter smiled calmly and said, "We drive in this all the time, Mother."

"Well, you won't get me back on the road until it clears, and then I'm heading for home!" I assured her.

"I was hoping you'd take me over to the garage to pick up my car."

"How far will we have to drive?"

"Just a few blocks," Carolyn said. "I'll drive. I'm used to this."

After several minutes, I had to ask, "Where are we going? This isn't the way to the garage!"

"We're going to my garage the long way," Carolyn smiled, "by way of the daffodils."

"Carolyn," I said sternly, "please turn around."

"It's all right, Mother, I promise. You will never forgive yourself if you miss this experience."

After about twenty minutes, we turned onto a small gravel road and I saw a small church. on the far side of the church, I saw a hand lettered sign that read, "Daffodil Garden." We got out of the car and each took a child's hand, and I followed Carolyn down the path. Then, we turned a corner of the path, and I looked up and gasped. Before me lay the most glorious sight. It looked as though someone had taken a great vat of gold and poured it down over the mountain in peak and slopes. The flowers were planted in majestic, swirling patterns, great ribbons and swaths of deep orange, white, lemon yellow, salmon, pink, saffron, and butter yellow. Each different-colored variety was planted as a group so that it swirled and flowed like its own river with its own unique hue. There were five acres of flowers.

"But who has done this?" I asked Carolyn.

"It's just one woman," Carolyn answered. "She lives on the property. That's her home" Carolyn pointed to a well-kept A-frame house that looked small and modest in the midst of all that glory. We walked up to the house.

On the patio, we saw a poster. ***"Answers to the Questions I Know You Are Asking"*** was the headline. The first answer was a simple one. "50,000 bulbs," it read. The second answer was, "One at a time, by one woman. Two hands, two feet, and very little brain." The third answer was, "Began in 1958." There it was, The Daffodil Principle.

For me, that moment was a life-changing experience I thought of this woman whom I had never met, who, more than forty years before, had begun, one bulb at a time to bring her vision of beauty and joy to an obscure mountaintop. Still, just planting one bulb at a time, year after year, had changed the world. This unknown woman had forever changed the world in which she lived. She had created something of ineffable (indescribable) magnificence, beauty, and inspiration. The principle her daffodil garden taught is one of the greatest principles of celebration. That is, learning to move toward our goals and desires one step at a time--often just one baby step at a time--and learning to love the doing, learning to use the accumulation of time. When we multiply tiny pieces of time with small increments of daily effort, we too will find we can accomplish magnificent things. We can change the world.

"It makes me sad in a way," I admitted to Carolyn. "What might I have accomplished if I had thought of a wonderful goal thirty-five or forty years ago and had worked away at it 'one bulb at a time' through all those years. Just think what I might have been able to achieve!"

My daughter summed up the message of the day in her usual direct way. "Start tomorrow," she said. It's so pointless to think of the lost hours of yesterdays. The way to make learning a lesson of celebration instead of a cause for regret is to only ask, "How can I put this to use today?"

So, stop waiting... Until your car or home is paid off. Until you get a new car or home. Until your kids leave the house. Until you go back to school. Until you finish school. Until you lose 10 lbs. Until you gain 10 lbs. Until you get married. Until you get a divorce. Until you have children. Until you retire. Until summer. Until spring. Until winter. Until fall. Until you die.

There is no better time than right now to be happy. Happiness is a journey, not a destination. So work like you don't need the money. Love like you've never been hurt, and dance like no one's watching.

sent by Kathy Currier

Darrell Scott's Testimony

I guess our national leaders didn't expect this, hmm? On Thursday, Darrell Scott, the father of Rachel Scott, a victim of the Columbine High School shootings in Littleton, Colorado, was invited to address the House Judiciary Committee's subcommittee. What he said to our national leaders during this special session of Congress was painfully truthful. They were not prepared for what he was to say, nor was it received well. It needs to be heard by every parent, every teacher, every politician, every sociologist, every psychologist, and every so-called expert! These courageous words spoken by Darrell Scott are powerful, penetrating, and deeply personal. There is no doubt that God sent this man as a voice crying in the wilderness. The following is a portion of the transcript:

"Since the dawn of creation there has been both good & evil in the hearts of men and women. We all contain the seeds of kindness or the seeds of violence. The death of my wonderful daughter, Rachel Joy Scott, and the deaths of that heroic teacher, and the other eleven children who died must not be in vain. Their blood cries out for answers.

"The first recorded act of violence was when Cain slew his brother Abel out in the field. The villain was not the club he used.. Neither was it the NCA, the National Club Association. The true killer was Cain, and the reason for the murder could only be found in Cain's heart. "In the days that followed the Columbine tragedy, I was amazed at how quickly fingers began to be pointed at groups such as the NRA. I am not a member of the NRA. I am not a hunter. I do not even own a gun. I am not here to represent or defend the NRA - because I don't believe that they are responsible for my daughter's death. Therefore I do not believe that they need to be defended. If I believed they had anything to do with Rachel's murder I would be their strongest opponent.

"I am here today to declare that Columbine was not just a tragedy-it was a spiritual event that should be forcing us to look at where the real blame lies! Much of the blame lies here in this room. Much of the blame lies behind the pointing fingers of the accusers themselves. I wrote a poem just four nights ago that expresses my feelings best. This was written way before I knew I would be speaking here today:

> Your laws ignore our deepest needs,
> Your words are empty air.
> You've stripped away our heritage,
> You've outlawed simple prayer.
> Now gunshots fill our classrooms,
> And precious children die.
> You seek for answers everywhere,
> And ask the question "Why?"
> You regulate restrictive laws,
> Through legislative creed.
> And yet you fail to understand,
> That God is what we need!

"Men and women are three-part beings. We all consist of body, soul, and spirit. When we refuse to acknowledge a third part of our make-up, we create a void that allows evil, prejudice, and hatred to rush in and reek havoc. Spiritual presences were present within our educational systems for most of our nation's history. Many of our major colleges began as theological seminaries. This is a historical fact. What has happened to us as a nation? We have refused to honor God, and in so doing, we open the doors to hatred and violence. And when something as terrible as Columbine's tragedy occurs -- politicians immediately look for a scapegoat such as the NRA. They immediately seek to pass more restrictive laws that contribute to erode away our personal and private liberties. We do not need more restrictive laws. Eric and Dylan would not have been stopped by metal detectors. No amount of gun laws can stop someone who spends months planning this type of massacre. The real villain lies within our own hearts. As my son Craig lay under that table in the school library and saw his two friends murdered before his very eyes, he did not hesitate to pray in school. I defy any law or politician to deny him that right! challenge every young person in America, and around the world, to realize that on April 20, 1999, at Columbine High School prayer was brought back to our schools. Do not let the many prayers offered by those students be in vain. Dare to move into the new millennium with a sacred disregard for legislation that violates your God-given right to communicate with Him. To those of you who would point your finger at the NRA, I give to you a sincere challenge. Dare to examine your own heart before casting the first stone! My daughter's death will not be in vain! The young people of this country will not allow that to happen!"

Do what the media did not - - let the nation hear this man's speech. Please send this out to everyone you can

A Daughter's Love

Her hair was up in a ponytail
Her favorite dress tied with a bow.
Today was Daddy's Day at school,
And she couldn't wait to go.
But her mommy tried to tell her,
That she probably should stay home.
Why the kids might not understand,
If she went to school alone.
But she was not afraid;
She knew just what to say.
What to tell her classmates
Of why he wasn't there today.
But still her mother worried,
For her to face this day alone.
And that was why once again,
She tried to keep her daughter home.
But the little girl went to school,
Eager to tell them all.
About a dad she never sees
A dad who never calls.
There were daddies along the wall in back,
For everyone to meet.
Children squirming impatiently,
Anxious in their seats.
One by one the teacher called,
A student from the class.
To introduce their daddy,
As seconds slowly passed.
At last the teacher called her name,
Every child turned to stare.
Each of them was searching,
For a man who wasn't there.
"Where's her daddy at?"
She heard a boy call out.

"She probably doesn't have one,"
Another student dared to shout.
And from somewhere near the back,
She heard a daddy say,
"Looks like another deadbeat dad,
Too busy to waste his day."
The words did not offend her,
As she smiled up at her Mom.
And looked back at her teacher,
Who told her to go on.
And with hands behind her back,
Slowly she began to speak.
And out from the mouth of a child,
Came words incredibly unique.
"My Daddy couldn't be here,
Because he lives so far away.
But I know he wishes he could be,
Since this is such a special day.
And though you cannot meet him,
I wanted you to know.
All about my daddy,
And how much he loves me so.
He loved to tell me stories
He taught me to ride my bike.
He surprised me with pink roses,
And taught me to fly a kite.
We used to share fudge sundaes,
And ice cream in a cone.
And though you cannot see him,
I'm not standing here alone.
"Cause my daddy's always with me,
Even though we are apart
I know because he told me,
He'll forever be in my heart"
With that, her little hand reached up,
And lay across her chest.
Feeling her own heartbeat,

Beneath her favorite dress.
And from somewhere in the crowd of dads,
Her mother stood in tears.
Proudly watching her daughter,
Who was wise beyond her years.
And when she dropped her hand back down,
Staring straight into the crowd.
She finished with a voice so soft,
But its message clear and loud.
"I love my daddy very much,
He's my shining star.
And if he could, he'd be here,
But heaven's just too far.
You see he was a fireman
And died just this past year
When airplanes hit the towers
And taught Americans to fear.
But sometimes when I close my eyes,
It's like he never went away."
And then she closed her eyes,
And saw him there that day.
And to her mother's amazement,
She witnessed with surprise.
A room full of daddies and children,
All starting to close their eyes.
Who knows what they saw before them,
Who knows what they felt inside.
Perhaps for merely a second,
They saw him at her side.
"I know you're with me Daddy,"
To the silence she called out.
And what happened next made believers,
Of those once filled with doubt.
Not one in that room could explain it,
For each of their eyes had been closed.
But there on the desk beside her,
Was a fragrant long-stemmed pink rose.

> And a child was blessed, if only for a moment,
> By the love of her shining bright star.
> And given the gift of believing,
> That heaven is never too far.
> *--Kelly Backhouse*

A Debt of Marbles

One day Mr. Miller was bagging some early potatoes for me at his produce stand. I noticed a small boy, delicate of bone and feature, ragged but clean, hungrily apprising a basket of freshly picked green peas. I paid for my potatoes but was also drawn to the display of fresh green peas. I am a pushover for creamed peas and new potatoes. Pondering the peas, I couldn't help overhearing the conversation between Mr. Miller and the ragged boy next to me.

"Hello Barry, how are you today?"

"H'lo, Mr. Miller. Fine, thank ya. Jus' admirin' them peas ... sure look good."

"They are good, Barry. How's your Ma?"

"Fine. Gittin' stronger alla' time."

"Good. Anything I can help you with?"

"No, Sir. Jus' admirin' them peas."

"Would you like to take some home?"

"No, Sir. Got nuthin' to pay for 'em with," answered Barry

"Well, what have you to trade me for some of those peas?" said Mr. Miller.

"All I got's my prize marble here."

"Is that right? Let me see it."

"Here 'tis. She's a dandy."

"I can see that. Hmmmmm, only thing is this one is blue and I sort of go for red. Do you have a red one like this at home?"

"Not zackley ... but almost."

"Tell you what. Take this sack of peas home with you and next trip this way let me look at that red marble."

"Sure will. Thanks Mr. Miller."

Mrs. Miller, who had been standing nearby, came over to help me. With a smile she said, "There are two other boys like him in our community, all three are in very poor circumstances. Jim just loves to bargain with them for peas, apples, tomatoes, or whatever. When they come back with their red marbles, and they always do, he decides he doesn't like red after all and he sends them home with a bag of produce for a green marble or an orange one, perhaps."

I left the stand smiling to myself, impressed with this man. A short time later I moved to Colorado but I never forgot the story of this man, the boys, and their bartering. Several years went by, each more rapid that the previous one. Just recently I had occasion to visit some old friends in that Idaho community and while I was there learned that Mr. Miller had died.

They were having his viewing that evening and knowing my friends wanted to go, I agreed to accompany them. Upon arrival at the mortuary we fell into line to meet the relatives of the deceased and to offer whatever words of comfort we could. Ahead of us in line were three young men. One was in an army uniform and the other two wore nice haircuts, dark suits and white shirts ... all very professional looking. They approached Mrs. Miller, standing composed and smiling by her husband's casket. Each of the young men hugged her, kissed her on the cheek, spoke briefly with her and moved on to the casket. Her misty light blue eyes followed them as, one by one, each young man stopped briefly and placed his own warm hand over the cold pale hand in the casket. Each left the mortuary awkwardly, wiping his eyes.

Our turn came to meet Mrs. Miller. I told her who I was and mentioned the story she had told me about the marbles. With her eyes glistening, she took my hand and led me to the casket. "Those three young men who just left were the boys I told you about. They just told me how they appreciated the things Jim "traded" them. Now, at last, when Jim could not change his mind about color or size ... they came to pay their debt."

"We've never had a great deal of the wealth of this world," she confided, "but right now, Jim would consider himself the richest man in Idaho." With loving gentleness she lifted the lifeless fingers of her deceased husband. Resting underneath were three exquisitely shined red marbles.

Moral: We will not be remembered by our words, but by our kind deeds. Life is not measured by the breaths we take, but by the moments that take our breath.

Today ... I wish you a day of ordinary miracles ....
A fresh pot of coffee you didn't make yourself ....
An unexpected phone call from an old friend ....
Green stoplights on your way to work.........
The fastest line at the grocery store ....
A good sing-along song on the radio ....
Your keys right where you left them
They say it takes a minute to find a special person,
An hour to appreciate them,
A day to love them,
But an entire life to forget them.
Send this to the people you'll never forget.

Do You Believe in Easter?

Edith Burns was a wonderful Christian who lived in San Antonio, Texas. She was the patient of a doctor by the name of Will Phillips. Dr. Phillips was a gentle doctor who saw patients as people. His favorite patient was Edith Burns.

One morning he went to his office with a heavy heart and it was because of Edith Burns. When he walked into that waiting room, there sat Edith with her big black Bible in her lap earnestly talking to a young mother sitting beside her. Edith

Burns had a habit of introducing herself in this way: "Hello, my name is Edith Burns. Do you believe in Easter?" Then she would explain the meaning of Easter and many times people would be saved.

Dr. Phillips went into the office and there he saw the head nurse, Beverly. Beverly had first met Edith when she was taking her blood pressure. Edith began by saying, "My name is Edith Burns. Do you believe in Easter?" Beverly said, "Why yes I do." Edith said, "Well, what do you believe about Easter?" Beverly said, "Well, it's all about egg hunts, going to church, and dressing up." Edith kept pressing her about the real meaning of Easter, and finally led her to a saving knowledge of Jesus Christ.

Dr. Phillips said, "Beverly, don't call Edith into the office quite yet. I believe there is another delivery taking place in the waiting room."

After being called back in the doctor's office, Edith sat down and when she took a look at the doctor she said, "Dr. Will, why are you so sad? Are you reading your Bible? Are you praying?"

Dr. Phillips said gently, "Edith, I'm the doctor and you're the patient." With a heavy heart he said, "Your lab report came back and it says you have cancer, and Edith, you're not going to live very long."

Edith said, "Why Will Phillips, shame on you. Why are you so sad? Do you think God makes mistakes? You have just told me I'm going to see my precious Lord Jesus, my husband, and my friends. You have just told me that I am going to celebrate Easter forever, and here you are having difficulty giving me my ticket!"

Dr. Phillips thought to himself, "What a magnificent woman this Edith Burns is!"

Edith continued coming to Dr. Phillips. Christmas came and the office was closed through January 3rd. On the day the office opened, Edith did not show up. Later that afternoon, Edith called Dr. Phillips and said she would have to be moving her story to the hospital and said, "Will, I'm very near home, so would you make sure that they put women in here next to me in my room who need to know about Easter."

Well, they did just that and women began to come in and share that room with Edith. Many women were saved. Everybody on that floor from staff to patients were so excited about Edith, that they started calling her Edith Easter; that is everyone except Phyllis Cross, the head nurse. Phyllis made it plain that she wanted nothing to do with Edith because she was a "religious nut." She had been a nurse in an army hospital. She had seen it all and heard it all. She was the original G.I. Jane. She had been married three times, she was hard, cold, and did everything by the book.

One morning the two nurses who were to attend to Edith were sick. Edith had the flu and Phyllis Cross had to go in and give her a shot. When she walked in, Edith had a big smile on her face and said, "Phyllis, God loves you and I love you, and I have been praying for you."

Phyllis Cross said, "Well, you can quit praying for me, it won't work. I'm not interested."

Edith said, "Well, I will pray and I have asked God not to let me go home until you come into the family."

Phyllis Cross said, "Then you will never die because that will never happen," and curtly walked out of the room.

Every day Phyllis Cross would walk into the room and Edith would say, "God loves you Phyllis and I love you, and I'm praying for you."

One day Phyllis Cross said she was literally drawn to Edith's room like a magnet would draw iron. She sat down on the bed and Edith said, "I'm so glad you have come, because God told me that today is your special day."

Phyllis Cross said, "Edith, you have asked everybody here the question, 'Do you believe in Easter?' but you have never ask me."

Edith said, "Phyllis, I wanted to many times, but God told me to wait until you asked, and now that you have asked." Edith Burns took her Bible and shared with Phyllis Cross the Easter Story of the death, burial and resurrection of Jesus Christ. Edith said, "Phyllis, do you believe in Easter? Do you believe that Jesus Christ is alive and that He wants to live in your heart?"

Phyllis Cross said, "Oh I want to believe that with all of my heart, and I do want Jesus in my life." Right there, Phyllis Cross prayed and invited Jesus Christ into her heart. For the first time Phyllis Cross did not walk out of a hospital room, she was carried out on the wings of angels.

Two days later, Phyllis Cross came in and Edith said, "Do you know what day it is?" Phyllis Cross said," Why Edith, it is Good Friday." Edith said, "Oh, no, for you every day is Easter. Happy Easter Phyllis!" Two days later, on Easter Sunday, Phyllis Cross came into work, did some of her duties and then went down to the flower shop and got some Easter lilies because she wanted to go up to see Edith and give her some Easter lilies and wish her a Happy Easter.

When she walked into Edith's room, Edith was in bed. That big black Bible was on her lap. Her hands were in that Bible. There was a sweet smile on her face. When Phyllis Cross went to pick up Edith's hand, she realized Edith was dead. Her left hand was on John 14:2 *"In my Father's house there are many mansions. I go to prepare a place for you, I will come again and receive you to Myself, that where I am, there you may be also."*

Her right hand was on Revelation 21:4, *"And God will wipe away every tear from their eyes, there shall be no more death nor sorrow, nor crying; and there shall be no more pain, for the former things have passed away."*

Phyllis Cross took one look at that dead body, and then lifted her face toward heaven, and with tears streaming down her cheeks, said, "Happy Easter, Edith - Happy Easter!"

Phyllis Cross left Edith's body, walked out of the room and over to a table where two student nurses were sitting. She said, "My name is Phyllis Cross. Do you believe in Easter?"

...Author Unknown

..oOo..

"And there shall be no night there; and they need no candle, neither light of the sun; for the Lord God giveth them light: and they shall reign forever and ever." (Rev. 22:5 KJV)

Do You Love Jesus?

Do You Love Him? This is a test: If you love Jesus share this
with at least 10 people...
I knelt to pray but not for long,
I had too much to do.
I had to hurry and get to work
For bills would soon be due.
So I knelt and said a hurried prayer,
And jumped up off my knees.
My Christian duty was now done
My soul could rest at ease.
All day long I had no time
To spread a word of cheer.
No time to speak of Christ to friends,
They'd laugh at me I'd fear.
No time, no time, too much to do,
That was my constant cry,
No time to give to souls in need
But at last the time, the time to die.
So I went before the Lord,
I came, I stood with downcast eyes.
For in his hands God held a book;
It was the book of life.
God looked into his book and said
"Your name I cannot find.
I once was going to write it down...
But never found the time"
<u>Now do you have the time to pass it on?</u>

Dr. Seuss; Computers

If a packet hits a pocket on a socket on a port,
and the bus is interrupted at a very last resort,

and the access of the memory makes your floppy disk abort,
then the socket packet pocket has an error to report.
If your cursor finds a menu item followed by a dash,
and the double-clicking icon puts your window in the trash,
and your data is corrupted 'cause the index doesn't hash,
then your situation's hopeless and your system's gonna crash!!!
If the label on the cable on the table at your house
says the network is connected to the button on your mouse,
but your packets want to tunnel to another protocol,
that's repeatedly rejected by the printer down the hall,
and your screen is all distorted by the side effects of gauss,
so your icons in the window are as wavy as a souse,
then you may as well reboot and go out with a bang,
'cuz sure as I'm a poet, the sucker's gonna hang.
When the copy of your floppy's getting sloppy in the disk,
and the macro code instructions cause unnecessary risk,
then you'll have to flash the memory and you'll want to RAM your ROM.
Quickly turn off the computer and be sure to tell your Mom!!
WELL! That certainly clears things up for me.

Drug Problem

We children (my brothers & sisters) had a "drug" problem when we were youngsters:

We were "drug" to church on Sunday morning.

We were "drug" to church for weddings and funerals.

We were "drug" to family reunions, no matter the weather.

We were "drug" to the bus stop to go to school every weekday.

We were "drug" by our ears when disrespectful to adults and teachers.

We were also "drug" to the woodshed when we disobeyed our parents.

Those "drugs" are still in our veins; and I believe they very much affect our behavior in what we do, say, and think. They are stronger than cocaine, crack, or heroin, and if today's kids had this kind of "drug" problem, perhaps America could be a better place.

"Eagles in a Storm"

Did you know that an eagle knows when a storm is approaching long before it breaks? The eagle will fly to some high spot and wait for the winds to come. When the storm hits, it sets its wings so that the wind will pick it up and lift it above the storm. While the storm rages below, the eagle is soaring above it.

The eagle does not escape the storm. It simply uses the storm to lift it higher. It rises on the winds that bring the storm.

When the storms of life come upon us -and all of us will experience them -we can rise above them by setting our minds and our belief toward God.

The storms do not have to overcome us. We can allow God's power to lift us above them. God enables us to ride the winds of the storm that bring sickness, tragedy, failure and disappointment in our lives. We can soar above the storm. Remember, it is not the burdens of life that weigh us down, it is how we handle them.

The Bible says, *"Those who hope in the Lord will renew their strength. They will soar on wings like eagles."* (Isaiah 40:31)

Take 60 seconds & prove to yourself the Power of Prayer! Simply say a small prayer for the person who sent you this, then send it on to five other people. Within hours, five people have prayed for you, and you caused a multitude of people to pray to God for other people.

Then sit back and watch the power of God work in your life for doing the thing that you know He loves.

Empty Bird Cage

(If this doesn't give you chills, nothing will..... It has been around before, but is worth reading again. Hope you are all as blessed as I was from this story.)

There once was a man named George Thomas, pastor in a small New England town. One Easter Sunday morning he came to the Church carrying a rusty, bent, old birdcage, and set it by the pulpit. Eyebrows were raised and, as if in response, Pastor Thomas began to speak...

"I was walking through town yesterday when I saw a young boy coming toward me swinging this bird cage. On the bottom of the cage were three little wild birds, shivering with cold and frightened. I stopped the lad and asked, "What you got there, son?"

"Just some old birds," came the reply.

"What are you gonna do with them?" I asked.

"Take 'em home and have fun with 'em," he answered. "I'm gonna tease 'em and pull out their feathers to make 'em fight. I'm gonna have a real good time."

"But you'll get tired of those birds sooner or later. What will you do?

"Oh, I got some cats," said the boy. "They like birds. I'll take 'em to them."

The pastor was silent for a moment. "How much do you want for those birds, son?"

"Huh?? !!! Why, you don't want them birds, mister. They're just plain old field birds. They don't sing. They ain't even pretty!"

"How much?" the pastor asked again.

The boy sized up the pastor as if he were crazy and said, "Ten dollars?"

The pastor reached in his pocket and took out a ten-dollar bill. He placed it in the boy's hand. In a flash, the boy was gone. The pastor picked up the cage and gently carried it to the end of the alley where there was a tree and a grassy spot.

Setting the cage down, he opened the door, and by softly tapping the bars persuaded the birds out, setting them free.

Well, that explained the empty birdcage on the pulpit, and then the pastor began to tell this story.... One day Satan and Jesus were having a conversation. Satan had just come from the Garden of Eden, and he was gloating and boasting.

"Yes, sir, I just caught the world full of people down there. Set me a trap, used bait I knew they couldn't resist. Got 'em all!"

"What are you going to do with them?" Jesus asked.

Satan replied, "Oh, I'm gonna have fun! I'm gonna teach them how to marry and divorce each other, how to hate and abuse each other, how to drink and smoke and curse. I'm gonna teach them how to invent guns and bombs and kill each other. I'm really gonna have fun!"

"And what will you do when you get done with them?" Jesus asked.

"Oh, I'll kill 'em," Satan glared proudly.

"How much do you want for them?" Jesus asked.

"Oh, you don't want those people. They ain't no good. Why, you'll take them and they'll just hate you. They'll spit on you, curse you and kill you. You don't want those people!!"

"How much? He asked again.

Satan looked at Jesus and sneered, "All your blood, tears and your life."

Jesus said, "DONE!" Then He paid the price.

The pastor picked up the cage, he opened the door and he walked from the pulpit....

P.S.: Isn't it funny how simple it is for people to trash God and then wonder why the world's going to hell? Isn't it funny how someone can say "I believe in God" but still follow Satan (who, by the way, also "believes" in God)? Isn't it funny how you can send a thousand jokes through e-mail and they spread like wildfire, but when you start sending messages regarding the Lord, people think twice about sharing?

Excuse Me...

One Sunday, a stranger found a nearby church, arrived there early, parked his car, and got out.

Another car pulled up along side him and the driver got out and said, "Excuse me, sir, I always park there!-- *You took my place!"*

The visitor went inside for Sunday School, found an empty seat, and sat down. A young lady from the church approached him and stated, "Sir, That's my seat... *You took my place."*

He was somewhat miffed by this rude welcome, but said nothing. After Sunday School, the man went into the sanctuary and sat down. Another member walked up to him and said, "That's where I always sit, you must be new here... *You're in my place!"* Even more disturbed by this treatment, he still said nothing.

Later as the congregation was praying for Christ to dwell among them, the visitor stood up, and his appearance began to change.... Horrible puncture scars were clearly visible on his forehead, on his hands and on his feet, which now wore sandals. Then his suit changed into a homespun robe. As He walked out someone noticed him and called out, "What happened to you?"

As a tear fell from His eye, He looked back and said, *"I took your place....."*

"And the King will tell them, 'I assure you, when you did it to one of the least of these my brothers and sisters, you were doing it to me'." (Matt 25:40 LB)

Failure

Failure is not fatal. Failure should be our teacher, not our undertaker.

"It should challenge us to new heights of accomplishments, not pull us to new depths of despair. From honest failure can come valuable experience." *(~William Arthur Ward~)*

"Far better it is to dare mighty things, to win glorious triumphs, even though checkered by failure, than to take rank with those poor spirits who neither enjoy much nor suffer much, because they live in the gray twilight that knows not victory nor defeat." *(~T. Roosevelt~)*

"Fall seven times, stand up eight." *(~Japanese proverb~)*
A MountainWings Moment #5097

Fair's Fair Football

This is a statement that was read over the PA system at the football game at Roane County High School, Kingston, Tennessee, by school Principal, Jody McLoud. I thought it was worth sharing with the world and hope you will forward it to all your friends. It shows clearly just how far this country has gone in the wrong direction.

"It has always been the custom at Roane County High School football games, to say a prayer and play the National Anthem, to honor God and Country, but due to a recent ruling by the Supreme Court, I am told that saying a Prayer is a violation of Federal Case Law. As I understand the law at this time,

I can use this public facility to approve of sexual perversion and call it "an alternate lifestyle," and if someone is offended, that's OK.

I can use it to condone sexual promiscuity, by dispensing condoms and calling it, "safe sex." If someone is offended, that's OK.

I can even use this public facility to present the merits of killing an unborn baby as a "viable means of birth control." If someone is offended, no problem.

I can designate a school day as "Earth Day" and involve students in activities to worship religiously and praise the goddess "Mother Earth" and call it "ecology."

I can use literature, videos and presentations in the classroom that depict people with strong, traditional Christian convictions as "simple minded" and "ignorant" and call it "enlightenment."

However, if anyone uses this facility to honor God and to ask Him to bless this event with safety and good sportsmanship, then Federal Case Law is violated. This appears to be inconsistent at best, and at worst, diabolical. Apparently, we are to be tolerant of everything and anyone, except God and His Commandments. Nevertheless, as a school principal, I frequently ask staff and students to abide by rules with which they do not necessarily agree. For me to do otherwise would be inconsistent at best, and at worst, hypocritical. I suffer from that affliction enough unintentionally. I certainly do not need to add an intentional transgression.

For this reason, I shall "Render unto Caesar that which is Caesar's," and refrain from praying at this time. However, if you feel inspired to honor, praise and thank God and ask Him, in the name of Jesus, to bless this event, please feel free to do so. As far as I know, that's not against the law----yet."

One by one, the people in the stands bowed their heads, held hands with one another and began to pray.

They prayed in the stands. They prayed in the team huddles. They prayed at the concession stand and they prayed in the Announcer's Box! The only place they didn't pray was in the Supreme Court of the United States of America - the Seat of "Justice" in the "one nation, under God."

Somehow, Kingston, Tennessee remembered what so many have forgotten. We are given the Freedom **OF** Religion, not the Freedom **FROM** Religion. Praise God that His remnant remains!

Celebrate Jesus in 2006 & 2007! Jesus said, *"If anyone is ashamed of me and my words, the Son of Man will be* ashamed of him when he comes in his glory and in the glory of the Father and of the holy angels." (Lk 9:26 NIV)

"Your hands made me and formed me; give me understanding to learn your commands. May those who fear you rejoice when they see me, for I have put my hope in your word. I know, Oh Lord, that your laws are righteous,
and in faithfulness you have afflicted me. May your unfailing love be my comfort, according to your promise to your servant. Let your compassion come to me that I may live, for your law is my delight." (Psalm 119:73-77 NIV).

The Filling Station

The old man sat in his gas station on a cold Christmas Eve. He hadn't been anywhere in years since his wife had passed away. He had no decorations, no tree, no lights. It was just another day to him. He didn't hate Christmas, just couldn't find a reason to celebrate. There were no children in his life. His wife had gone.

He was sitting there looking at the snow that had been falling for the last hour and wondering what it was all about when the door opened and a homeless man stepped through. Instead of throwing the man out, George, Old George as he was known by his customers, told the man to come and sit by the space heater and warm-up.

"Thank you, but I don't mean to intrude," said the stranger. "I see you're busy. I'll just go"

"Not without something hot in your belly," George turned and opened a wide mouth Thermos and handed it to the stranger. "It ain't much, but it's hot and tasty. Stew. Made it myself. When you're done there's coffee and it's fresh." Just at that moment he heard the "ding" of the driveway bell. "Excuse me, be right back," George said.

There in the driveway was an old 53 Chevy. Steam was rolling out of the front. The driver was panicked. "Mister can you help me!" said the driver with a deep Spanish accent. "My wife is with child and my car is broken."

George opened the hood. It was bad. The block looked cracked from the cold; the car was dead. "You ain't going anywhere in this thing," George said as he turned away.

"But mister. Please help...."The door of the office closed behind George as he went in. George went to the office wall and got the keys to his old truck, and went back outside. He walked around the building and opened the garage, started the truck and drove it around to where the couple was waiting.

"Here, you can borrow my truck," he said. "She ain't the best thing you ever looked at, but she runs real good."

George helped put the woman in the truck and watched as it sped off into the night. George turned and walked back inside the office.

"Glad I loaned em the truck. Their tires were shot too. That 'ol truck has brand new tires........" George thought he was talking to the stranger, but the man had gone. The thermos was on the desk, empty with a used coffee cup beside it.

"Well, at least he got something in his belly," George thought. George went back outside to see if the old Chevy would start. It cranked slowly, but it started. He pulled it into the garage where the truck had been. He thought he would tinker with it for something to do. Christmas Eve meant no customers. He discovered the block hadn't cracked, it was just the bottom hose on the radiator.

"Well, I can fix this," he said to himself. So he put a new one on. "Those tires ain't gonna get 'em through the winter either." He took the snow treads off of his wife's old Lincoln. They were like new and he wasn't going to drive the car.

As he was working he heard a shot being fired. He ran outside and beside a police car an officer lay on the cold ground. Bleeding from the left shoulder, the officer moaned, "Help me."

George helped the officer inside as he remembered the training he had received in the Army as a medic. He knew the wound needed attention.

"Pressure to stop the bleeding," he thought. The laundry company had been there that morning and had left clean shop towels. He used those and duct tape to bind the wound. "Hey, they say duct tape can fix anythin'," he said, trying to make the policeman feel at ease. "Something for pain," George thought. All he had was the pills he used for his back. "These ought to work." He put some water in a cup and gave the policeman the pills.

"You hang in there. I'm going to get you an ambulance." George said, but the phone was dead. "Maybe I can get one of your buddies on that there talk box out in your police car." He went out only to find that a bullet had gone into the dashboard destroying the two way radio. He went back in to find the policeman sitting up.

"Thanks," said the officer. "You could have left me there. The guy that shot me is still in the area."

George sat down beside him. "I would never leave an injured man in the Army and I ain't gonna leave you." George pulled back the bandage to check for bleeding. "Looks worse than what it is. Bullet passed right through 'ya. Good thing it missed the important stuff though. I think with time your gonna be right as rain."

George got up and poured a cup of coffee. "How do you take it?" he asked.

"None for me," said the officer.

"Oh, yer gonna drink this. Best in the city." Then George added: "Too bad I ain't got no donuts." The officer laughed and winced at the same time.

The front door of the office flew open. In burst a young man with a gun. "Give me all your cash! Do it now!" the young man yelled. His hand was shaking and George could tell that he had never done anything like this before.

"That's the guy that shot me!" exclaimed the officer.

87

"Son, why are you doing this?" asked George. "You need to put the cannon away. Somebody else might get hurt."

The young man was confused. "Shut up old man, or I'll shoot you, too. Now give me the cash!"

The cop was reaching for his gun. "Put that thing away," George said to the cop. "We got one too many in here now." He turned his attention to the young man. "Son, it's Christmas Eve. If you need the money, well then, here. It ain't much but it's all I got. Now put that pee shooter away." George pulled $150 out of his pocket and handed it to the young man, reaching for the barrel of the gun at the same time. The young man released his grip on the gun, fell to his knees and began to cry.

"I'm not very good at this am I? All I wanted was to buy something for my wife and son," he went on. "I've lost my job. My rent is due. My car got repossessed last week..."

George handed the gun to the cop. "Son, we all get in a bit of squeeze now and then. The road gets hard sometimes, but we make it through the best we can." He got the young man to his feet, and sat him down on a chair across from the cop. "Sometimes we do stupid things." George handed the young man a cup of coffee. "Being stupid is one of the things that makes us human. Comin' in here with a gun ain't the answer. Now sit there and get warm and we'll sort this thing out."

The young man had stopped crying. He looked over to the cop. "Sorry I shot you. It just went off. I'm sorry officer."

"Shut up and drink your coffee." the cop said. George could hear the sounds of sirens outside. A police car and an ambulance skidded to a halt. Two cops came through the door, guns drawn.

"Chuck! You ok?" one of the cops asked the wounded officer.

"Not bad for a guy who took a bullet. How did you find me?"

"GPS locator in the car. Best thing since sliced bread. Who did this?" the other cop asked as he approached the young man.

Chuck answered him, "I don't know. The guy ran off into the dark. Just dropped his gun and ran."

George and the young man both looked puzzled at each other. "That guy works here," the wounded cop continued.

"Yep," George said. "Just hired him this morning. Boy lost his job."

The paramedics came in and loaded Chuck onto the stretcher.

The young man leaned over the wounded cop and whispered, "Why?"

Chuck just said, "Merry Christmas, boy. And you too, George, and thanks for everything."

"Well, looks like you got one doozy of a break there. That ought to solve some of your problems." George went into the back room and came out with a box. He pulled out a ring box. "Here you go. Something for the little woman. I don't think Martha would mind. She said it would come in handy some day."

The young man looked inside to see the biggest diamond ring he ever saw. "I can't take this," said the young man. "It means something to you."

"And now it means something to you," replied George. "I got my memories. That's all I need." George reached into the box again. A toy airplane, a racing car and a little metal truck appeared next. They were toys that the oil company had left for him to sell. "Here's something for that little man of yours."

The young man began to cry again as he handed back the $150 that the old man had handed him earlier.

"And what are you supposed to buy Christmas dinner with? You keep that, too. Count it as part of your first week's pay." George said. "Now git home to your family."

The young man turned with tears streaming down his face. "I'll be here in the morning for work, if that job offer is still good."

"Nope. I'm closed Christmas day," George said. "See ya the day after."

George turned around to find that the stranger had returned. "Where'd you come from? I thought you left?"

"I have been here. I have always been here," said the stranger. "You say you don't celebrate Christmas. Why?"

"Well, after my wife passed away I just couldn't see what all the bother was. Puttin' up a tree and all seemed a waste of a good pine tree. Bakin' cookies like I used to with Martha just wasn't the same by myself and besides I was getting a little chubby."

The stranger put his hand on George's shoulder. "But you do celebrate the holiday, George. You gave me food and drink and warmed me when I was cold and hungry. The woman with child will bear a son and he will become a great doctor. The policeman you helped will go on to save 19 people from being killed by terrorists. The young man who tried to rob you will become a rich man and share his wealth with many people. That is the spirit of the season and you keep it as good as any man."

George was taken aback by all this stranger had said. "And how do you know all this?" asked the old man.

"Trust me, George. I have the inside track on this sort of thing. And when your days are done you will be with Martha again." The stranger moved toward the door. "If you will excuse me, George, I have to go now. I have to go home where there is a big celebration planned."

George watched as the man's old leather jacket and his torn pants turned into a white robe. A golden light began to fill the room. "You see, George, it's My birthday. Merry Christmas."

...*Author Unknown*   (...from *MountainWings.com - The Daily Inspirational Email*)

A Fire of Desire
By Walt Banko

Christmas tree, O Christmas tree, cut down in prime
Decorated with ornaments and lights, you look fine.
We're glad you're here for all to see,
Children most thrilled will jump with glee.
Christmas tree, O Christmas tree that everyone can see

Enjoy the season wherever you be.
In homes, halls, foyers and Malls
Under your branches we find trucks and dolls.
Visualize Santa riding aloft on his sled,
Then the vision of Christ on the Cross where He bled.

Peace on earth and good will to men'
To the turkey that applies, and also the hen
Here's hoping these thoughts make a little sense,
Brain works clearly; but, sometimes is dense.
Come in, out of a cold and blustery night
Where dancing flames are so right.
That which is prone most to desire
Comes out of the warmth of a flickering fire.
Out of the muck and confusion of thought
The best presents of all cannot be bought.

FIRE WALKING

By Bonnie Fulkerson

Health is not the absence of disease
But the facing of your problems and dealing with them.

THOUGH I WALK THROUGH THE VALLEY OF THE SHADOW OF DEATH, I WILL FEAR NO EVIL FOR I KNOW THAT YOU ARE WITH ME. YOU ARE WITH ME WHEN I LAY FEELING EMPTY INSIDE, WONDERING WHY I SHOULD GO ON? YOU ARE WITH ME WHEN I LAY
SHEDDING SILENT TEARS, THE BEATING OF MY HEART THE ONLY SOUND IN THE DARKNESS. YOU ARE WITH ME WHEN I FEEL LIKE SCREAMING, WANTING ONLY TO BE LEFT ALONE. YOU ARE WITH ME WHEN I FEEL LIKE KILLING, WISHING HIS NECK WAS WITHIN MY GRASP. YOU ARE WITH ME WHERE I LAY LOOKING UP FROM THE BOTTOM OF THAT DEEP

BLACK HOLE LONGING FOR THE PATCH OF LIGHT AT ITS TOP. YOU ARE WITH ME WHEN THE PAIN BECOMES SO UNBEARABLE I MUST FACE THE TRUTH AND STOP HOLDING RELIGION UP AS A WALL BETWEEN US. YOU ARE WITH ME WHERE I LAY, MEDICS WORKING OVER ME, TEACHING ME HUMILITY WITH THE UNCONTROLABLE FORCE OR YOUR POWER. YOU ARE WITH ME WHEN I HAVE LEARNED TO VALUE MYSELF AS MUCH AS YOU VALUE ME. YOU ARE MY ROD AND MY STAFF, YOU LEAD ME WHERE I SHOULD GO. YOUR TRUTH IS MY TRUTH AND YOU HAVE TAUGHT ME TO SAY, **"I WILL BE SILENT NO-MORE FOREVER"!**

First Grader's Insight

It's hard to believe these were actually done by first graders, but there are some good ones nonetheless. A first grade teacher collected well-known proverbs. She gave each child in her class the first half of a proverb and asked them to come up with the remainder of the proverb. Their insight may surprise you:

Better to be safe than..................punched by a 5th grader.
Strike while the ....bug is close.
It's always darkest before.........…...........Daylight Savings Time.
Never underestimate the power of...........................termites.
You can lead a horse to water but...…...................….......how?
Don't bite the hand that........................…..............looks dirty.
No news is.........................…….........................impossible.
A miss is as good as a...................…...........................Mr.
You can't teach an old dog new...…..........................….math.
If you lie down with dogs, you'll................stink in the morning.
Love all, trust........................……..............................me.
The pen is mightier than the..................................…..pigs.
An idle mind is.........…................…...........the best way to relax.

Where there's smoke there's..................................pollution.
Happy is the bride who........................gets all the presents.
A penny saved is..not much.
Two's company, three's........................the Musketeers.
Don't put off till tomorrow what..........you put on to go to bed.
Laugh and the whole world laughs with you, cry and............. you have to blow your nose.
None are so blind as.................................Stevie Wonder.
Children should be seen and not.............spanked or grounded.
If at first you don't succeed........................get new batteries.
You get out of something what you....see pictured on the box.
When the blind leadeth the blind..................get out of the way.
Better late than..pregnant.

For A Glass of Milk

One day, a poor boy who was selling goods from door to door to pay his way through school found he had only one thin dime left, and he was hungry. He decided he would ask for a meal at the next house. However, he lost his nerve when a lovely young woman opened the door. Instead of a meal, he asked for a drink of water.

She thought he looked hungry so brought him a large glass of milk. He drank it slowly and then asked, "How much do I owe you?"

"You don't owe me anything," she replied. "Mother has taught us never to accept pay for a kindness."

He said, "Then I thank you from my heart." As Howard Kelly left that house, he not only felt stronger physically, but his faith in God and man was strong also. He had been ready to give up and quit.

Many year's later that same young woman became critically ill. The local doctors were baffled. They finally sent her to the big city where they called in specialists to study her rare disease.

Dr. Howard Kelly was called in for the consultation. When he heard the name of the town she came from, a strange light filled his eyes. Immediately he rose and went down the hall of the hospital to her room. Dressed in his doctor's gown he went in to see her. He recognized her at once. He went back to the consultation room determined to do his best to save her life.

From that day he gave special attention to her case. After a long struggle, the battle was won. Dr. Kelly requested the business office to pass the final bill to him for approval. He looked at it, then wrote something on the edge and the bill was sent to her room.

She feared to open it, for she was sure it would take the rest of her life to pay for it all. Finally she looked and something caught her attention on the side of the bill. She read these words, "Paid in full with one glass of milk"   (Signed) *Dr. Howard Kelly.*

Tears of joy flooded her eyes as her happy heart prayed: "Thank You, God, that Your love has spread abroad through human hearts and hands."

From the Heart of God

I just had to write to tell you how much I love you and care for you. Yesterday, I saw you walking and laughing with your friends; I hoped that soon you'd want Me to walk along with you, too. So, I painted you a sunset to close your day and whispered a cool breeze to refresh you. I waited, but you never called... I just kept on loving you.

As I watched you fall asleep last night, I wanted so much to touch you. I spilled moonlight onto your face, trickling down your cheeks as so many tears have. You didn't even think of me; I wanted so much to comfort you.   The next day I exploded a brilliant sunrise into glorious morning for you. But, you woke up late and rushed off to work. And you didn't even notice. My sky became cloudy and My tears were the rain.

I love you. Oh, if you'd only listen. I really love you. I try to say it in the quiet of the green meadows and in the blue sky. The wind whispers My love throughout the treetops and spills it into the vibrant colors of all the flowers. I shout it to you in the thunder of the great waterfalls and compose love songs for birds to sing to you. I warm you with the clothing of My sunshine and perfume the air with nature's sweet scents. My love for you is deeper than any ocean and greater than any need in your heart. If you'd only realize how much I care.

My Dad sends His love. I want you to meet Him; He cares too. Fathers are just that way. So, please call on Me soon. No matter how long it takes, I'll wait… because I love you.

Your Friend, Jesus

Giver God
By Patricia Clark

Praise your name.
Thank you for the day.
Praise your name.
Happens it's a sunny day.
This day is about the love
You lavish on our life.
Gifts You've spread about
Colorful and so bright.
Lavish love all around
For me in which to bathe.
Thank you glorious Giver God
This day I'll praise your name

God Brings You To It

If God brings you to it, He will bring you through it.
In happy moments, praise God.
In difficult moments, seek God.
In quiet moments, worship God.
In painful moments, trust God.
Every moment, thank God.
Pass this message to seven people. You will receive a miracle tomorrow (Just do it)

God Lives Under the Bed

(Don't start reading this one until you've got more than 2 or 3 minutes to just "scan" over it. It deserves some time for reflection)-
Unknown Author

My brother Kevin thinks God lives under his bed. At least that's what I heard him say one night. He was praying out loud in his dark bedroom, and I stopped outside his closed door to listen. "Are you there, God?" he asked, "Where are you? Oh, I see. Under the bed."

I giggled softly and tiptoed off to my own room.

Kevin's unique perspectives are often a source of amusement. But that night something else lingered long after the humor. I realized for the first time the very different world Kevin lives in.

He was born 30 years ago, mentally disabled.. He reasons and communicates with the capabilities of a 7-year-old, and he always will.

He will probably always believe that God lives under his bed, that Santa Claus is the one who fills the space under our tree every Christmas, and that airplanes stay up in the sky because angels carry them.

Kevin is up before dawn each day, off to work at a workshop for the disabled, home to walk our cocker spaniel, return to eat his favorite macaroni and cheese for dinner, and later to bed. The only variations in the entire scheme are laundry, when he hovers excitedly over the washing machine like a mother with her newborn child. He does not seem dissatisfied. He lopes out to the bus every morning at 7:05, eager for a day of simple work. He wrings his hands excitedly while the water boils on the stove before dinner, and he stays up late twice a week to gather our dirty laundry for his next day's laundry chores.

And Saturdays-oh, the bliss of Saturdays! That's the day my Dad takes Kevin to the airport to have a soft drink, watch the planes land, and speculate loudly on the destination of each passenger inside. "That one's goin' to Chi-car-go!" Kevin shouts as he claps his hands. His anticipation is so great he can hardly sleep on Friday nights. And so goes his world of daily rituals and weekend field trips. He doesn't know what it means to be discontented.

His life is simple. He will never know the entanglements of wealth of power, and he does not care what brand of clothing he wears or what kind of food he eats. His needs have always been met, and he never worries that one day they may not be. His hands are diligent. Kevin is never so happy as when he is working. When he unloads the dishwasher or vacuums the carpet, his heart is completely in it. He does not shrink from a job when it is begun, and he does not leave a job until it is finished.

But when his tasks are done, Kevin knows how to relax. He is not obsessed with his work or the work of others. His heart is pure. He still believes everyone tells the truth, promises must be kept, and when you are wrong, you apologize instead of argue. Free from pride and unconcerned with appearances. Kevin is not afraid to cry when he is hurt, angry or sorry. He is always transparent, always sincere. And he trusts God.

Not confined by intellectual reasoning, when he comes to Christ, he comes as a child. Kevin seems to know God - to really be friends with Him in a way that is difficult for an "educated" person to grasp. God seems like his closest companion.

In my moments of doubt and frustrations with my Christianity, I envy the security Kevin has in his simple faith. It is then that I am most willing to admit that he has some divine knowledge that rises above my mortal questions. It is then I realize that perhaps he is not the one with the handicap - I am! My obligations, my fear, my pride, my circumstances -- they all become disabilities when I do not trust them to God's care.

Who knows if Kevin comprehends things I can never learn? After all, he has spent his whole life in that kind of innocence, praying after dark and soaking up the goodness and love of God.

And one day, when the mysteries of heaven are opened, and we are all amazed at how close God really is to our hearts, I'll realize that God heard the simple prayers of a boy who believed that God lived under his bed. Kevin won't be surprised at all!

When you receive this, say a prayer. That's all you have to do. There is nothing attached. This is powerful. Just send this to four people and do not break this, please.

Prayer is one of the best free gifts we receive. There is no cost, but a lot of rewards. **FRIENDS ARE ANGELS WHO LIFT US TO OUR FEET WHEN OUR WINGS HAVE TROUBLE REMEMBERING HOW TO FLY.**

God's Diet

......And God populated the earth with broccoli, cauliflower, spinach and yellow vegetables of all kinds, so Man and Woman would live long and healthy lives. *and Satan created McDonald's and brought forth the 99 cent double cheeseburger and Satan said to Man, "You want fries with that?" Man said, "Super-size them," and gained pounds.*

And God said, "Try my crispy salad." *and Satan added creamy dressings, bacon bits and shredded cheese, and* there was ice cream for dessert, and Woman gained pounds.

And God said, "I have sent you healthy heart vegetables and olive oil with which to cook them." **Then Satan brought out chicken-fried steak so big it needed its own platter, and Man gained pounds and his cholesterol went thru the roof.**

God brought forth running shoes and Man resolved to lose those extra pounds, and Satan created remote controls for cable TV so Man would not have to toil to change channels between ESPN and ESPN2, and Man gained pounds.

God said, "You're running up score, Devil," so God made the potato, naturally low in fat and brimming with nutrition, *but Satan peeled off the healthful skin and sliced the starchy center into chips and deep-fat fried them, and then he created sour cream dip. And Man clutched his remote control and ate the potato chips swaddled in cholesterol, and Satan saw and said, "It is good." And Man went into cardiac arrest.*

God sighed and created the quadruple bypass. *And Satan created HMO's...*

God's Grace

<u>GETTING THERE</u> A man dies and goes to Heaven. Of course, St. Peter meets him at the Pearly Gates. St. Peter says, "Here's how it works. You need 100 points to make it into heaven. You tell me all the good things you've done, and I give you a certain number of points for each item, depending on how good it was. When you reach 100 points, you get in." "Okay," the man says, "I was married to the same woman for 50 years and never cheated on her, even in my heart."

"That's wonderful," says St. Peter, "that's worth three points!". "Three points?" he says, slightly concerned. "Well, I attended church all my life and supported its ministry with my tithe and service." "Terrific!" says St. Peter. "That's certainly worth a point."

"One point!?!" he moans, now really getting worried. "I started a soup kitchen in my city and worked in a shelter for homeless veterans." "Fantastic, that's good for two more points," he says... "Two points!" the man cries. "At this rate the only way I get into Heaven is by the grace of God!"

St. Peter nods and says, "Bingo, 100 points! Come on in!"
(Reprint from Vol. One)

Good Deeds Pay

I've been thinking; (I do a lot of that since I retired) I wondered what would happen in this world if each one of us did a good deed every day for someone else. Yes, even for a complete stranger. I have found it to be very interesting. No, I don't do one every day, but that's my goal.

On a trip up north last year, I was cleaning my windshield before leaving our motel in Spokane WA. I noticed the car's windshield next to me was covered with bugs. They were from Texas. When I finished cleaning mine, I stepped over to clean theirs, and the owner caught me in the act. He couldn't believe that someone would do that. He really appreciated it. I told him about my goal and he thought it was an excellent idea. He said he would also give it a try. The responses may surprise you.

A few months back my wife and I stopped by our favorite Chinese restaurant. As we were getting ready to order, I couldn't help but overhear a conversation going on a couple of booths behind us. A little old man was explaining to the waiter that he was hungry but had no money. I flagged the waiter over to our table and told him to give the person anything he wanted and put it on my bill. I figured he couldn't possibly eat enough to tap me out. His portion came to only $4.25. The old guy never knew who paid it and I thought that was the end of that.

Later that night, I played in a poker game and had one of my rare winning nights. I won one hundred times the amount that I gave to that stranger. It was almost to the penny. When I mentioned it to the other players, they asked that I hold off on any good deeds the day we play cards.

Whenever I do something for someone else, I seem to get paid back much more than I give. I guess that's the way it works down here. Give it a try. Besides the satisfaction of doing something nice for someone, you never know. You may reap more than you sow. Hallelujah! *by **T. Steffanson**, Portland Fire Bureau*

Good Morning!

As you got up this morning, I watched you, and hoped you would talk to me, even if it was just a few words, asking my opinion or thanking me for something good that happened in your life yesterday. But I noticed you were too busy, trying to find the right outfit to wear.

When you ran around the house getting ready, I knew there would be a few minutes for you to stop and say hello, but you were too busy. At one point you had to wait, fifteen minutes with nothing to do except sit in a chair. I thought you would talk to me then, but instead you ran to the phone and called a friend to get the latest gossip.

I watched patiently all day long. With all your activities I guess you were too busy to say anything to me. I noticed that before lunch you looked around, maybe you felt embarrassed to talk to me, that is why you didn't bow your head. You glanced three or four tables over and you noticed some of your friends talking to me briefly before they ate, but you didn't. That's okay. There is still more time left, and I hope that you will talk to me yet.. You went home and it seems as if you had lots of things to do. After a few of them were done, you turned on the TV. I don't know if you like TV or not, just about anything goes there and you spend a lot of time each day in front of it not thinking about anything, just enjoying the show. I waited patiently again as you watched the TV and ate your meal, but again you didn't talk to me. Bedtime-I guess you felt too tired.. After you said goodnight to your family you plopped into bed and fell asleep in no time.

That's okay because you may not realize that I am always there for you. I've got patience, more than you will ever know. I even want to teach you how to be patient with others as well. I love you so much that I wait everyday for a nod, prayer or thought or a thankful part of your heart. It is hard to have a one-sided conversation. Well, you are getting up once again.

And once again I will wait, with nothing but love for you. Hoping that today you will give me some time. Have a nice day!

Your friend, GOD

Graham Interview

Jane Clayson of the "Early Show" asked Anne Graham (Billy Graham's daughter) how "God could let something like this happen" (referring to the Twin towers) . Anne Graham gave an extremely profound and insightful response.

She said "I believe that God is deeply saddened by this just as we are, but for years we have been telling God to get out of our schools, to get out of our government, and to get out of our lives and being the gentlemen that He is, I believe that He calmly backed out. How can we expect God to give us His blessing and His protection if we DEMAND He leave us alone? "

Grandmas & Grandkids

An elderly woman and her little grandson, whose face was sprinkled with bright freckles, spent the day at the zoo. Lots of children were waiting in line to get their cheeks painted by a local artist who was decorating them with tiger paws.

"You've got so many freckles, there's no place to paint!" a girl in the line said to the little fella. Embarrassed, the little boy dropped his head.

His grandmother knelt down next to him "I love your freckles. When I was a little girl I always wanted freckles, she said, while tracing her finger across the child's cheek. "Freckles are beautiful!"

The boy looked up, "Really?"

"Of course," said the grandmother. "Why, just name me one thing that's prettier than freckles."

The little boy thought for a moment, peered intensely into his grandma's face, and softly whispered, "Wrinkles."

.oOo

A grandmother was telling her little granddaughter what her own childhood was like. "We used to skate outside on a pond. I had a swing made from a tire; it hung from a tree in our front yard. We rode our pony. We picked wild raspberries in the woods.

The little girl was wide-eyed, taking this in. At last she said, "I sure wish I'd gotten to know you sooner."

.oOo.

My grandson was visiting one day when he asked, Grandma, do you know how you and God are alike?" I mentally polished my halo while I asked, "No, how are we alike?" "You're both old," he said.

.oOo.

When my grandson asked me how old I was, I teasingly replied "I'm not sure." "Look in your underwear, Grandma," he advised. "Mine says I'm four."

.oOo.

A Sunday school class was studying the Ten Commandments. They were ready to discuss the last one. The teacher asked if anyone could tell her what it was. Susie raised her hand, stood tall, and quoted, "Thou shall not take the covers off thy neighbor's wife."

.oOo.

Our five-year-old son Mark couldn't wait to tell his friend about the movie we had watched on television, "20,000 Leagues Under the Sea." The scenes with the submarine and the giant octopus had kept him wide-eyed.

In the middle of the telling, my husband interrupted Mark, "What caused the submarine to sink?" With a look of incredulity Mark replied, "Dad, it was the 20,000 leaks!!"

.oOo.

A second grader came home from school and said to her mother, "Mom, guess what? We learned how to make babies today." The mother, more than a little surprised, tried to keep her cool. "That's interesting," she said. "How do you make babies?" "It's simple," replied the girl. "You just change "y" to "i" and add "es."   (Wouldn't an English teacher love that one?)

.oOo.

" Give me a sentence about a public servant," said a teacher. The small boy wrote: "The fireman came down the ladder pregnant." The teacher took the lad aside to correct him. "Don't you know what pregnant means?" she asked. Sure," said the young boy confidently. "It means carrying a child."

.oOo.

A grandmother was surprised by her 7 year old grandson one morning. He had made her coffee. She drank what was the worst cup of coffee in her life. When she got to the bottom, there were three of those little green Army men in the cup. She said "Honey, what are these army men doing in my coffee?"

Her grandson said, "Grandma, it says on TV, "The best part of waking up is soldiers in your cup!"

.oOo.

A nursery school teacher was delivering a station wagon full of kids home one day when a fire truck zoomed past. Sitting in the front seat of the fire truck was a Dalmatian dog. The children started discussing the dog's duties.

"They use him to keep crowds back," said one youngster. "No," said another, "he's just for good luck" A third child brought the argument to a close..."They use the dogs", she said firmly, "to find the fire hydrant."

Grandpa's Hands

Grandpa, some ninety plus years, sat feebly on the patio bench. He didn't move, just sat with his head down staring at his hands. When I sat down beside him he didn't acknowledge my presence and the longer I sat I wondered if he was OK. Finally, not really wanting to disturb him but wanting to check on him at the same time, I asked him if he was OK. He raised his head and looked at me and smiled.

"Yes, I'm fine, thank you for asking," he said in a clear strong voice.

"I didn't mean to disturb you, grandpa, but you were just sitting here staring at your hands and I wanted to make sure you were OK."

"Have you ever looked at your hands, he asked. I mean really looked at your hands?"

I slowly opened my hands and stared down at them. I turned them over, palms up and then palms down. "No, I guess I had never really looked at my hands," I said, as I tried to figure out the point he was making.

Grandpa smiled and related this story: "Stop and think for a moment about the hands you have; how they have served you well throughout your years. These hands, though wrinkled, shriveled and weak have been the tools I have used all my life to reach out and grab and embrace life. They braced and caught my fall when as a toddler I crashed upon the floor. They put food in my mouth and clothes on my back. As a child my mother taught me to fold them in prayer. They tied my shoes and pulled on my boots. They dried the tears of my children and caressed the love of my life. They held my rifle and wiped my tears when I went off to war. They have been dirty, scraped and raw, swollen and bent. They were uneasy and clumsy when I tried to hold my newborn son. Decorated with my wedding band, they showed the world that I was married and loved someone special. They wrote the letters home and trembled and shook when I buried my parents and spouse and walked my daughter down the aisle. Yet, they were strong and sure when I dug my buddy out of a foxhole and lifted a plow off of my best friends foot.

"They have held children, consoled neighbors, and shook in fists of anger when I didn't understand. They have covered my face, combed my hair, and washed and cleansed the rest of my body. They have been sticky, wet, bent, broken, dried, and raw. To this day when not much of anything else of me works real well, these hands hold me up, lay me down, and continue to fold in prayer. These hands are the mark of where I've been and the ruggedness of my life.

"But more importantly, it will be these hands that God will reach out and take when He leads me home. And with my hands He will lift me to His side and there I will use these hands to touch the face of Christ!"

"Am I OK? Yes, I certainly am."   *from Adrianne G.*

The Greatest Golfer In The World!

"Who's the greatest golfer in the world?" That's the question the golf instructor asked my son. As I walked in the door, the golf instructor recognized me. He was the same instructor who taught golf to my late father. He taught me. I was bringing my son to be taught.

He looked at my son, not quite five, and asked him a question that anyone following the golf world would know. He expected the universal answer. *(One man has revolutionized the sport of golf. Virtually every major sport has dropped in participation while golf has skyrocketed. The rocket that has carried the sport upward is one young man).*

The golf pro figured that my son should know that. "Who's the greatest golfer in the world?" My son without blinking an eye or missing a beat instantly answered. He knew without hesitation or doubt. "My daddy," he answered.

The instructor smiled, understanding both the correctness and error of the answer. I smiled, realizing the responsibility placed within my hands for the shaping of a young mind.

Do you realize to someone, especially if you have children, you are the greatest in the world? YOU are the greatest influence, the greatest guide, and the one your children are most likely to imitate, not the celebrity. Makes you feel like a Tiger doesn't it? *(~A MountainWings Original 114]~)*

A Grizzled Atheist

An Atheist was taking a walk through the woods. *What majestic trees! What powerful rivers! What beautiful animals!* he thought.

As he was walking alongside the river he heard a rustling in the bushes behind him. He turned to look. He saw a seven-foot grizzly charge towards him. He ran as fast as he could up the path. He looked over his shoulder and saw that the bear was closing in on him. He tripped and fell on the ground. He rolled over to pick himself up but saw the bear right on top of him, reaching for him with his left paw and raising his right paw to strike him.

At that instant the Atheist cried out: "Oh my God!..."

Time stopped. The bear froze. The forest was silent. As a bright light shone upon the man, a voice came out of the sky:

"You deny my existence for all of these years, teach others I don't exist, and even credit creation to a cosmic accident. Do you expect me to help you out of this predicament? Am I to count you as a believer?"

The Atheist looked directly into the light, "It would be hypocritical of me to suddenly ask You to treat me as a Christian now, but perhaps could you make the BEAR a Christian?"

"Very well," said the voice.

The light went out. The sounds of the forest resumed. And then the bear dropped his right paw, brought both paws together and bowed his head and spoke: "Lord, bless this food, which I am about to receive from thy bounty through Christ our Lord, Amen."

He Is... ...

He is the First and Last, the Beginning and the End!
He is the keeper of Creation and the Creator of all!
He is the Architect of the universe and
The Manager of all times.
He always was, He always is, and He always will be...
Unmoved, Unchanged, Undefeated, and never Undone!
He was bruised and brought healing!
He was pierced and eased pain!
He was persecuted and brought freedom!
He was dead and brought life!
He is risen and brings power!
He reigns and brings Peace!
The world can't understand him,
The armies can't defeat Him,
The schools can't explain Him, and
The leaders can't ignore Him.
Herod couldn't kill Him,
The Pharisees couldn't confuse Him, and
The people couldn't hold Him!
Nero couldn't crush Him,

Hitler couldn't silence Him,
The New Age can't replace Him, and
Donahue can't explain Him away!
He is light, love, longevity, and Lord.
He is goodness, Kindness, Gentleness, and God.
He is Holy, Righteous, mighty, powerful, and pure.
His ways are right,   His word is eternal,
His will is unchanging, and   His mind is on me.
He is my Redeemer,   He is my Savior,
He is my guide, and   He is my peace!
He is my Joy,   He is my comfort,
He is my Lord, and   He rules my life!
I serve Him because His bond is love,
His burden is light, and
His goal for me is abundant life.
I follow Him because He is the wisdom of the wise,
The power of the powerful,
The ancient of days, the ruler of rulers,
The leader of leaders, the overseer of the overcomers, and
The sovereign Lord of all that was and is and is to come.
And if that seems impressive to you, try this for size.
His goal is a relationship with ME!
He will never leave me,   Never forsake me,
Never mislead me,   Never forget me,
Never overlook me, and
Never cancel my appointment in His appointment book!
When I fall, He lifts me up!   When I fail, He forgives!
When I am weak, He is strong!
When I am lost, He is the way!
When I am afraid, He is my courage!
When I stumble, He steadies me!
When I am hurt, He heals me!
When I am broken, He mends me!
When I am blind, He leads me!
When I am hungry, He feeds me!
When I face trials, He is with me!
When I face persecution, He shields me!

When I face problems, He comforts me!
When I face loss, He provides for me!
When I face Death, He carries me Home!
He is everything for everybody, everywhere,
Every time, and every way.
He is God, He is faithful.   I am His, and He is mine!
My Father in heaven can whip the father of this world.
If you're wondering why I feel so secure, understand this...
He said it and that settles it.
God is in control, I am on His side, and
That means all is well with my soul.
Everyday is a blessing for GOD Is!

I love the Lord and thank Him for all that he does in my life, therefore, I am passing this on. Yes I do love Jesus. He is my source of existence and my Savior. He keeps me functioning each and everyday. Without Him, I will be nothing. *"Without Him, I am nothing but with Him I can do all things."*   Philippians 4:13

Heaven, Please

Mommy went to Heaven,
But I need her here today,
My tummy hurts and I fell down,
I need her right away,
Operator can you tell me how
To find her in this book?
Is heaven in the yellow part,
I don't know where to look.
I think my daddy needs her too,
At night I hear him cry.
I hear him call her name sometimes,
But I really don't know why.

Maybe if I call her,
She will hurry home to me.
Is Heaven very far away,
Is it across the sea?
She's been gone a long, long time
She needs to come home now!
I really need to reach her,
I simply don't know how.
Help me find the number please,
Is it listed under "Heaven"?
I can't read these big big words,
I am only seven.
I'm sorry operator,
I didn't mean to make you cry,
Is your tummy hurting too,
Or is there something in your eye?
If I call my church
Maybe they will know.
Mommy said when we need help
That's where we should go.
Thank you operator,
I'll give them a call.

Highway 109

A drunk man in an Oldsmobile
They said had run the light
That caused the six-car pileup
On 109 that night.
When broken bodies lay about
And blood was everywhere,
The sirens screamed out elegies,
For death was in the air.
A mother, trapped inside her car,

Was heard above the noise;
Her plaintive plea near split the air:
"Oh, God, please spare my boys!"
She fought to loose her pinned hands;
She struggled to get free,
But mangled metal held her fast
In grim captivity.
Her frightened eyes then focused
On where the back seat once had been,
But all she saw was broken glass and
Two children's seats crushed in.
Her twins were nowhere to be seen;
She did not hear them cry,
And then she prayed they'd been thrown free,
"Oh, God, don't let them die!"
Then firemen came and cut her loose,
But when they searched the back,
They found therein no little boys,
But the seat belts were intact.
They thought the woman had gone mad
And was traveling alone,
But when they turned to question her,
They discovered she was gone.
Policemen saw her running wild
And screaming above the noise
In beseeching supplication,
"Please help me find my boys!
They're four years old and wear blue shirts;
Their jeans are blue to match."
One cop spoke up,
"They're in my car,
And they don't have a scratch.
They said their daddy put them there
And gave them each a cone,
Then told them both to wait for Mom
To come and take them home.
I've searched the area high and low,

But I can't find their dad.
He must have fled the scene,
I guess, and that is very bad."
The mother hugged the twins and said,
While wiping at a tear,
"He could not flee the scene, you see,
For he's been dead a year."
The cop just looked confused and asked,
"Now, how can that be true?"
The boys said, "Mommy, Daddy came
And left a kiss for you.
He told us not to worry
And that you would be all right,
And then he put us in this car with
The pretty, flashing light.
We wanted him to stay with us,
Because we miss him so,
But Mommy, he just hugged us tight
And said he had to go.
He said someday we'd understand
And told us not to fuss,
And he said to tell you, Mommy,
He's watching over us."
The mother knew without a doubt
That what they spoke was true,
For she recalled their dad's last words,
"I will watch over you."
The firemen's notes could not explain
The twisted, mangled car,
And how the three of them escaped
Without a single scar.
But on the cop's report was scribed,
In print so very fine,
An angel walked the beat tonight
On Highway 109.
He who has a thousand friends has not a friend to spare

The 7 Second Prayer Just repeat this phrase and see how God moves... "Lord, I love you and I need you, come into my heart, and bless me, my family, my home, and my friends, in Jesus' name. Amen."

History Forgotten

This is worth remembering, because it is true. It's familiar territory, but those of you that graduated from school after the early 60's were probably never taught this. Our courts have seen to that!

Did you know that 52 of the 55 signers of "The Declaration of Independence" were orthodox, deeply committed, Christians? That they all believed in the Bible as the divine truth, the God of scripture, and His personal intervention. It is the same Congress that formed the American Bible Society, immediately after creating the Declaration of Independence, the Continental Congress voted to purchase and import 20,000 copies of Scripture for the people of this nation.

Patrick Henry, who is called the firebrand of the American Revolution, is still remembered for his words, "Give me liberty or give me death"; but in current textbooks, the context of these words is omitted. Here is what he actually said: "An appeal to arms and the God of hosts is all that is left us. But we shall not fight our battle alone. There is a just God that presides over the destinies of nations. The battle, sir, is not to the strong alone. Is life so dear or peace so sweet as to be purchased at the price of chains and slavery? Forbid it Almighty God. I know not what course others may take, but as for me, give me liberty, or give me death."

These sentences have been erased from our textbooks. Was Patrick Henry a Christian? The following year, 1776, he wrote this: "It cannot be emphasized too strongly or too often that this great Nation was founded not by religionists, but by Christians;

not on religions, but on the Gospel of Jesus Christ. For that reason alone, people of other faiths have been afforded freedom of worship here."

Consider these words that **Thomas Jefferson** wrote in the front of his well-worn Bible: "I am a real Christian, that is to say, a disciple of the doctrines of Jesus. I have little doubt that our whole country will soon be rallied to the unity of our creator." He was also the chairman of the American Bible Society, which he considered his highest and most important role.

On July 4, 1821, **President John Adams** said, "The highest glory of the American Revolution was this: "It connected in one indissoluble bond the principles of civil government with the principles of Christianity."

Calvin Coolidge, the 30th President of the United States reaffirmed this truth, when he wrote, "The foundations of our society and our government rest so much on the teachings of the Bible that it would be difficult to support them if faith in these teachings would cease to be practically universal in our country."

In 1782, the United States Congress voted this resolution: "The Congress of the United States recommends and approves the Holy Bible for use in all schools."

William Holmes McGuffey is the author of the McGuffey Reader, which was used for over 100 years in our public schools with over 125 million copies sold until it was stopped in 1963. **President Abraham Lincoln** called him the "Schoolmaster of the Nation."

Listen to these words of Mr. McGuffey: "The Christian religion is the religion of our country. From it are derived our nation, on the character of God, on the great moral Governor of the universe. On its doctrines are founded the peculiarities of our free Institutions. From no source has the author drawn more conspicuously than from the sacred Scriptures. From all these extracts from the Bible, I make no apology."

Of the first 108 universities founded in America, 106 were distinctly Christian, including the first, Harvard University, chartered in 1636. In the original Harvard Student Handbook, rule number 1 was that students seeking entrance must know

Latin and Greek so that they could study the Scriptures: "Let every student be plainly instructed and earnestly pressed to consider well, the main end of his life and studies, is, to know God and Jesus Christ, which is eternal life, John 17:3; and therefore to lay Jesus Christ as the only foundation for our children to follow the moral principles of the Ten Commandments."

James Madison, the primary author of the Constitution of the United States, said this: "We have staked the whole future of all our political constitutions upon the capacity of each of ourselves to govern ourselves by the moral principles of the Ten Commandments."

Today, we are asking God to bless America. But, how can He bless a Nation that has departed so far from Him? Prior to September 11, He was not welcome in America. Most of what you read in this article has been erased from our textbooks. Revisionists have rewritten history to remove the truth about our country's Christian roots.

You are encouraged to share with others, so that the truth of our nation's history will be told. John 3:16. For God so loved the world, that he gave his only begotten Son, that whoever believes in Him shall not perish but have eternal life!

This information shared is only a drop of cement to help secure a foundation that is crumbling daily in a losing war that most of the country doesn't even know is raging on, in, and around them...

Please do your bit and share this with as many as possible and make the ill-informed aware of what they once had.

The Holiday

In Florida, an atheist became incensed over the preparation for Easter and Passover holidays and decided to contact the local ACLU about the discrimination inflicted on atheists by the constant celebrations afforded to Christians and Jews with all their holidays while the atheists had no holiday to celebrate.

The ACLU jumped on the opportunity to once again pick up the cause of the godless and assigned their sharpest attorneys to the case. The case was brought before a wise judge who after listening to the long, passionate presentation of the ACLU lawyers, promptly banged his gavel and declared, "Case dismissed!"

The lead ACLU lawyer immediately stood and objected to the the ruling and said, "Your honor, how can you possibly dismiss this case? Surely the Christians have Christmas, Easter, and many other observances. And the Jews--why in addition to Passover they have Yom Kippur and Hanukkah... and yet my client and all other atheists have no such holiday!"

The judge leaned forward in his chair and simply said, "Obviously you and your client are too confused to know about, or for that matter, even celebrate the atheists' holiday!"

The ACLU lawyer pompusly said, "We are aware of no such holiday for atheists. Just when might that be, your honor?'

The judge said, "Well it comes every year on exactly the same date - April 1st!"

The fool says in his heart, "There is no God."

Homeless Visitor

I sat, with two friends, in the picture window of a quaint restaurant just off the corner of the Town Square. The food and the company were both especially good that day. As we talked, my attention was drawn outside, across the street. There, walking into town, was a man who appeared to be carrying all his worldly goods on his back. He was carrying, a well-worn sign that read, "I will work for food." My heart sank. I brought him to the attention of my friends and noticed that others around us had stopped eating to focus on him. Heads moved in a mixture of sadness and disbelief. We continued with our meal, but his image lingered in my mind.

We finished our meal and went our separate ways. I had errands to do and quickly set out to accomplish them. I glanced toward the town square, looking somewhat half-heartedly for the strange visitor. I was fearful, knowing that seeing him again would call some response.

I drove through town and saw nothing of him. I made some purchases at a store and got back in my car. Deep within me, the Spirit of God kept speaking to me: "Don't go back to the office until you've at least driven once more around the square." Then with some hesitancy, I headed back into town.

As I turned the square's third corner. I saw him. He was standing on the steps of the storefront church, going through his sack. I stopped and looked; feeling both compelled to speak to him, yet wanting to drive on. The empty parking space on the corner seemed to be a sign from God: an invitation to park. I pulled in, got out and approached the town's newest visitor.

"Looking for the pastor?" I asked.

"Not really," he replied, "just resting."

"Have you eaten today?"

"Oh, I ate something early this morning."

"Would you like to have lunch with me?"

"Do you have some work I could do for you?"

"No work," I replied. "I commute here to work from the city, but I would like to take you to lunch."

"Sure," he replied with a smile. As he began to gather his things, I asked some surface questions.

"Where you headed?"

"St. Louis."

"Where you from?"

"Oh, all over; mostly Florida."

"How long you been walking?"

"Fourteen years," came the reply. I knew I had met someone unusual.

We sat across from each other in the same restaurant I had left earlier. His face was weathered slightly beyond his 38 years.

His eyes were dark yet clear, and he spoke with an eloquence and articulation that was startling. He removed his jacket to reveal a bright red T-shirt that said, "Jesus is The Never Ending Story."

Then Daniel's story began to unfold. He had seen rough times early in life. He'd made some wrong choices and reaped the consequences. Fourteen years earlier, while packing across the country, he had stopped on the beach in Daytona. He tried to hire on with some men who were putting up a large tent and some equipment. A concert, he thought. He was hired, but the tent would not house a concert but revival services, and in those services he saw life more clearly. He gave his life over to God. "Nothing's been the same since," he said, " I felt the Lord telling me to keep walking, and so I did, some 14 years now."

"Ever think of stopping?" I asked.

"Oh, once in a while, when it seems to get the best of me. But God has given me this calling. I give out Bibles. That's what's in my sack. I work to buy food and Bibles, and I give them out when His Spirit leads."

I sat amazed. My homeless friend was not homeless. He was on a mission and lived this way by choice. The question burned inside for a moment and then I asked: "What's it like to walk into a town carrying all your things on your back and to show your sign?"

"Oh, it was humiliating at first. People would stare and make comments. Once someone tossed a piece of half-eaten bread and made a gesture that certainly didn't make me feel welcome. But then it became humbling to realize that God was using me to touch lives and change people's concepts of other folks like me." My concept was changing, too. We finished our dessert and gathered his things. Just outside the door, he paused. He turned to me and said, "Come Ye blessed of my Father and inherit the kingdom I've prepared for you. For when I was hungry you gave me food, when I was thirsty you gave me drink, a stranger and you took me in." I felt as if we were on holy ground.

"Could you use another Bible?" I asked. He said he preferred a certain translation. It traveled well and was not too heavy. It was also his personal favorite.

"I've read through it 14 times," he said.

"I'm not sure we've got one of those, but let's stop by our church and see." I was able to find my new friend a Bible that would do well, and he seemed very grateful. "Where are you headed from here?"

"Well, I found this little map on the back of this amusement park coupon."

"Are you hoping to hire on there for awhile?"

"No, I just figure I should go there. I figure someone under that star right there needs a Bible, so that's where I'm going next." He smiled, and the warmth of his spirit radiated the sincerity of his mission. I drove him back to the Town Square where we'd met two hours earlier, and as we drove, it started raining. We parked and unloaded his things.

"Would you sign my autograph book?" he asked. "I like to keep messages from folks I meet." I wrote in his little book that his commitment to his calling had touched my life. I encouraged him to stay strong. And I left him with a verse of scripture, **"I know the plans I have for you," declared the Lord, "plans to prosper you and not to harm you. Plans to give you a Future and a hope."** (Jeremiah 29:11 NIV)

"Thanks, man," he said. "I know we just met and we're really just strangers, but I love you."

"I know," I said, "I love you, too." "The Lord is good!" "Yes, He is. How long has it been since someone hugged you?" I asked.

"A long time," he replied. And so on the busy street corner in the drizzling rain, my new friend and I embraced, and I felt deep inside that I had been changed. He put his things on his back, smiled his winning smile and said, "See you in the New Jerusalem."

"I'll be there!" was my reply. He began his journey again. He headed away with his sign dangling from his bedroll and pack of Bibles. He stopped, turned and said, "When you see something that makes you think of me, will you pray for me?"

"You bet," I shouted back, "God bless." "God bless." And that was the last I saw of him.

Late that evening as I left my office, the wind blew strong. The cold front had settled hard upon the town. I bundled up and hurried to my car. As I sat back and reached for the emergency brake, I saw them... a pair of well-worn brown work gloves neatly laid over the length of the handle. I picked them up and thought of my friend and wondered if his hands would stay warm that night without them. Then I remembered his words: "If you see something that makes you think of me, will you pray for me?" Today his gloves lie on my desk in my office. They help me to see the world and its people in a new way, and they help me remember those two hours with my unique friend and to pray for his ministry. "See you in the New Jerusalem," he said. Yes, Daniel, I know I will... If this story touched you, forward it to a friend!

"I shall pass this way but once. Therefore, any good that I can do or any kindness that I can show, let me do it now, for I shall not pass this way again." Let's continue to pray for one another. God bless you and have a nice day!

The Hospital Window:

Two men, both seriously ill, occupied the same hospital room. One man was allowed to sit up in his bed for an hour each afternoon to help drain the fluid from his lungs. His bed was next to the room's only window. The other man had to spend all his time flat on his back. The men talked for hours on end. They spoke of their wives and families, their homes, their jobs, their involvement in the military service, where they had been on vacation.

Every afternoon when the man in the bed by the window could sit up, he would pass the time by describing to his roommate all the things he could see outside the window. The man in the other bed began to live for those one hour periods where his world would be broadened and enlivened by all the activity and color of the world outside. The window overlooked a park with a lovely lake. Ducks and swans played on the water while children sailed their model boats. Young lovers walked arm in arm amidst flowers of every color and a fine view of the city skyline could be seen in the distance. As the man by the window described all this in exquisite detail, the man on the other side of the room would close his eyes and imagine the picturesque scene.

One warm afternoon the man by the window described a parade passing by. Although the other man couldn't hear the band - he could see it in his mind's eye as the gentleman by the window portrayed it with descriptive words.

Days and weeks passed.

One morning, the day nurse arrived to bring water for their baths only to find the lifeless body of the man by the window, who had died peacefully in his sleep. She was saddened and called the hospital attendants to take the body away.

As soon as it seemed appropriate, the other man asked if he could be moved next to the window. The nurse was happy to make the switch, and after making sure he was comfortable, she left him alone. Slowly, painfully, he propped himself up on one elbow to take his first look at the real world outside. He strained to slowly turn to look out the window beside the bed. It faced a blank wall.

The man asked the nurse what could have compelled his deceased roommate who had described such wonderful things outside this window. The nurse responded that the man was blind and could not even see the wall. She said, "Perhaps he just wanted to encourage you."

Epilogue: There is tremendous happiness in making others happy, despite our own situations... Shared grief is half the sorrow, but happiness when shared, is doubled...If you want to feel rich, just count all the things you have that money can't buy...Today is a gift, that's why it is called the present.

The Hug

It was one of those mornings. You know the type. Things are tense. Our infant son had been up all night. My wife's eyes (along with the rest of her) were weary. My oldest son, the five-year-old, wasn't feeling his best either. He was slow getting ready for school. He understandably didn't feel like going. It was just one of those mornings. You know the type.

As I drove him to school, he was quiet. When parents are tense and tired, the children feel it. They know by word and gesture when their acts and attitudes are less tolerated. After being fussed at, he was sullen. It was one of those mornings. You know the type.

I walked him to his classroom as usual. He walked in, removed his coat and hung it up. I usually give my son a hug before I leave him in class. I knew today he really needed a big hug, and maybe, so did I. He came forward with his arms outstretched. I bowed down, clasped my arms around him, closed my eyes and hugged him tight. Normally, I would only hug him for two or three seconds but on this morning, I held him tight as the seconds ticked by like dashed lines on the highway.

All of a sudden, I felt him get heavier. Still clinging to my son, I opened my eyes. I understood why he had gotten heavier. His feet were off the ground. He had curled his legs up and his heels were only inches away from his backside. He clung. I clung. Sometimes in life no words are needed.

As he folded his legs up and trusted his father to carry all of his weight, he didn't get heavier to my spirit. I actually felt lighter. It was a ritual repeated countless times through countless years from countless parents to countless children. The touch and embrace between a parent and a child, make them both feel more secure. It was one of those mornings. You know the type.

~A MountainWings Original~ #2121

I Asked God...

I asked God to take away my habit. God said, **"No. It is not for me to take away, but for you to give it up."**

I asked God to make my handicapped child whole. God said, **"No. His spirit is whole, his body is only temporary."**

I asked God to grant me patience. God said, **"No. Patience is a byproduct of tribulations; it isn't granted, it is learned."**

I asked God to give me happiness. God said, **"No. I give you blessings; Happiness is up to you."**

I asked God to spare me pain. God said, **"No. Suffering draws you apart from worldly cares and brings you closer to me."**

I asked God to make my spirit grow. God said, **"No. You must grow on your own, but I will prune you to make you fruitful.".**

I asked God for all the things that I might enjoy in life. God said, **"No. I will give you life, so that you may enjoy all things."**

I ask God to help me LOVE others, as much as He loves me. God said... "**Ahhhh, finally you have the idea**".

THIS DAY IS YOURS DON'T THROW IT AWAY May God Bless You, "To the world you might be one person, but to one person you just might be the world"

Ice Cream For the Soul

Last week I took my children to a restaurant. My six-year-old son asked if he could say grace. As we bowed our heads he said, "God is good. God is great. Thank you for the food, and I would even thank you more if Mom gets us ice cream for dessert. And Liberty and Justice for all! Amen!"

Along with the laughter from the other customers, nearby I heard a woman remark, "That's what's wrong with this country. Kids today don't even know how to pray. Asking God for ice-cream! Why, I never!"

Hearing this, my son burst into tears and asked me, "Did I do it wrong? Is God mad at me?" As I held him and assured him that he had done a terrific job and God was certainly not mad at him, an elderly gentleman approached the table.

He winked at my son and said, "I happen to know that God thought that was a great prayer."

"Really?" my son asked.

"Cross my heart." Then in theatrical whisper he added (indicating the woman whose remark had started this whole thing), "Too bad she never asks God for ice cream. A little ice cream is good for the soul sometimes."

Naturally, I bought my kid's ice cream at the end of the meal. My son stared at his for a moment and then did something I will remember the rest of my life.

He picked up his sundae and without a word walked over and placed it in front of the woman. With a big smile he told her, "Here, this is for you. Ice cream is good for the soul sometimes, and my soul is good already."

'Jesus' Is Watching You

A burglar broke into a house one night. He shined his flashlight around, looking for valuables, and when he picked up a CD player to place in his sack, a strange, disembodied voice echoed from the dark saying, "Jesus is watching you."

He nearly jumped out of his skin, clicked his flashlight out, and froze. When he heard nothing more after a bit, he shook his head, promised himself a vacation after the next big score, then clicked the light on and began searching for more valuables.

Just as he pulled the stereo out so he could disconnect the wires, clear as a bell he heard, "Jesus is watching you." Freaked out, he shone his light around frantically, looking for the source of the voice. Finally, in the corner of the room, his flashlight beam came to rest on a parrot.

"Did you say that?" He hissed at the parrot.

"Yep," the parrot confessed, then squawked, "I'm just trying to warn you."

The burglar relaxed. "Warn me, huh? Who in the world are you?"

"Moses," replied the bird.

"Moses?" the burglar laughed. "What kind of people would name a bird Moses?"

"The same kind of people that would name their Rottweiler Jesus."

Fourth of July Poem
by Al Allaway

Happy Birthday, to our Uncle Sam,
Hoping you'd get us out of a jam!

Once in schools, on a knee we could pray,
To Almighty GOD; have it Your way…

Founding Fathers did agree,
That our God has made us free.

But now, there are people offended
By His Holy Word… They've pretended

It's fiction not really existing.
So, now your help we are enlisting,

Whisper in the High Court's ear,
Make this a Jubilee year.

Kansas Senate Prayer

I thought you might enjoy this interesting prayer given in Kansas at the opening session of their Senate. It seems prayer still upsets some people.

When Minister Joe Wright was asked to open the new session of the Kansas Senate, everyone was expecting the usual generalities, but this is what they heard:

"Heavenly Father, we come before you today to ask your forgiveness and to seek your direction and guidance. We know Your Word says, "Woe to those who call evil good," but that is exactly what we have done. We have lost our spiritual equilibrium and reversed our values. We confess that. We have ridiculed the absolute truth of Your Word and called it Pluralism. We have exploited the poor and called it the lottery, We have rewarded laziness and called it welfare, We have killed our unborn and called it choice, We have shot abortionists and called it justifiable, We have neglected to discipline our children and called it building self-esteem, We have abused power and called it politics, We have coveted our neighbor's possessions and called it ambition, We have polluted the air with profanity and pornography and called it freedom of expression, We have ridiculed the time-honored values of our forefathers and called it enlightenment. Search us, Oh, God, and know our hearts today; cleanse us from every sin and set us free. Guide and bless these men and women who have been sent: to direct us to the center of Your will and to openly ask these things in the name of Your Son, the living Savior, Jesus Christ. Amen!"

The response was immediate. A number of legislators walked out during the prayer in protest. The majority, however, remained and 'brought the house down' with their applause.

Keepers

I grew up in the fifties with practical parents – a Mother, God love her, who washed aluminum foil after she cooked in it, then reused it. She was the original recycle queen, before they had a name for it... And a Father who was happier getting old shoes fixed than buying new ones.

Their marriage was good, their dreams focused. Their best friends lived barely a wave away. I can see them now, Dad in trousers, tee shirt and a hat and Mom in a house dress, lawn mower in one hand, dishtowel in the other.

It was the time for fixing things -- a curtain rod, the kitchen radio, screen door, the oven door, the hem in a dress.

Things we keep... It was a way of life, and sometimes it made me crazy. All that re-fixing, re-heating, renewing, I wanted just once to be wasteful. Waste meant affluence. Throwing things away meant there'd always be more.

But then my Mother died, and on that clear summer's night, in the warmth of the hospital room, I was struck with the pain of learning that sometimes there isn't any 'more.'

Sometimes, what we care about most gets all used up and goes away...never to return. So...while we have it...it's best we love it.....and care for it.....and fix it when it's broken.....and heal it when it's sick.

This is true.....for marriage.....and old cars.....and children with bad report cards.....and dogs with bad hips..... and good friends....and sisters...... aging parents.....and grandparents.

We keep them because they are worth it, because we are worth it.

Some things we keep... Like a best friend that moved away -- or – a classmate we grew up with. There are just some things that make life important, like people we know who are special.....and so, we keep them close! Now send this to all those people that are "keepers" in your life...like you!!

Kids Letters to God

Dear God, Thank you for the baby brother but what I asked for was a puppy. I never asked for anything before. You can look it up. Joyce

Dear Mr. God, I wish you would not make it so easy for people to come apart. I had to have 3 stitches and a shot. Janet

Dear God, I didn't think orange went with purple until I saw the sunset you made on Tuesday night. That was really cool. Carol

God, I read the bible. What does begat mean? Nobody will tell me.   Love, Alison

Dear God, Is it true my father won't get in Heaven if he uses his golf words in the house?   Anita

Dear God, I bet it's very hard for you to love all of everybody in the whole world. There are only 4 people in our family and I can never do it.   Nan

Dear God, Did you really mean, Do Unto Others As They Do Unto You? If you did then, I'm going to get even with my brother.   Darla

Dear God, I like the story about Noah the best of all of them. You really made up some good ones. I like walking on water, too.   Glenn

Dear God, My Grandpa says you were around when he was a little boy. How far back do you go?   Love, Dennis

Dear God, Do you draw the lines around the countries? If you don't, who does?   Nan

Dear God, It's O. K. that you made different religions but don't you get mixed up sometimes?   Arnold

Dear God, Did you mean for giraffes to look like that or was it an accident?   Norma

Dear God, In bible times, did they really talk that fancy? Jennifer

Dear God, I am doing the best I can. Really.   Frank

Dear God, What does it mean you are a jealous God? I thought you had everything you wanted.   Jane

Dear God, How come you did all those miracles in the old days and don't do any now?   Billy

Dear God, Please send Dennis Clark to a different summer camp this year.   Peter

Dear God, You don't have to worry about me. I always look both ways before I cross the street.   Dean

Dear God, My brother told me about how you are born but it just doesn't sound right. What do you say?   Marsha

Dear God, If you watch in Church on Sunday I will show you my new shoes.   Barbara

Dear God, Is Reverend Coe a friend of yours, or do you just know him through the business?   Donny

Dear God, In Sunday School they told us what you do for a job. Who does it when you are on vacation?   Jane

Dear God, I do not think anybody could be a better God than you. Well, I just want you to know that. I am not just saying that because you are already God.   Charles

Dear God, it is great the way you always get the stars in the right place. Why can't you do that with the moon? Jeff

The Letter

Ruth went to her mail box and there was only one letter. She picked it up and looked at it before opening, but then she looked at the envelope again. There was no stamp, no postmark, only her name and address. She read the letter:

> **Dear Ruth:**
> *I'm going to be in your neighborhood Saturday afternoon and I'd like to stop by for a visit.*
> *Love Always, Jesus*

Her hands were shaking as she placed the letter on the table. "Why would the Lord want to visit me? I'm nobody special. I don't have anything to offer." With that thought, Ruth remembered her empty kitchen cabinets. "Oh my goodness, I really don't have anything to offer. I'll have to run down to the store and buy something for dinner." She reached for her purse and counted out its contents. Five dollars and forty cents. "Well, I can get some bread and cold cuts, at least."

She threw on her coat and hurried out the door. A loaf of French bread, a half-pound of sliced turkey, and a carton of milk...leaving Ruth with grand total twelve cents to last her until Monday. Nonetheless, she felt good as she headed home, her meager offerings tucked under her arm.

"Hey lady, can you help us, lady?" Ruth had been so absorbed in her dinner plans, she hadn't even noticed two figures huddled in the alleyway. A man and a woman, who were dressed in little more than rags. "Look lady, I ain't got a job, ya know, and my wife and I have been living out here on the street, and, well, now it's getting cold and we're getting kinda hungry and, well, if you could help us. Lady, we'd really appreciate it."

Ruth looked at them both. They were dirty, they smelled bad and frankly, she was certain that they could get some kind of work if they really wanted to. "Sir, I'd like to help you, but I'm a poor woman myself. All I have is a few cold cuts and some bread, and I'm having an important guest for dinner tonight and I was planning on serving that to Him."

"Yeah, well, okay lady, I understand. Thanks anyway." The man put his arm around the woman's shoulders, turned and headed back into the alley.

As she watched them leave, Ruth felt a familiar twinge in her heart. "Sir, wait!" The couple stopped and turned as she ran down the alley after them. "Look, why don't you take this food. I'll figure out something else to serve my guest."

She handed the man her grocery bag. "Thank you lady. Thank you very much!" "Yes, thank you!" It was the man's wife, and Ruth could see now that she was shivering.

"You know, I've got another coat at home. Here, why don't you take this one." Ruth unbuttoned her jacket and slipped it over the woman's shoulders. Then smiling, she turned and walked back to the street...without her coat and with nothing to serve her guest.

Ruth was chilled by the time she reached her front door, and worried too. The Lord was coming to visit and she didn't have anything to offer Him. She fumbled through her purse for the door key. But as she did, she noticed another envelope in her mailbox. "That's odd. The mailman doesn't usually come twice in one day." She took the envelope out of the box and opened it.

> *Dear Ruth:*
>
> *It was so good to see you again. Thank you for the lovely meal. And thank you, too, for the beautiful coat.*
>
> *Love Always*
>
> > *Jesus*

The air was still cold, but even without her coat, Ruth no longer noticed.

Letter From Heaven

Sally jumped up as soon as she saw the Surgeon come out of the operating room. The Surgeon said, "I'm sorry, we did all we could."

Sally moaned, "Why do little children get cancer, doesn't GOD care anymore? GOD, where were you when my son needed you?"

The Surgeon said, "One of the nurses will be out in a few minutes to let you spend time with your son's remains before it's transported to the university".

Sally asked that the nurse stay with her while she said Good-bye to her son. Sally ran her fingers through his thick red curly hair.

Sally said, "It was Jimmy's idea to give his body to the university for study. He said it might help somebody else," and that is what he wanted. I said, No at first, but Jimmy said, "Mom I won't be using it after I die, maybe it will help some other little boy to be able to spend one more day with his mother. My Jimmy had a heart of Gold, always thinking of someone else and always wanting to help others if he could".

When Sally got home, she laid down across Jimmy's bed and cried herself to sleep holding his pillow. She woke up about midnight and laying beside of her on the bed, was a letter folded up. She opened the letter, it said:

Dear Mom,
I know your going to miss me, but don't think that I will ever forget you or stop loving you because I'm not around to say I LOVE YOU. I'll think of you every day mom and I'll love you even more each day.
If you want to adopt a little boy so you won't be so lonely, he can have my room and my old stuff to play with.
If you decide to get a girl instead, she probably wouldn't like the same things as us boys do, so you will have to buy her dolls and stuff girls like. Don't be sad when you think about me, this is really a great place.
Grandma and Grandpa met me as soon as I got here and showed me around some, but it will take a long time to see everything here. The angels are so friendly, I love to watch them fly. Jesus doesn't look like any of the pictures I saw of Him, but I knew it was Him as soon as I saw Him.
Jesus took me to see GOD! And guess what, Mom? I got to sit on GOD'S knee and talk to Him like I was somebody important. I told God that I wanted to write you a letter and tell you Good-bye and everything, but I knew that wasn't allowed. God handed me some paper and His own personal pen to write you this letter with. I think Gabriel is the name of the angel that is going to drop this letter off to you .
God said for me to give you the answer to one of the questions you asked Him about. Where was He when I needed him? God said, "The same place He was when

*Jesus was on the cross. He was right there,
as He always is with all His children.
Oh, by the way Mom, nobody else can see what is
written on this paper but you. To everyone else, it
looks like a blank piece of paper. I have to give
God His pen back now, he has some more names to
write in the Book Of Life.
Tonight I get to sit at the table with Jesus for
Supper. I'm sure the food will be great. I almost
forgot to let you know - Now I don't hurt anymore,
the cancer is all gone. I'm glad because I couldn't
stand that pain anymore and God couldn't stand to
see me suffer the pain either, so He sent The Angel of
Mercy to get me. Signed with love from:
God, Jesus & Me.*

A Letter from Yakima County Jail

Dear Chaplain Campfield;

My name is Mary. Before I came to jail, I was hurt, angry, selfish, hurtful to others (family) and myself. I had no goals, motivation, direction or discipline. I did not respect myself or others. My focus was on me, and all I cared about was numbing myself by getting high. Now, I have a new focus, my Father God who knows all my problems and questions and I know He understands and gives me the ability to ask him daily for wisdom, knowledge, understanding, patience, tolerance, kindness, and most importantly, love.

I am now saying, "Father, Thy will, not mine be done". Here in jail, people come to me and ask me questions about God. I conduct Bible studies and I give hope to others by my passion and faith in the Lord. I want to learn more, it makes me feel food to help others. I'm starting to love myself; I thank God for all my blessings everyday. I'm starting to see thinks and realize things through God's point of view.

Chaplain Campfield, you have shown us, and especially me how to communicate about my days here and what the Lord is doing in my life. I am no longer on my own, I have a family finally! I need that, I want that, I deserve that, and I know that only God can and will make that possible. That's what brings me peace and joy now. I will become involved in a church and continue to get an education and hopefully volunteer. Thank you for the experience I will ever appreciate it, I will continue to respect my authorities and myself as the Lord would want me to. Thank you for bringing God into my life. Praising the Lord all ways, Mary.

The Little Green Snake (Humor)

Need a Laugh? Read about… **a Little Green Snake:**
A couple in Sweetwater, Texas had a lot of potted plants, and during a recent cold spell, the wife was bringing a lot of them indoors to protect them from a possible freeze. It turned out that a little green garden grass snake was hidden in one of the plants and when it had warmed up, it slithered out and the wife saw it go under the sofa. She let out a very loud scream.

The husband who was taking a shower ran out into the living room naked to see what the problem was. She told him there was a snake under the sofa. He got down on the floor on his hands and knees to look for it.

About that time the family dog came and cold-nosed him on the leg. He thought the snake had bitten him and he fainted. His wife thought he had a heart attack, so she called an ambulance. The attendants rushed in and loaded him on the stretcher and started carrying him out.

About that time the snake came out from under the sofa and the Emergency Medical Technician saw it and dropped his end of the stretcher. That's when the man broke his leg and why he is in the hospital.

The wife still had the problem of the snake in the house, so she called on a neighbor man. He volunteered to capture the snake. He armed himself with a rolled-up newspaper and began poking under the couch.

Soon he decided it was gone and told the woman, who sat down on the sofa in relief. But in relaxing, her hand dangled in between the cushions, where she felt the snake wriggling around. She screamed and fainted, the snake rushed back under the sofa, and the neighbor man, seeing her laying there passed out, tried to use CPR to revive her.

The neighbor's wife, who had just returned from shopping at the grocery store, saw her husband's mouth on the woman's mouth and slammed her husband in the back of the head with a bag of canned goods, knocking him out and cutting his scalp to a point where it needed stitches. An ambulance was again called and it was determined that the injury required hospitalization.

The noise woke the woman from her dead faint and she saw her neighbor lying on the floor with his wife bending over him, so she assumed he had been bitten by the snake. She went to the kitchen, brought back a small bottle of whiskey, and began pouring it down the man's throat.

By now the police had arrived. They saw the unconscious man, smelled the whiskey, and assumed that a drunken fight had occurred. They were about to arrest them all, when the two women tried to explain how it all happened over a little green snake. They called an ambulance, which took away the neighbor and his sobbing wife.

Just then the little snake crawled out from under the couch. One of the policemen drew his gun and fired at it. He missed the snake and hit the leg of the end table that was on one side of the sofa. The table fell over and the lamp on it shattered. As the bulb broke, it started a fire in the drapes.

The other policeman tried to beat out the flames and fell through the window into the yard on top of the family dog, who startled, jumped up and raced out into the street, where an oncoming car swerved to avoid it and smashed into the parked police car and set it on fire. Meanwhile the burning drapes had spread to the walls and the entire house was blazing.

Neighbors had called the fire department and the arriving fire-truck had started raising his ladder as they were halfway down the street. The rising ladder tore out the overhead wires and put out the electricity and disconnected the telephones in a ten-square city block area.

Time passed --------- Both men were discharged from the hospital, the house was re-built, the police acquired a new car, and all was right with their world ------- And the little green snake is still hiding under the sofa.

(Our Pastor read this story just before he did a preach about "not jumping to conclusions).

Long-stemmed Thorns

Sandra felt as low as the heels of her Birkenstocks as she pushed against a November wind gust and the florist shop door. Her life had been easy, like a spring breeze. Then in the fourth month of her second pregnancy, a minor automobile accident stole her ease. During this Thanksgiving week she would have delivered a son. She grieved over her loss. As if that weren't enough her husband's company threatened a transfer. Then her sister, whose holiday visit she coveted, called saying she could not come. What's worse, Sandra's friend infuriated her by suggesting her grief was a God-given path to maturity that would allow her to empathize with others who suffer. Had she lost a child? -No-she has no idea what I'm feeling, thought Sandra with a shudder. Thanksgiving? Thankful for what? She wondered. For a careless driver whose truck was hardly scratched when he rear-ended her? For an airbag that saved her life but took that of her child?

"Good afternoon, can I help you?" The flower shop clerk's approach startled her. "Sorry," said Jenny, "I just didn't want you to think was ignoring you." "I....I need an arrangement," stammered Sandra.

"For Thanksgiving?" Sandra nodded. "Do you want beautiful but ordinary, or would you like to challenge the day with a customer favorite I call the Thanksgiving Special." Jenny saw Sandra's curiosity and continued. "I'm convinced that flowers tell stories, that each arrangement insinuates a particular feeling.. Are you looking for something that conveys gratitude this Thanksgiving?" "Not exactly!" Sandra blurted. "Sorry, but in the last five months, everything that could go wrong has." Sandra regretted her outburst but was surprised when Jenny said, "I have the perfect arrangement for you." The door's small bell suddenly rang.

"Barbara! Hi, let me get your order," Jenny said. She politely excused herself from Sandra and walked toward a small workroom.. She quickly reappeared carrying a massive arrangement of greenery, bows, and long-stemmed thorny roses. Only, the ends of the rose stems were neatly snipped, no flowers. "Want this in a box?" Jenny asked.

Sandra watched for Barbara's response. Was this a joke? Who would want rose stems and no flowers! She waited for laughter, for someone to notice the absence of flowers atop the thorny stems, but neither woman did. "Yes, please. It's exquisite," Barbara replied with an appreciative smile. "You'd think after three years of getting the special, I'd not be so moved by its significance, but I can feel it right here, all over again." She gently tapped her chest. "My family will love this one. Thanks."

Sandra stared. Why so normal a conversation about so strange an arrangement? She wondered. "Uh," said Sandra, pointing.. "That lady just left it, ah...uh.." "Yes?" "Well, you gave her no flowers!" "Right, I cut off the flowers."

"Cut them off?"

"Off. Yep. That's the Special. I call it the Thanksgiving Thorns Bouquet." "I just cannot believe people would pay for that!" In spite of herself she chuckled. "Do you really want to know why?" "I couldn't leave this shop without knowing. I'd think of nothing else!" "That might be good," mused Jenny. "Well," she continued, "Barbara came into the shop three years ago feeling very much like you feel today. She thought she had very little to be thankful for. She had lost her father to cancer, the family business was failing, her son was into drugs, and she faced major surgery."

"Ooooh!" murmured Sandra. "That same year, I had lost my husband," Jenny went on.. "I assumed complete responsibility for the shop and for the first time, spent the holidays alone. I had no children, no husband, no family nearby, and too great a debt to allow any travel." "What did you do?" "I learned to be thankful for thorns."

Sandra's eyebrows lifted. "Thorns?"

I'm a Christian, Sandra. I've always thanked God for good things in life and I never thought to ask Him why good things happened to me, but, when bad stuff hit, did I ever ask! It took time to learn that dark times are important. I always enjoyed the 'flowers' of life but it took thorns to show me the beauty of God's comfort. You know, the Bible says that God comforts us when we're afflicted and from His consolation we learn to comfort others." Sandra sucked in her breath as she thought about the very thing her friend had tried to tell her. "I guess the truth is I don't want comfort. I've lost a baby and I'm angry with God." She started to ask Jenny to "go on" when the door's bell diverted their attention. "Hey, Phil!" shouted Jenny as a balding, rotund man entered the shop. She softly touched Sandra's arm and moved to welcome him. He tucked her under his side for a warm hug. "I'm here for twelve thorny long-stemmed stems!" Phil laughed, heartily. "I figured as much," said Jenny, "and I've got them ready." She lifted a tissue-wrapped arrangement from the refrigerated cabinet.

"Beautiful," exclaimed Phil. "My wife will love them!" Sandra could not resist asking. "These are for your wife? Do you mind me asking, why thorns?" "In fact, I'm glad you asked," Phil replied. "Four years ago my wife and I nearly divorced. After forty years, we were in a real mess, but with the Lord's guidance, we slogged through, problem by rotten problem. God rescued our marriage- our love, really. Last year at Thanksgiving I stopped in here for flowers. I must have mentioned surviving a tough process because Jenny told me that for a long time she kept a vase of rose stems--- stems!---as a reminder of what she learned from "thorny" times. That was good enough for me. I took home stems. My wife and I decided to label each one for a specific thorny situation and give thanks for what the problem taught us." Phil paid Jenny, thanked her again and as he left, said to Sandra, "I highly recommend the Special!" "I don't know if I can be thankful yet for the thorns in my life."

Sandra said to Jenny. "It is still...too fresh." "Well," Sandra replied carefully, "my experience says that thorns make roses more precious. We treasure God's providential care more during trouble than at any other time. Remember, it was a crown of thorns that Jesus wore so we might know His love. Do not resent the thorns." Tears rolled down Sandra's cheeks. For the first time since the accident she loosened her grip on resentment. "I'll take those twelve long-stemmed thorns, please." she managed to choke out. "I hoped you would," Jenny said. "I'll have them ready in a minute. Then, every time you see them, remember to appreciate both good and hard times. We grow through both."

"Thank you. What do I owe you?" "Nothing. Nothing but a promise to allow our Lord to heal your heart. The first year's arrangement is always on me." Jenny smiled and handed a card to Sandra. "I'll attach a card like this to your arrangement but maybe you'd like to read it first." It said: "My God, I have never thanked Thee for my thorns! I have thanked Thee a thousand times for my roses, but never once for my thorns. Teach me the glory of the cross I bear, teach me the value of my thorns. Show me that I have climbed to Thee by the path of pain. Show me that my tears have made my rainbow!

Look At Me!

(When an old lady died in the geriatric ward of a hospital near Dundee, Scotland, it was felt that she had left nothing of value. Then the nurses, going through her possessions, found this poem. Its quality so impressed the staff that copies were made and distributed to every nurse in the hospital. One nurse took her copy to Ireland. The old lady's sole bequest to posterity has since appeared in the Christmas edition of the News Magazine of the North Ireland Association for Mental Health. A slide presentation has also been made based on the poem.)

LOOK AT ME!

What do you see, nurses, what do you see,
What are you thinking when you're looking at me?
A crabby old woman, not very wise,
Uncertain of habit, with faraway eyes.
Who dribbles her food and makes no reply
When you say in a loud voice, "I do wish you'd try!"
Who seems not to notice the things that you do,
And forever is losing a stocking or shoe.
Who, resisting or not, lets you do as you will
With bathing and feeding, the long day to fill.
Is that what you're thinking? Is that what you see?
Then open your eyes, nurse; you're not looking at me.
I'll tell you who I am as I sit here so still,
As I use at your bidding, as I eat at your will.
I'm a small child of ten with a father and mother,
Brothers and sisters, who love one another.
A young girl of sixteen, with wings on her feet,
Dreaming that soon now a lover she'll meet.
A bride soon at twenty-my heart gives a leap,
Remembering the vows that I promised to keep.
At twenty-five now, I have young of my own
Who need me to guide and a secure happy home.

A woman of thirty, my young now grown fast,
Bound to each other with ties that should last.
At forty my young sons have grown and are gone,
But my man's beside me to see I don't mourn.
At fifty once more babies play round my knee,
Again we know children, my loved one and me.
Dark days are upon me, my husband is dead;
I look at the future, I shudder with dread.
For my young are all rearing young of their own,
And I think of the years and the love that I've known.
I'm now an old woman and nature is cruel;
'Tis jest to make old age look like a fool.
The body, it crumbles, grace and vigor depart,
There is now a stone where I once had a heart.
But inside this old carcass a young girl still dwells,
And now and again my battered heart swells.
I remember the joys, I remember the pain,
And I'm loving and living life over again.
I think of the years - all too few, gone too fast
And accept the stark fact that nothing can last.
So open your eyes, nurses, open and see,
Not a crabby old woman; look closer-see ME!!

Remember this poem when you next meet an old person. We will all be there one day.

Lord's Prayer

(Eavesdrop on a conversation God had with a lady who was trying to pray in rote)...

"Our Father which art in heaven ... "   ***"Yes?"***
"Don't interrupt me. I'm praying."   ***"But you called me."***
"Called you? I didn't call you. I'm praying. Our Father which art in heaven ..."   ***"There ... you did it again."***

"Did what?" **"Called me. You said, Our Father which art in heaven. Here I am. What's on your mind?"**

"But I didn't mean anything by it. I was, you know, just saying my prayers for the day. I always say the Lord's Prayer. It makes me feel good, kind of like getting a duty done." **"All right. Go on."**

"Hallowed be thy name ..." **"Hold it! What do you mean by that?"**

"By what?" **"By 'hallowed be thy name'?"**

"It means ... it means ... good grief! I don't know what it means. How should I know? It's just a part of the prayer. By the way, what does it mean?" **"It means honored ... holy ... wonderful."**

"Hey, that makes sense. I never thought about what 'hallowed' meant before... Thy kingdom come, Thy will be done, on earth as it is in heaven." **"Do you really mean that?"**

"Sure, why not?" **"What are you doing about it?"**

"Doing? Nothing, I guess! I just think it would be kind of neat if you got control of everything down here like you have up there." **"Have I got control of you?"**

"Well ... I go to church." **"That isn't what I asked you. What about your bad temper? You've really got a problem there, you know. And then there's the way you spend your money ... all on yourself. And what about the kind of books you read?"**

"Stop picking on me! I'm just as good as some of the rest of those people at the church." **"Excuse me. I thought you were praying for my will to be done. If that is to happen, it will have to start with the ones who are praying for it ... like you, for example."**

"Oh, all right. I guess I do have some hang-ups. Now that you mention it, I could probably name some others." **"So could I."**

"I haven't thought about it very much until now, but I really would like to cut out some of those things. I would like to ... you know ... be really free." **"Good ... now we're getting** *somewhere! We'll work together, you and I. Some victories can truly be won. I'm proud of you."*

"Look, Lord, I need to finish up here. This is taking a lot longer than it usually does... Give us this day, our daily bread." *"You need to cut out the bread. You're overweight as it is."*

"Hey, wait a minute! What is this ... 'Criticize me day?' Here I was doing my religious duty, and all of a sudden you break in and remind me of all my hang-ups." *"Praying is a dangerous thing. You could wind up changed, you know That's what I'm trying to get across to you. You called me, and here I am. It's too late to stop now. Keep praying. I'm interested in the next part of your prayer ... (pause). Well ... go on!"*

"I'm scared to." *"Scared? Of what?"*

"I know what You'll say." *"Try me and see."*

"Forgive us our sins, as we forgive those who sin against us." *"What about Sarah?"*

"See? I knew it! I knew you would bring her up! Why Lord, she's told lies about me, spread stories about my family. She never paid back the debt she owes me. I've sworn to get even with her!" *"But your prayer? What about your prayer?"*

"I didn't mean it." *"Well, at least you're honest. But it's not much fun carrying that load of bitterness around inside, is it?"*

"No, but I'll feel better as soon as I get even. Boy, have I got some plans for that neighbor. She'll wish she had never moved into this neighborhood." *"You won't feel any better. You'll feel worse. Revenge isn't sweet. Think of how unhappy you already are. But I can change all that."*

"You can? How?" *"Forgive Sarah. Then I'll forgive you. Then the hate and sin will be Sarah's problem and not yours. You will have settled your heart."*

"Oh, you're right. You always are. And more than I want to revenge Sarah, I want to be right with you. Sarah, I want to be right with you ... (pause) ...(sigh). All right! All right! I forgive her! Help her to find the right road in life, Lord. She's bound to be awfully miserable now that I think about it. Anybody who goes around doing the things she does to others has to be out of it. Someway, somehow, show her the right way." ***"There now! Wonderful! How do you feel?"***

"Hmmmm ... well, not bad. Not bad at all. In fact, I feel pretty great! You know, I don't think I'll have to go to bed uptight tonight for the first time since I can remember. Maybe I won't be so tired from now on because I'm not getting enough rest." ***"You're not through with your prayer. Go on."***

"Oh, all right. And lead us not into temptation, but deliver us from evil." ***"Good! Good! I'll do that. Just don't put yourself in a place where you can be tempted."***

"What do you mean by that?" ***Don't turn on the TV when you know the laundry needs to be done and the house needs to be picked up. Also, about the time you spend having coffee with your friends ... if you can't influence the conversation to positive things, perhaps you should re-think the value of those friendships. Another thing, your neighbors and friends shouldn't be your standard for "keeping up with." And please don't use me for an escape hatch."***

"I don't understand the last part." ***"Sure you do. You've done it a lot of times. You get caught in a bad situation. You get into trouble and then you come running to me. "Lord, help me out of this mess, and I promise you I'll never do it again." You remember some of those bargains you tried to make with me?"***

"Yes and I'm ashamed, Lord. I really am." ***"Which bargain are you remembering?"***

"Well, there was the night that Jim was gone and the children and I were home alone. The wind was blowing so hard I thought the roof would go any minute and tornado warnings were out. I remember praying, 'Oh God, if you spare us, I'll never skip my devotions again." ***"I protected you, but you didn't keep your promise, did you?"***

"I'm sorry, Lord. I really am. Up until now I thought that if I just prayed the Lord's Prayer every day, then I could do what I liked. I didn't expect anything to happen like it did." ***"Go ahead and finish your prayer."***

"For Thine is the kingdom, and the power, and the glory forever. Amen." ***"Do you know what would bring me glory? What would really make me happy?"***

"No, but I'd like to know. I now want to please you. I can see what a mess I've made of my life. And I can see how great it would be to really be one of your followers." ***"You just answered the question."***

"I did?" ***"Yes. The thing that would bring me glory is to have people like you truly love me. And I see that happening between us. Now that some of these old sins are exposed and out of the way, well, there is no telling what we can do together."***

"Lord, let's see what we can make of me, okay?" ***"Yes, let us see."***

Love Defined...

A group of professional people posted this question to a group of 4 to 8 year olds. "What does love mean?" the answers they got were broader and deeper than anyone could have imagined. See what you think...

"When my grandma got arthritis, she couldn't bend over and paint her toenails anymore. So my grandpa does it for her now all the time, even when his hands got arthritis too. That's love. *Rebecca- age 8*

"When someone loves you, the way they say your name is different. You just know that your name is safe in their mouths. *Billy- age 4*

"Love is when a girl puts on perfume and a boy puts on shaving cologne and they go out and smell each other. *Kari- age 5*

"Love is when you go out to eat and give somebody most of your French fries without making them give you any of theirs. *Chrissy- age 6*

"Love is what makes you smile when you're tired. *Terri- age 4*

"Love is when my mommy makes coffee for my daddy and she takes a sip before giving it to him, to make sure the taste is OK. *Danny- age 7*

"Love is when you kiss all the time. Then when you get tired of kissing, you still want to be together and you talk more. My mommy and daddy are like that. They look gross when they kiss. *Emily- age 8*

"Love is what's in the room with you at Christmas if you stop opening presents and listen. *Bobby- age 7* (wow!)

"If you want to learn to love better, you should start with a friend who you hate. *Nikka- age 6*

"Love is when you tell a guy you like his shirt, then he wears it everyday. *Noelle- age 7*

"Love is like a little old woman and a little old man who are still friends even after they know each other so well. *Tommy- age 6*

"During my piano recital, I was on stage and I was scared. I looked at all the people watching me and saw my daddy waving and smiling. He was the only one doing that. I wasn't scared anymore. *Cindy- age 8*

"Love is when mommy gives daddy the best piece of chicken. *Elaine- age 5*

"Love is when mommy sees daddy smelly and sweaty and still says he is handsomer than Robert Redford. *Chris- age 7*

"Love is when your puppy licks your face even after you left him alone all day. *Mary Ann- age 4*

'When you love somebody, your eyelashes go up and down and little stars come out of you. *Karen- age 7*

"You really shouldn't say "I LOVE YOU" unless you mean it. But if you mean it, you should say it a lot. People forget. *Jessica- age 8*

And the winner was a 4 year old child whose next door neighbor was an elderly man who had just lost his wife. When the child saw the man cry, the little boy went over into the man's yard and climbed on top of the man's lap and just sat there. When the boy's mother asked him what he'd said to the neighbor, the little boy said "Nothing, I just helped him cry."

The Majority Rules!
Samuel Thompson wrote:

I don't believe in Santa Claus, but I'm not going to sue somebody for singing a Ho-Ho-Ho song in December. I don't agree with Darwin but I didn't go out and hire a lawyer when my high school teacher taught his theory of evolution. Life, liberty or your pursuit of happiness will not be endangered because someone says a 30-second prayer before a football game. So what's the big deal? It's not like somebody is up there reading the entire book of Acts. They're just talking to a God they believe in and asking him to grant safety to the players on the field and the fans going home from the game.

"But it's a Christian prayer," some will argue. Yes, and this is the United States of America, a country founded on Christian principles. And we are in the Bible Belt. According to our very own phone book, Christian churches outnumber all others better than 200-to-1. So what would you expect -- somebody chanting Hare Krishna? If I went to a football game in Jerusalem, I would expect to hear a Jewish prayer. If I went to a soccer game in Baghdad, I would expect to hear a Muslim prayer. If I went to a ping pong match in China, I would expect to hear someone pray to Buddha. And I wouldn't be offended. It wouldn't bother me one bit. When in Rome...

"But what about the atheists?" is another argument. What about them? Nobody is asking them to be baptized. We're not going to pass the collection plate. Just humor us for 30 seconds. If that's asking too much, bring a Walkman or a pair of ear plugs. Go to the bathroom. Visit the concession stand. Call your lawyer. Unfortunately, one or two will make that call. One or two will tell thousands what they can and cannot do. I don't think a short prayer at a football game is going to shake the world's foundations.

Christians are just sick and tired of turning the other cheek while our Courts strip us of all our rights. Our parents and grandparents taught us to pray before eating, to pray before we go to sleep. Our Bible tells us just to pray without ceasing.

Now a handful of people and their lawyers are telling us to cease praying. God, help us. And if that last sentence offends you, well..........just sue me. The silent majority has been silent too long... it's time we let that one or two who scream loud enough to be heard, that the vast majority don't care what they want... it is time the majority rules!

It's time we tell them, you don't have to pray.. you don't have to say the Pledge of allegiance, you don't have to believe in God or attend services that honor Him. That is your right, and we will honor your right... but by golly you are no longer going to take our rights away... we are fighting back... and we WILL WIN! After all, the God you have the right to denounce is on our side!

God bless us one and all, especially those who denounce Him... God bless America, despite all her faults.. still the greatest nation of all..... God bless our service men and women who are fighting to protect our right to pray and worship God...

Make 2003 and 2004 the years the silent majority is heard and we put God back as the foundation of our families and institutions. Keep looking up...... In God WE Trust

If you agree with this, please pass it on.

Manger Story
(Get your Kleenex)

In 1994, two Americans answered an invitation from the Russian Department of Education to teach morals and ethics (based on Biblical principles) in the public schools. They were invited to teach at prisons, businesses, the fire and police departments and a large orphanage. About 100 boys and girls who had been abandoned, abused, and left in the care of a government-run program were in the orphanage. They relate the following story in their own words:

It was nearing the holiday season, 1994, time for our orphans to hear, for the first time, the traditional story of Christmas. We told them about Mary and Joseph arriving in Bethlehem. Finding no room in the inn, the couple went to a stable, where the baby Jesus was born and placed in a manger.

Throughout the story, the children and orphanage staff sat in amazement as they listened. Some sat on the edges of their stools, trying to grasp every word. Completing the story, we gave the children three small pieces of cardboard to make a crude manger. Each child was given a small paper square, cut from yellow napkins I had brought with me. No colored paper was available in the city. Following instructions, the children tore the paper and carefully laid strips in the manger for straw. Small squares of flannel, cut from a worn-out nightgown an American lady was throwing away as she left Russia, were used for the baby's blanket. A doll-like baby was cut from tan felt we had brought from the United States.

The orphans were busy assembling their manger as I walked among them to see if they needed any help.

All went well until I got to one table where little Misha sat. He looked to be about 6 years old and had finished his project. As I looked at the little boy's manger, I was startled to see not one, but two babies in the manger.

Quickly, I called for the translator to ask the lad why there were two babies in the manger. Crossing his arms in front of him and looking at this completed manger scene, the child began to repeat the story very seriously. For such a young boy, who had only heard the Christmas story once, he related the happenings accurately-until he came to the part where Mary put the baby Jesus in the manger.

Then Misha started to ad-lib. He made up his own ending to the story as he said, "And when Maria laid the baby in the manger, Jesus looked at me and asked me if I had a place to stay. I told him I have no mamma and I have no papa, so I don't have any place to stay.

"Then, Jesus told me I could stay with him. But I told him I couldn't, because I didn't have a gift to give him like everybody else did."

"But I wanted to stay with Jesus so much, so I thought about what I had that maybe I could use for a gift. I thought that maybe if I kept him warm, that would be a good gift. So I asked Jesus, 'If I keep you warm, will that be a good enough gift?'

"And Jesus told me, 'If you keep me warm, that will be the best gift anybody ever gave me.' "So I got into the manger, and then Jesus looked at me and he told me I could stay with him--- for always."

As little Misha finished his story, his eyes brimmed full of tears that splashed down his little cheeks. Putting his hand over his face, his head dropped to the table and his shoulders shook as he sobbed and sobbed. The little orphan had found someone who would never abandon nor abuse him, someone who would stay with him - FOR ALWAYS.

Mary Had a Little Lamb
Think carefully about what you will be reading.

Mary had a little lamb,
His fleece was white as snow.
And everywhere that Mary went,
The Lamb was sure to go.
He followed her to school each day,
T'wasn't even in the rule.
It made the children laugh and play,
To have a Lamb at school.
And then the rules all changed one day,
Illegal it became;
To bring the Lamb of God to school,
Or even speak His Name!
Every day got worse and worse,

And days turned into years.
Instead of hearing children laugh,
We heard gun shots and tears.
What must we do to stop the crime,
That's in our schools today?
Let's let the Lamb come back to school,
And teach our kids to pray!

The Mayonnaise Jar & Coffee

When things in your life seem almost too much to handle, when 24 hours in a day are not enough, remember the mayonnaise jar...and the coffee...

A professor stood before his philosophy class and had some items in front of him. When the class began, wordlessly, he picked up a very large and empty mayonnaise jar and proceeded to fill it with golf balls. He then asked the students if the jar was full. They agreed that it was.

So the professor then picked up a box of pebbles and poured them into the jar. He shook the jar lightly. The pebbles rolled into the open areas between the golf balls. He then asked the students again if the jar was full. They agreed it was.

He next picked up a box of sand and poured it into the jar. Of course, the sand filled up everything else. He asked once more if the jar was full. The students responded with an unanimous "Yes."

The professor then produced two cups of coffee from under the table and poured the entire contents into the jar, effectively filling the empty space between the sand. The students laughed.

"Now," said the professor, as the laughter subsided, " I want you to recognize that this jar represents your life. The golf balls are the important things: your God, family, your children, your health, your friends, and your favorite passions-things that if everything else was lost and only they remained, your life would still be full.

The pebbles are the other things that matter like your job, your house, and your car. The sand is everything else-the small stuff.

"If you put the sand into the jar first," he continued, "There is no room for the pebbles or the golf balls. The same goes for life. If you spend all your time and energy on the small stuff, you will never have room for the things that are important to you. Pay attention to the things that are critical to your happiness. Play with your children. Take time to get medical checkups. Take your partner out to dinner. Play another 18. There will always be time to clean the house and fix the disposal. Take care of the golf balls first, the things that really matter. Set your priorities. The rest is just sand."

One of the students raised her hand and inquired what the coffee represented. The professor smiled. "I'm glad you asked. It just goes to show you that no matter how full your life may seem, there's always room for a couple of cups of coffee with a friend."

Please share this with someone you care about. Have a blessed day!!!

Mikey

Howard County Sheriff Jerry Marr got a disturbing call one Saturday afternoon a few months ago. His 6-year-old grandson Mikey had been hit by a car while fishing in Greentown with his dad. The father and son were near a bridge by the Kokomo Reservoir when a woman lost control of her car, slid off the bridge and hit Mikey at a rate of about 50 mph.

Sheriff Marr had seen the results of accidents like this and feared the worst. When he got to Saint Joseph Hospital, he rushed through the emergency room to find Mikey conscious and in fairly good spirits

"Mikey, what happened?" Sheriff Marr asked. Mikey replied,

"Well, Papaw, I was fishin' with Dad, and some lady runned me over, I flew into a mud puddle, and broke my fishin' pole and I didn't get to catch no fish!" As it turned out, the impact propelled Mikey about 500 feet, over a few trees and an embankment and in the middle of a mud puddle. His only injuries were to his right femur bone which had broken in two places. Mikey had surgery to place pins in his leg. Otherwise the boy is fine. Since all the boy could talk about was that his fishing pole was broken, the Sheriff went out to Wal-mart and bought him a new one while he was in surgery so he could have it when he came out.

The next day the Sheriff sat with Mikey to keep him company in the hospital. Mikey was enjoying his new fishing pole and talked about when he could go fishing again as he cast into the trash can. When they were alone, Mikey, just a matter-of-fact, said,

"Papaw, did you know Jesus is real?"

"Well, "the Sheriff replied, a little startled. "Yes, Jesus is real to all who believe in him and love him in their hearts."

"No," said Mikey. "I mean Jesus is REALLY real."

"What do you mean?" asked the Sheriff.

"I know he's real 'cause I saw him." said Mikey, still casting into the trash can.

"You did?" said the Sheriff.

"Yep," said Mikey. "When that lady runned me over and broke my fishing pole, Jesus caught me in his arms and laid me down in the mud puddle."

GIVES YOU GLORY BUMPS DOESN'T IT!
I asked the Lord to bless you
As I prayed for you today
To guide you and protect you
As you go along your way
His love is always with you

His promises are true
And when we give Him all our cares
You know He will see us through
So when the road you're traveling on
Seems difficult at best Just remember I'm here praying
And GOD WILL DO THE REST.

Mom is an Angel

The soul of a yet unborn baby asked God, "They tell me you are sending me to earth tomorrow, but how am I going to live there being so small and helpless?"

"Your angel will be waiting for you and will take care of you."

The child further inquired, "But tell me, here in heaven I don't have to do anything but sing and smile to be happy."

God said, "Your angel will sing for you and also smile for you. And you will feel your angel's love and be very happy."

Again the child asked, "And how am I going to be able to understand when people talk to me if I don't know the language?"

God said, "Your angel will tell you the most beautiful and sweet words you will ever hear, and with much patience and care, your angel will teach you how to speak."

"And what am I going to do when I want to talk to you?"

God said, "Your angel will place your hands together and will teach you how to pray."

"Who will protect me?"

God said, "Your angel will defend you even if it means risking its life."

"But I will always be sad because I will not see you anymore."

God said, "Your angel will always talk to you about Me and will teach you the way to come back to Me, even though I will always be next to you."

At that moment there was much peace in Heaven, but voices from Earth could be heard and the child hurriedly asked, "God, if I am to leave now, please tell me my angel's name."

"You will simply call her, "Mom."

Lift a mother's spirit; send this to every mother you know.

Montana Easter
by Jacky Allaway

The sun was shining, the cool breeze blowing and I was sitting on the steps marveling at the beauty of the forsythia in bloom, I laid back on the concrete patio letting the wind dry the sweat from my head..... Spring, yes, it is a lot of work, cleaning the leaves that have blown into the garden beds and in every nook and cranny of the yard. Spring brings thoughts of new life, the earth bringing forth her seed, the birds building nests, the baby chicks for sale in the stores, cheeping out their cheery songs.

As a child I remembered going to the little post office in our extremely small Montana town, being greeted at the opening of the door with the fragrance of the baby chicks that had just arrived in the mail. Smelling the fresh odor of life and hearing the cheeping, which I'm sure, must have been almost deafening to the workers in the back. This was a particularly interesting spring because I was so excited about Easter coming....the fun, the CANDY, the new clothes, the Bible stories in celebration of our Saviors birth and looking forward to my first sunrise service followed by the Church Breakfast...ummmm.

The excitement that year met a deep abyss when my older brother informed me of a dastardly ritual held each year by one of God's own creations....the bunny rabbit. It seems that the rabbit did not lay eggs! Imagine my shock when I realized that all this time I had held them in such high esteem only to find out that they had put little chickens into servitude to lay hundreds of eggs. Then steal them to give out as their own gift to little children such as myself. This little girl was broken-hearted and found herself praying for the life of that thieving creature. Then to find out that the Easter eggs we found and ate were actually - almost, little baby chicks....argh! My life was over. So young, so deceived...how could I eat another egg?

Surely, we all have memories similar to my experience, hopefully you have recovered as well as I have....but I must admit, bunnies aren't as cute and eggs are still hard to swallow. However, the true significance to Easter is not so much the bunnies, and chicks, the eggs, the fun, the candy, ...but more in the value of the new life springing forth.

Memories took me back to one particular spring in which we had a terrible snowstorm that had come quite late and most unexpectedly. A young couple had moved to our town, purchased a farm and bought a flock of sheep. They had a rough time the first year and shared many of their experiences with us. They were looking forward to the new baby lambs as a promise of better things to come. But the storm of freezing temperatures, high winds and blizzard conditions gave them a bleak outlook that year. The sheep were in the fields and he could not get them to come in because the winds were so loud they could not hear his calling to them. Being very shortsighted, they would not follow each other because they could not see through the blowing snowstorm.

It was too early on Monday morning and we awoke to the hopes that there would be no school, it was too dark, too stormy and surely there would be a day off. The phone call came from the young couple in desperate need of helpers to come aid them in gathering in the lambs before they would freeze to death in the blizzard. The Pastor had them call for the youth group to see if they could organize a line of searchers to walk the fields with flashlights and find the sheep and their young.

We showed up well padded and each carrying our own flashlights. The crew lined up arms length apart with strict instruction not to stray, as the conditions were extremely hazardous. We were already frozen and had not yet left the sanctity of the barn...in full determination to save his livelihood; we put our head into the wind, embarking on the mission. The trucks came behind but we could barely see their lights, the flashlights were only visible a few feet ahead and no one could hear the voice of another. Soon the line would break as a little lamb was being lifted to the truck, here a sheep and another, sometimes there would be many in a group...most of them without the lambs. We knew their only hope was to be found before it was too late, every little clump of snow was checked to see if it was a lamb, it often was.

After an hour, (it seemed like several), we were taken back to the shed to warm up and take some hot cocoa...I never tasted such fantastic cocoa in my life, it took two cups to warm the tummy. Back again into the truck and out further in the fields to scour the fields for the sheep. We didn't stop until daylight and more people showed up to help.

That year the young couple did loose some sheep but not as many lambs as they expected, they were so grateful for our help that we were all invited back to the shearing. It was awesome to see the big burly sheep shoving and bawling until they were led to the hands of the Shearer and suddenly they were as docile as if they had been drugged. So many Scriptures came alive for me in that season...learning about the sheep how the sheep follow the voice of the shepherd, but conditions had made that impossible. How, often the little lambs stray...the shepherd valued so greatly the life of one little lamb, searched for them, gathered them and placed them in warm blankets then placed them under lamps in the barn to keep them alive. How the sheep sometimes abandoned their young, and how another would adopt them as their own.

But most vividly was ..."and He was led as a sheep to the slaughter; and as a sheep before his Shearer is dumb, so he opened not his mouth."

Yes, Easter comes from the death of winter into the new life of spring, reminding us that our Savior gave up his life for us, suffered death, hell and the grave. It is the majestic power of God - the LOVE that passed through heaven and earth and under the earth to take the life of the perfect sacrifice from the bonds of darkness and to raise Him up. It brings forth for us the new life we can now live IN CHRIST.

This Season of Celebration as we glory in the vibrancy of the many colors of spring, the fragrance of fresh earth being tilled, the smell of the birthing of new baby animals, the song of the birds singing a promise of a new day...let us allow each picture to bring to us the image of the love or our Creator, the resurrection of His Son and our hope of an eternal life with Him.

More than Enough

At an airport, I overheard a father and his daughter in their last moments together. They had announced her plane's departure and standing near the door she said, "Daddy, our life together has been more than enough. Your love is all I ever needed. I wish you enough too, Daddy."

They kissed good-bye and she left. He walked over towards the window where I was seated. Standing there I could see he wanted and needed to cry. I tried not to intrude on his privacy, but he welcomed me in by asking, "Did you ever say good-bye to someone knowing it would be forever?"

"Yes, I have," I replied. Saying that brought back memories I had of expressing my love and appreciation for all my Dad had done for me. Recognizing that his days were limited, I took the time to tell him face to face how much he meant to me. So I knew what this man was experiencing.

"Forgive me for asking, but why is this a forever good-bye?" I asked.

"I am old and she lives much too far away. I have challenges ahead and the reality is, her next trip back will be for my funeral," he said.

"When you were saying good-bye I heard you say, 'I wish you enough,' may I ask what that means?" He began to smile. "That's a wish that has been handed down from other generations. My parents used to say it to everyone." He paused for a moment and looking up as if trying to remember it in detail, he smiled even more. "When we said, 'I wish you enough,' we were wanting the other person to have a life filled with enough good things to sustain them". He continued and then, turning toward me, he shared the following as if he were reciting it from memory:

I wish you enough sun to keep your attitude bright.

I wish you enough rain to appreciate the sun more.

I wish you enough happiness to keep your spirit alive.

I wish you enough pain so that the smallest joys in life appear much bigger.

I wish you enough gain to satisfy your wanting.

I wish you enough loss to appreciate all that you possess.

I wish you enough "Hellos" to get you through the final "Good-bye." He then began to sob and walked away.

My friends and loved ones, I wish you enough!

They say, "It takes a minute to find a special person, an hour to appreciate them, a day to love them, but an entire lifetime to forget them." NEVER FORGET!

Share this phrase with the people you'll never forget.

sent by Mike Thomas

Morning Talk With God

Good morning! This is God. Today I will be handling all of your problems. Please remember that I do not need your help. If the devil happens to deliver a situation to you that you cannot handle, do not attempt to resolve it. Kindly put it in the SFJTD, (Something For Jesus To Do) box. It will be addressed in My time, not yours. Once the matter is placed into the box, do not hold on to it or attempt to remove it. Holding on or removal will delay the resolution. Rest My child. If you need Me, I am here 24 hours a day and I am only a prayer away. Have a great day!

Love, God

My Perfect Squelch

I have been guilty of looking at others my own age and thinking, "surely I cannot look that old". I'm sure you've done the same...

While waiting for my first appointment in the reception room of a new dentist, I noticed her certificate, which bore her full name. Suddenly, I remembered that a tall, beautiful girl with the same name had been in my high school class some 40 years ago. Upon seeing her, however, I quickly discarded any such thought. This fat, gray-haired old woman with the deeply lined face was too old to have been my classmate!

After she had examined my teeth, I asked her if she had attended the local high school.

"Yes," she replied.

"When did you graduate?" I asked.

She answered, "In 1957."

"You were in my class!" I exclaimed.

She looked at me closely and then asked, "What did you teach?"

My Spiritual Attorney

After living what I felt was a "decent" life, my time on earth came to the end. The first thing I remember is sitting on a bench in the waiting room of what I thought to be a court house. The doors opened and I was instructed to come in and have a seat by the defense table.

As I looked around I saw the "prosecutor." He was a villainous looking gent who snarled as he stared at me. He definitely was the most evil person I have ever seen.

I sat down and looked to my left and there sat My Attorney, a kind and gentle looking man whose appearance seemed so familiar to me, I felt I knew Him. The corner door flew open and there appeared the Judge in full flowing robes. He commanded an awesome presence as He moved across the room. I couldn't take my eyes off of Him. As He took His seat behind the bench, He said, "Let us begin."

The prosecutor rose and said, "My name is Satan and I am here to show you why this sinner belongs in hell." He proceeded to tell of lies that I told, things that I stole, and in the past when I cheated others. Satan told of other horrible perversions that were once in my life and the more he spoke, the further down in my seat I sank. I was so embarrassed that I couldn't look at anyone, even my own Attorney, as the Devil told of sins that even I had completely forgotten about. As upset as I was at Satan for telling all these things about me,

I was equally upset at My Attorney who sat there silently not offering any form of defense at all. I know I had been guilty of those things, but I had done some good in my life -- couldn't that at least equal out part of the harm I'd done? Satan finished with a fury and said, "This sinner belongs in hell, and is guilty of all that I have charged and there is not a person who can prove otherwise."

When it was His turn, My Attorney first asked if He might approach the bench. The Judge allowed this over the strong objection of Satan, and beckoned Him to come forward. As He got up and started walking, I was able to see Him in His full splendor and majesty. I realized why He seemed so familiar; this was Jesus representing me, my Lord and my Savior.

He stopped at the bench and softly said to the Judge, "Hi, Dad," and then He turned to address the court. "Satan was correct in saying that this man had sinned, I won't deny any of these allegations. And, yes, the wage of sin is death, and this sinner deserves to be punished." Jesus took a deep breath and turned to His Father with outstretched arms and proclaimed, "However, I died on the cross so that this person might have eternal life and he has accepted Me as his Savior, so he is Mine." My Lord continued with, "His name is written in the book of life and no one can snatch him from Me. Satan still does not understand. This man is not to be given justice, but rather mercy."

As Jesus sat down, He quietly paused, looked at His Father and said, "There is nothing else that needs to be done. I've done it all."

The Judge lifted His mighty hand and slammed the gavel down. The following words resounded from His lips... "This man is free. The penalty for him has already been paid in full. Case dismissed."

As my Lord embraced me and led me away, I could hear Satan ranting and raving, "I won't give up, I will win the next one."

I asked Jesus, as He gave me my instructions where to go next, "Have you ever lost a case?" Christ lovingly smiled and said, "Everyone that has come to Me and asked Me to represent them has received the same verdict as you, "PAID IN FULL."

"Stop telling God how big your storm is. Instead, tell the storm how big your God is!"

My Sunshine

"You are My Sunshine, My only Sunshine" (Be prepared to get watery eyes!)

Like any good mother, when Karen found out that another baby was on the way, she did what she could to help her 3-year-old son, Michael, prepare for a new sibling. They found out that the new baby was going be a girl, and day after day, night after night, Michael sang to his sister in mommy's tummy. He was building a bond of love with his little sister before he even met her.

The pregnancy progressed normally for Karen, an active member of the Panther Creek United Methodist Church in Morristown, Tennessee. In time, the labor pains came. Soon it was every five minutes, every three, every minute. But serious complications arose during delivery and Karen found herself in hours of labor. Would a C-section be required? Finally, after a long struggle, Michael's little sister was born. But she was in very serious condition. With a siren howling in the night, the ambulance rushed the infant to the neonatal intensive care unit at St. Mary's Hospital, Knoxville, Tennessee.

The days inched by. The little girl got worse. The pediatrician had to tell the parents that there was very little hope. Be prepared for the worst. Karen and her husband contacted a local cemetery about a burial plot. They had fixed up a special room in their house for their new baby but now they found themselves having to plan for a funeral. Michael, however, kept begging his parents to let him see his sister. I want to sing to her, he kept saying.

Week two in the intensive care unit looked as if a funeral would come before the week was over. Michael kept nagging about singing to his baby sister, but kids are never allowed in Intensive Care. Karen decided to take Michael whether they liked it or not. If he didn't see his sister right then, he may never see her alive. She dressed him in an oversized scrub suit and marched him into ICU. He looked like a walking laundry basket. The head nurse recognized him as a child and bellowed, "Get that kid out of here now. No children are allowed."

The mother rose up strong in Karen, and the usually mild-mannered lady glared steel-eyed right into the head nurse's face, her lips a firm line. "He is not leaving until he sings to his sister" she stated. Then Karen towed Michael to his sister's bedside. He gazed at the tiny infant losing the battle to live. After a moment, he began to sing.

In the pure-hearted voice of a 3-year-old, Michael sang: "You are my sunshine, my only sunshine, you make me happy when skies are gray."

Instantly the baby girl seemed to respond. The pulse rate began to calm down and become steady. "Keep on singing, Michael," encouraged Karen with tears in her eyes.

"You never know, dear, how much I love you, please don't take my sunshine away." As Michael sang to his sister, the baby's ragged, strained breathing became as smooth as a kitten's purr.

"Keep on singing, sweetheart." Karen begged.

"The other night, dear, as I lay sleeping, I dreamed I held you in my arms". Michael's little sister began to relax as rest, healing rest, seemed to sweep over her.

"Keep on singing, Michael." Tears had now conquered the face of the bossy head nurse. Karen glowed.

"You are my sunshine, my only sunshine. Please don't take my sunshine away..." The next, day...the very next day...the little girl was well enough to go home. Woman's Day Magazine called it The Miracle of a Brother's Song. The medical staff just called it a miracle. Karen called it a miracle of God's love. NEVER GIVE UP ON THE PEOPLE YOU LOVE. LOVE IS SO INCREDIBLY POWERFUL.

by Frances Milhous

Neat Prayer

(Please take a moment to relax your mind and humble your heart to focus on Christ. Allow God, to be the only person on your mind while you read this prayer. If we can take the time to read long jokes, stories, etc., we should give the same respect to this prayer. Friends that pray together, stay together.)

Dear Lord, I thank You for this day. I thank You for my being able to see and to hear this morning. I'm blessed because You are a forgiving God and an understanding God. You have done so much for me and You keep on blessing me. Forgive me this day for everything I have done, said or thought that was not pleasing to you. I ask now for Your forgiveness.

Please keep me safe from all danger and harm. Help me to start this day with a new attitude and plenty of gratitude. Let me make the best of each and every day to clear my mind so that I can hear from You.

Please broaden my mind that I can accept all things.

Let me not whine and whimper over things I have no control over. Let me continue to see sin through God's eyes and acknowledge it as evil. And when I sin, let me repent, and confess with my mouth my wrongdoing, and receive the forgiveness of God.

And when this world closes in on me, let me remember Jesus' example -to slip away and find a quiet place to pray. It's the best response when I'm pushed beyond my limits. I know that when I can't pray, You listen to my heart. Continue to use me to do Your will.

Continue to bless me that I may be a blessing to others. Keep me strong that I may help the weak. Keep me uplifted that I may have words of encouragement for others. I pray for those that are lost and can't find their way. I pray for those that are misjudged and misunderstood. I pray for those who don't know You intimately. I pray for those that will delete this without sharing it with others. I pray for those that don't believe. But I thank you that I believe.

I believe that God changes people and God changes things. I pray for all my sisters and brothers. For each and every family member and their households. I pray for husbands and wives who struggle with the need for understanding and the need to be understood. Heal our marriages and help us to remember again that you have called us to love one another with an everlasting love. I pray that we learn to accept our differences and rejoice in our commonalties. I pray for peace, love and joy in their homes that they are out of debt and all their needs are met.

I pray that every eye that reads this knows there is no problem, circumstance, or situation greater than God. Every battle is in Your hands for You to fight. I pray that these words be received into the hearts of every eye that sees them and every mouth that confesses them willingly. And on that day when we stand before you let us be able to say, we set our face like a flint, looking not to the left or the right, we fought the good fight , we stayed the course and we now have the eternal reward.   This is my prayer. In Jesus' Name, Amen.

Know that you are already blessed by the person whom sent this to you.

The "New" Bible

(This is great. Pay special attention to the wording and spelling).

<u>The Bible</u> If you know the Bible, even a little, you'll find this hilarious! It comes from a Catholic elementary school. Kids were asked questions about the Old and New Testaments. The following statements about the Bible, were written by children. They have not been retouched or corrected (i.e., incorrect spelling has been left in).

In the first book of the bible, Guinessis, God got tired of creating the world, so he took the Sabbath off.

Noah's wife was called Joan of Ark. Noah built an ark, which the animals come on to in pears.

Lot's wife was a pillar of salt by day, but a ball of fire by night.

The Jews were a proud people and they had trouble with the unsympathetic Genitals.

Samson was a strongman who let himself be led astray by a Jezebel like Delilah.

Samson slayed the Philistines with the axe of the Apostles.

By the Red Sea, the Hebrews made unleavened bread which is bread without any ingredients.

After the Egyptians were drowned, Moses went up on Mount Cyanide to get the ten ammendments.

The first commandment was when Eve told Adam to eat the apple.

The seventh commandment is thou shalt not admit adultery.

Moses died before he ever reached Canada. Then Joshua led the Hebrews in the battle of Geritol.

The greatest miracle in the Bible is when Joshua told his son to stand still and he obeyed him.

David was a Hebrew king skilled at playing the liar. He fought with the Finklesteins, a race of people.

Solomon, one of David's sons, had 300 wives and 700 porcupines.

When Mary heard that she was the mother of Jesus, she sang the Magna Carta.

When the three wise guys from the east side arrived, they found Jesus in the manager.

Jesus was born because Mary had an immaculate contraption.

St. John the blacksmith dumped water on his head.

Jesus enunciated the Golden Rule, which says to do one to others before they do one to you.

It was a miracle when Jesus rose from the dead and managed to get the tombstone off the entrance.

The people who followed the lord were called the 12 decibels.

The epistles were the wives of the apostles.

One of the oppossums was St. Matthew who was also a taximan.

St. Paul cavorted to Christianity. He preached holy acrimony, which is; another name for marriage.

Christians have only one spouse. This is called monotony.

New School Prayer

(This was supposed to have been written by a teen in Bagdad, Arizona!)

Now I sit me down at school,
Where praying is against the rule..
For this great nation under God,
Finds mention of Him very odd.
If Scripture now the class recites,
It violates the Bill of Rights..
And anytime my head I bow
Becomes a Federal matter now.
Our hair can be purple, orange, or green,
That's no offense; it's a freedom scene.
The law is specific, the law is precise.
Prayers spoken aloud are a serious vice.
For praying in a public hall
Might offend someone with no faith at all.
In silence alone we must meditate,
God's name is prohibited by the state.
We're allowed to cuss and dress like freaks,
And pierce our noses, tongues and cheeks.
They've outlawed guns, but FIRST the Bible.
To quote the Good book makes me liable.
We can elect a pregnant Senior Queen,
And the 'unwed daddy,' our Senior King.
It's "inappropriate" to teach right from wrong,
We're taught that such "judgments" do not belong.
We can get our condoms and birth controls,
Study witchcraft, vampires and totem poles.
But the Ten Commandments are not allowed,
No word of God must reach this crowd.
It's scary here I must confess,
When chaos reigns the school's a mess..
So, Lord, this silent plea I make:
Should I be shot; My soul please take!   Amen

Jesus said, "If you are ashamed of me, I will be ashamed of you before my Father.
I have called you friends, for everything that I have learned from my Father I have made known to you.." -[John 15:15]

Night Watch

A nurse took the tired, anxious serviceman to the bedside. "Your son is here," she said to the old man. She had to repeat the words several times before the patient's eyes opened. Heavily sedated because of the pain of his heart attack, he dimly saw the young uniformed Marine standing outside he oxygen tent. He reached out his hand.

The Marine wrapped his toughened fingers around the old man's limp ones, squeezing a message of love and encouragement. The nurse brought a chair so that the Marine could sit beside the bed. All through the night the young Marine sat there in the poorly lighted ward, holding the old man's hand and offering him words of love and strength.

Occasionally, the nurse suggested that the Marine move away and rest awhile. He refused. Whenever the nurse came into the ward, the Marine was oblivious of her and of the night noises of the hospital - the clanking of the oxygen tank, the laughter of the night staff members exchanging greetings, the cries and moans of the other patients.

Now and then she heard him say a few gentle words. The dying man said nothing, only held tightly to his son all through the night. Along towards dawn, the old man died. The Marine released the now lifeless hand he had been holding and went to tell the nurse. While she did what she had to do, he waited. Finally, she returned.

She started to offer words of sympathy, but the Marine interrupted her.

"Who was that man?" he asked.

The nurse was startled; "He was your father," she answered.

"No, he wasn't," the Marine replied. "I never saw him before in my life."

"Then why didn't you say something when I took you to him?"

"I knew right away there had been a mistake, but I also knew he needed his son, and his son just wasn't here. When I realized that he was too sick to tell whether or not I was his son, knowing how much he needed me. I stayed."

The next time someone needs you...be there.   STAY. You'll be glad you did.

The Old Man and His Dog
Better get a tissue for this one! It's long but you'll enjoy it.

"Watch out! You nearly broad-sided that car!" My father yelled at me. "Can't you do anything right?"

Those words hurt worse than blows. I turned my head toward the elderly man in the seat beside me, daring me to challenge him. A lump rose in my throat as I averted my eyes. I wasn't prepared for another battle.

"I saw the car, Dad. Please don't yell at me when I'm driving." My voice was measured and steady, sounding far calmer than I really felt.

Dad glared at me, then turned away and settled back.

At home I left Dad in front of the television and went outside to collect my thoughts. Dark, heavy clouds hung in the air with a promise of rain. The rumble of distant thunder seemed to echo my inner turmoil. What could I do about him? Dad had been a lumberjack in Washington and Oregon. He had enjoyed being outdoors and had reveled in pitting his strength against the forces of nature. He had entered grueling lumberjack competitions, and had placed often. The shelves in his house were filled with trophies that attested to his prowess.

The years marched on relentlessly. The first time he couldn't lift a heavy log, he joked about it; but later that same day I saw him outside alone, straining to lift it. He became irritable whenever anyone teased him about his advancing age, or when he couldn't do something he had done as a younger man.

Four days after his sixty-seventh birthday, he had a heart attack. An ambulance sped him to the hospital while a paramedic administered CPR to keep blood and oxygen flowing. At the hospital, Dad was rushed into an operating room. He was lucky; he survived.

But something inside Dad died. His zest for life was gone. He obstinately refused to follow doctors orders. Suggestions and offers of help were turned aside with sarcasm and insults. The number of visitors thinned, then finally stopped altogether. Dad was left alone.

My husband, Rick, and I asked Dad to come live with us on our small farm. We hoped the fresh air and rustic atmosphere would help him adjust.

Within a week after he moved in, I regretted the invitation. It seemed nothing was satisfactory. He criticized everything I did. I became frustrated and moody. Soon I was taking my pent-up anger out on Rick. We began to bicker and argue.

Alarmed, Rick sought out our pastor and explained the situation. The clergyman set up weekly counseling appointments for us. At the close of each session he prayed, asking God to soothe Dad's troubled mind. But the months wore on and God was silent.

A raindrop struck my cheek. I looked up into the gray sky. Somewhere up there was "God." Although I believe a Supreme Being had created the universe, I had difficulty believing that God cared about the tiny human beings on this earth. I was tired of waiting for a God who did not answer.

Something had to be done and it was up to me to do it. The next day I sat down with the phone book and methodically called each of the mental health clinics listed in the Yellow Pages. I explained my problem in vain to each of the sympathetic voices that answered.

Just when I was giving up hope, one of the voices suddenly exclaimed, "I just read something that might help you! Let me go get the article."

I listened as she read. The article described a remarkable study done at a nursing home. All of the patients were under treatment for chronic depression. Yet their attitudes had improved dramatically when they were each given responsibility for a pet dog.

That afternoon I drove to the animal shelter. After I filled out a questionnaire, a uniformed officer led me to the kennels. The odor of disinfectant stung my nostrils as I moved down the row of pens. Each contained five to seven dogs. Long-haired dogs, curly-haired dogs, black dogs, spotted dogs - all jumped up, trying to reach me. I studied each one but rejected one after the other for various reasons, too big, too small, too much hair.

As I neared the last pen a dog in the shadows of the far corner struggled to his feet, walked to the front of the run and sat down. It was a pointer, one of the dog world's aristocrats. But this was a caricature of the breed. Years had etched his face and muzzle with shades of gray. His hipbones jutted out in lopsided triangles. But it was his eyes that caught and held my attention. Calm and clear, they beheld me unwaveringly.

I pointed to the dog. "Can you tell me about him?"

The officer looked, then shook his head in puzzlement. "He's a funny one. Appeared out of nowhere and sat in front of the gate. We brought him in, figuring someone would be right down to claim him. That was two weeks ago and we've heard nothing. His time is up tomorrow." He gestured helplessly.

As the words sank in I turned to the man in horror. "You mean you're going to kill him?"

"Ma'am," he said gently, "that's our policy. We don't have room for every unclaimed dog."

I looked at the pointer again. The calm brown eyes awaited my decision. "I'll take him," I said.

I drove home with the dog on the front seat beside me. When I reached the house I honked the horn twice. I was helping my prize out of the car when Dad shuffled onto the front porch. "Ta-da! Look what I got for you, Dad!" I said excitedly.

Dad looked, then wrinkled his face in disgust. "If I had wanted a dog I would have gotten one. And I would have picked out a better specimen than that bag of bones. Keep it! I don't want it." Dad waved his arm scornfully and turned back toward the house.

Anger rose inside me. It squeezed together my throat muscles and pounded into my temples. "You'd better get used to him, Dad. He's staying!"

Dad ignored me.

"Did you hear me, Dad?" I screamed.

At those words Dad whirled angrily, his hands clenched at his sides, his eyes narrowed and blazing with hate. We stood glaring at each other like duelists, when suddenly the pointer pulled free from my grasp. He wobbled toward my dad and sat down in front of him. Then slowly, carefully, he raised his paw.

Dad's lower jaw trembled as he stared at the uplifted paw. Confusion replaced the anger in his eyes. The pointer waited patiently. Then Dad was on his knees hugging the animal. It was the beginning of a warm and intimate friendship.

Dad named the pointer Cheyenne. Together he and Cheyenne explored the community. They spent long hours walking down dusty lanes. They spent reflective moments on the banks of streams, angling for tasty trout. They even started to attend Sunday services together, Dad sitting in a pew and Cheyenne lying quietly at his feet.

Dad and Cheyenne were inseparable throughout the next three years. Dad's bitterness faded, and he and Cheyenne made many friends.

Then late one night I was startled to feel Cheyenne's cold nose burrowing through our bed covers. He had never before come into our bedroom at night. I woke Rick, put on my robe and ran into my father's room. Dad lay in his bed, his face serene. But his spirit had left quietly sometime during the night.

Two days later my shock and grief deepened when I discovered Cheyenne lying dead beside Dad's bed. I wrapped his still form in the rag rug he had slept on. As Rick and I buried him near a favorite fishing hole, I silently thanked the dog for the help he had given me in restoring Dad's peace of mind.

The morning of Dad's funeral dawned overcast and dreary. This day looks like the way I feel, I thought, as I walked down the aisle to the pews reserved for family. I was surprised to see the many friends Dad and Cheyenne had made filling the church.

The pastor began his eulogy. It was a tribute to both Dad and the dog who had changed his life. And then the pastor turned to Hebrews 13:2. "Be not forgetful to entertain strangers..."

I've often thanked God for sending that angel," he said.

For me, the past dropped into place, completing a puzzle that I had not seen before: the sympathetic voice that had just read the right article... Cheyenne's unexpected appearance at the animal shelter. His calm acceptance and complete devotion to my father...and the proximity of their deaths.

And suddenly I understood. I knew that God had answered my prayers after all.

~by Catherine Moore~ (Mountain Wings # 5088)

The Old Telephone

When I was quite young, my father had one of the first telephones in our neighborhood. I remember the polished, old case fastened to the wall. The shiny receiver hung on the side of the box. I was too little to reach the telephone, but used to listen with fascination when my mother talked to it.

Then I discovered that somewhere inside the wonderful device lived an amazing person. Her name was "Information Please" and there was nothing she did not know. Information Please could supply anyone's number and the correct time.

My personal experience with the genie-in-a-bottle came one day while my mother was visiting a neighbor. Amusing myself at the tool bench in the basement, I whacked my finger with a hammer, the pain was terrible, but there seemed no point in crying because there was no one home to give sympathy.

I walked around the house sucking my throbbing finger, finally arriving at the stairway. The telephone! Quickly, I ran for the footstool in the parlor and dragged it to the landing. Climbing up, I unhooked the receiver in the parlor and held it to my ear.

"Information, please" I said into the mouthpiece just above my head.

A click or two and a small clear voice spoke into my ear. "Information."

"I hurt my finger..." I wailed into the phone, the tears came readily enough now that I had an audience.

"Isn't your mother home?" came the question.

"Nobody's home but me," I blubbered.

"Are you bleeding?" the voice asked.

"No," I replied. "I hit my finger with the hammer and it hurts."

"Can you open the icebox?" she asked. I said I could. "Then chip off a little bit of ice and hold it to your finger," said the voice.

After that, I called "Information Please" for everything. I asked her for help with my geography, and she told me where Philadelphia was. She helped me with my math. She told me my pet chipmunk that I had caught in the park just the day before, would eat fruit and nuts.

Then, there was the time Petey, our pet canary, died. I called, "Information Please," and told her the sad story. She listened, and then said things grown-ups say to soothe a child.

But I was not consoled. I asked her, "Why is it that birds should sing so beautifully and bring joy to all families, only to end up as a heap of feathers on the bottom of a cage?"

She must have sensed my deep concern, for she said quietly, "Paul always remember that there are other worlds to sing in.'

Somehow I felt better. Another day I was on the telephone, "Information Please."

"Information," said in the now familiar voice.

"How do I spell fix?" I asked.

All this took place in a small town in the Pacific Northwest.

When I was nine years old, we moved across the country to Boston. I missed my friend very much. "Information Please" belonged in that old wooden box back home and I somehow never thought of trying the shiny new phone that sat on the table in the hall.

As I grew into my teens, the memories of those childhood conversations never really left me. Often, in moments of doubt and perplexity I would recall the serene sense of security I had then I appreciated now how patient, understanding, and kind she was to have spent her time on a little boy.

A few years later, on my way west to college, my plane put down in Seattle. I had about a half-hour or so between planes. I spent 15 minutes or so on the phone with my sister, who lived there now.

Then without thinking what I was doing, I dialed my hometown operator and said, "Information Please."

Miraculously, I heard the small, clear voice I knew so well.

"Information." I hadn't planned this, but I heard myself saying, "Could you please tell me how to spell fix?"

There was a long pause. Then came the soft spoken answer, "I guess your finger must have healed by now."

I laughed, "So it's really you," I said. "I wonder if you have any idea how much you meant to me during that time?"

I wonder," she said, "if you know how much your calls meant to me. I never had any children and I used to look forward to your calls."

I told her how often I had thought of her over the years and I asked if I could call her again when I came back to visit my sister.

"Please do", she said. "Just ask for Sally."

Three months later I was back in Seattle. A different voice answered, "Information."

I asked for Sally.

"Are you a friend?" she said.

"Yes, a very old friend," I answered.

"I'm sorry to have to tell you this," she said. "Sally had been working part-time the last few years because she was sick. She died five weeks ago."

Before I could hang up she said, "Wait a minute, did you say your name was Paul?"

"Yes." I answered.

"Well, Sally left a message for you. She wrote it down in case you called. Let me read it to you."

The note said, "Tell him there are other worlds to sing in. He'll know what I mean."

I thanked her and hung up. I knew what Sally meant.

Never underestimate the impression you may make on others. Whose life have you touched today?

May you find the joy and peace you long for. Life is a journey ... NOT a guided tour.

Beautiful One-liners

1. Give God what's right -- not what's left.
2. Man's way leads to a hopeless end -- God's way leads to an endless hope.
3. A lot of kneeling will keep you in good standing.
4. He who kneels before God can stand before anyone.
5. In the sentence of life, the devil may be a comma--but never let him be the period.
6. Don't put a question mark where God puts a period.
7. Are you wrinkled with burden? Come to the church for a face-lift.

8. When praying, don't give God instructions - just report for duty.

9. Don't wait for six strong men to take you to church.

10. We don't change God's message – His message changes us.

11. The church is prayer-conditioned.

12. When God ordains, He sustains.

13. WARNING: Exposure to the Son may prevent burning.

14. Plan ahead -- It wasn't raining when Noah built the ark.

15. Most people want to serve God, but only in an advisory position.

16. Suffering from truth decay? Brush up on your Bible.

17. Exercise daily -- walk with the Lord.

18. Never give the devil a ride – he will always want to drive

19. .Nothing else ruins the truth like stretching it.

20. Compassion is difficult to give away because it keeps coming back.

21. He who angers you controls you.

22. Worry is the darkroom in which negatives can develop.

23. Give Satan an inch & he'll be a ruler.

24. Be ye fishers of men -- you catch them & He'll clean them.

Only a Mother...

Only a mother can listen to the same knock-knock joke 27 times without hollering, "Nobody's home!"

Only a mother will unwind 56 feet of toilet paper so her little darling can have the empty roll to make her a Mother's Day present.

Only a mother knows the exact temperature a crayon will melt on the dashboard.

Only a mother will try to hide a leafy green vegetable in a cookie.

Only a mother sees a Picasso in the scribbles decorating the refrigerator.

Only a mother knows all the verses to "This Old Man."

Only a mother can deal out emergency lunch money from the dryer lint filter.

Only a mother can find her last good pair of pantyhose hitching a wagon to a tricycle.

Only a mother is limber enough to wrestle a fitted sheet onto the top bunk bed.

Only a mother will attempt to grow hydroponic tomatoes in one night for a last-minute science project.

Only a mother has a bathtub filled with little yellow duckies.

Only a mother will notice that there are only four pieces of pie for five people and promptly announce that she never did care for pie.

Dear Ann Landers: While going through some papers, I came across a yellowed clipping from one of your columns printed in 1966. I have two sons and five grandchildren, all of whom live nearby. They are always "too busy" to call or stop by. I hope you will print this letter again and ask them to remember us. -- Frustrated Grandma in Ft. Lauderdale, Fla.

Dear Grandma: Several readers have asked me to reprint this one. Here it is: Dear Ann Landers: Today is my mother's birthday. For the first time since I was a little girl, I cannot give her a gift. After I married, we lived only a mile apart. I always managed to run in and drop off a present I had picked up at the last minute. Sometimes I didn't even wait long enough to have it gift-wrapped. No matter what it was, she'd smile and say, "You knew exactly what I wanted, didn't you, dear?"

Then I'd head for the door, and she would sigh, "I wish you could sit down and visit for a little while. You are always in such a hurry." My stock answer was, "I wish I could, Mom, and I will, one of these days ... we'll have a really good visit, but today, I have so many things to do, I must get going." For the life of me, I can't remember what I was doing that was so important, but I was always running.

"One of these days" will never come because Mom passed away last week. For the very first time in her wonderful, unselfish life, she was the one who didn't have time for me. She had a massive heart attack and went so fast, I'm not sure she heard me say, "I love you, Mom."

Time has a sneaky way of slipping away. We all get so involved in our own little worlds, and before you know it, the tomorrows are yesterdays. If I can encourage just one person to stop, no matter how busy, and find an hour to visit his or her mother, it will be the best gift I could give my mom. And it will be the best present your readers could give theirs. -- I'll Miss Her Forever ...Only A Mother.

Penicillin.

His name was Fleming, and he was a poor Scottish farmer.

One day, while trying to make a living for his family, he heard a cry for help coming from a nearby bog. He dropped his tools and ran to the bog. There, mired to his waist in black muck, was a terrified boy, screaming and struggling to free himself. Farmer Fleming saved the lad from what could have been a slow and terrifying death.

The next day, a fancy carriage pulled up to the Scotsman's sparse surroundings. An elegantly dressed nobleman stepped out and introduced himself as the father of the boy Farmer Fleming had saved. "I want to repay you," said the nobleman. "You saved my son's life."

"No, I can't accept payment for what I did," the Scottish farmer replied waving off the offer. At that moment, the farmer's own son came to the door of the family hovel.

"Is that your son?" the nobleman asked.

"Yes," the farmer replied proudly.

"I'll make you a deal. Let me provide him with the level of education my own son will enjoy. If the lad is anything like his father, he'll no doubt grow to be a man we both will be proud of ".

And that he did. Farmer Fleming's son attended the very best schools and in time, graduated from St. Mary's Hospital Medical School in London, and went on to become known throughout the world as the noted Sir Alexander Fleming, the discoverer of Penicillin.

Years afterward, the same nobleman's son who was saved from the bog was stricken with pneumonia. What saved his life this time?   Penicillin.

The name of the nobleman? Lord Randolph Churchill. His son's name?   Sir Winston Churchill.

Someone once said: What goes around comes around.

Work, like you don't need the money.

Love, like you've never been hurt.

Dance, like nobody's watching.

Sing, like nobody's listening.

Pennies From Heaven

You always hear the usual stories of pennies on the sidewalk being good luck, gifts from angels, etc. This is the first time I've ever heard this twist on the story. Gives you something to think about.

Several years ago, a friend of mine and her husband were invited to spend the weekend at the husband's employer's home. My friend, Arlene, was nervous about the weekend. The boss was very wealthy, with a fine home on the waterway, and cars costing more than her house.

The first day and evening went well, and Arlene was delighted to have this rare glimpse into how the very wealthy live. The husband's employer was quite generous as a host, and took them to the finest restaurants. Arlene knew she would never have the opportunity to indulge in this kind of extravagance again, so was enjoying herself immensely.

As the three of them were about to enter an exclusive restaurant that evening, the boss was walking slightly ahead of Arlene and her husband. He stopped suddenly, looking down on the pavement for a long, silent moment.

Arlene wondered if she was supposed to pass him. There was nothing on the ground except a single darkened penny that someone had dropped, and a few cigarette butts. Still silent, the man reached down and picked up the penny.

He held it up and smiled, then put it in his pocket as if he had found a great treasure. How absurd! What need did this man have for a single penny? Why would he even take the time to stop and pick it up?

Throughout dinner, the entire scene nagged at her. Finally, she could stand it no longer. She causally mentioned that her daughter once had a coin collection, and asked if the penny he had found had been of some value.

A smile crept across the man's face as he reached into his pocket for the penny and held it out for her to see. She had seen many pennies before! What was the point of this?

"Look at it." He said. "Read what it says."

She read the words "United States of America."

"No, not that; read further."

"One cent?" "No, keep reading."

"In God we Trust?" "Yes!" "And?"

"And if I trust in God, the name of God is holy, even on a coin. Whenever I find a coin I see that inscription. It is written on every single United States coin, but we never seem to notice it!

God drops a message right in front of me telling me to trust Him? Who am I to pass it by? When I see a coin, I pray, I stop to see if my trust IS in God at that moment. I pick the coin up as a response to God; that I do trust in Him. For a short time, at least, I cherish it as if it were gold. I think it is God's way of starting a conversation with me.

Lucky for me, God is patient and pennies are plentiful!

When I was out shopping today, I found a penny on the sidewalk. I stopped and picked it up, and realized that I had been worrying and fretting in my mind about things I cannot change. I read the words, "In God We Trust," and had to laugh. Yes, God, I get the message.

It seems that I have been finding an inordinate number of pennies in the last few months, but then, pennies are plentiful!

And, God is patient... Have a blessed day!!

From: Stan & Dottie Roser

Perspective

One day a very wealthy father took his son on a trip to the country for the sole purpose of showing his son how it was to be poor. They spent a few days and nights on the farm of what would be considered a very poor family. After their return from the trip, the father asked his son how he liked the trip.

"It was great, Dad," the son replied.

"Did you see how poor people can be?" the father asked.

"Oh Yeah," said the son.

"So what did you learn from the trip?" asked the father.

The son answered, "I saw that we have one dog and they had four. We have a pool that reaches to the middle of our garden and they have a creek that has no end. We have imported lanterns in our garden and they have the stars at night. Our patio reaches to the front yard and they have the whole horizon. We have a small piece of land to live on and they have fields that go beyond our sight. We have servants who serve us, but they serve others. We buy our food, but they grow theirs. We have walls around our property to protect us, they have friends to protect them."

The boy's father was speechless. Then his son added, "It showed me how poor we are." Too many times we forget what we have and concentrate on what we don't have. What is one person's worthless object is another's prize possession. It is all based on one's perspective. Makes you wonder what would happen if we all gave thanks to the Creator for all the bounty we have been provided by Him, instead of worrying about wanting more.

Take joy in all He has given each and every one of us, especially rejoice in our friends.

Phoenix Fire Department or The Littlest Firefighter
(Rated: "4-1/2 tissues")

In Phoenix, Arizona, a 26-year-old mother stared down at her six-year-old son, who was dying of terminal leukemia. Although her heart was filled with sadness, she also had a strong feeling of determination. Like any parent, she wanted her son to grow up and fulfill all his dreams. Now that was no longer possible. The leukemia would see to that. But she still wanted her son's dreams to come true.

She took her son's hand and asked, "Billy, did you ever think about what you wanted to be once you grew up? Did you ever dream and wish what you would do with your life?"

"Mommy, I always wanted to be a fireman when I grew up."

Mom smiled back and said, "Let's see if we can make your wish come true." Later that day she went to her local fire department in Phoenix, Arizona, where she met Firefighter Bob, who had a heart as big as Phoenix. She explained her son's final wish and asked if it might be possible to give her six-year-old son a ride around the block on a fire engine.

Firefighter Bob said, "Look, we can do better than that, if you'll have your son ready at seven o'clock Wednesday morning, we'll make him an honorary Firefighter for the whole day. He can come down to the fire station, eat with us, go out on all the fire calls, the whole nine yards! And if you'll give us his sizes, we'll get a real fire uniform for him, with a real fire hat-not a toy one-with the emblem of the Phoenix Fire Department on it, a yellow slicker like we wear and rubber boots. They're all manufactured right here in Phoenix, so we can get them fast."

Three days later Firefighter Bob picked up Billy, dressed him in his fire uniform and escorted him from his hospital bed to the waiting hook and ladder truck. Billy got to sit on the back of the truck and help steer it back to the fire station. He was in heaven. There were three fire calls in Phoenix that day and Billy got to go out on all three calls. He rode in the different fire engines, the paramedic's van, and even the fire chief's car. He was also videotaped for the local news program. Having his dream come true, with all the love and attention that was lavished upon him, so deeply touched Billy that he lived three months longer than any doctor thought possible.

One night all of his vital signs began to drop dramatically and the head nurse, who believed in the hospice concept that no one should die alone, began to call the family members to the hospital. Then she remembered the day Billy had spent as a firefighter, so she called the Fire Chief and asked if it would be possible to send a fireman in uniform to the hospital to be with Billy as he made his transition.

The chief replied, "We can do better than that. We'll be there in five minutes. Will you please do me a favor? "When you hear the sirens screaming and see the lights flashing, will you announce over the PA system that there is not a fire? It's just the fire department coming to see one of its finest members one more time. And will you open the window to his room?"

About five minutes later a hook and ladder truck arrived at the hospital and extended its ladder up to Billy's third floor open window. 16 firefighters climbed up the ladder into Billy's room. With his mother's permission, they hugged him and held him and told him how much they loved him. With his dying breath, Billy looked up at the fire chief and said, "Chief, am I really a firefighter now?"

"Billy, you are! And the Head Chief, Jesus, is holding your hand," the chief said.

With those words, Billy smiled and said, "I know, He's been holding my hand all day, and the angels have been singing." He closed his eyes one last time.

The Pink Dress

There was this little girl sitting by herself in the park. Everyone passed by her and never stopped to see why she looked so sad. Dressed in a worn pink dress, barefoot and dirty, the girl just sat and watched the people go by. She never tried to speak. She never said a word. Many people passed by her, but no one would stop.

The next day I decided to go back to the park in curiosity to see if the little girl would still be there. Yes, she was there, right in the very spot where she was yesterday, and still with the same sad look in her eyes. Today I was to make my own move and walk over to the little girl. For as we all know, a park full of strange people is not a place for young children to play alone. As I got closer I could see the back of the little girl's dress. It was grotesquely shaped. I figured that was the reason people just passed by and made no effort to speak to her.

Deformities are a low blow to our society and, heaven forbid if you make a step toward assisting someone who is different. As I got closer, the little girl lowered her eyes slightly to avoid my intent stare. As I approached her, I could see the shape of her back more clearly. She was grotesquely shaped in a humped over form. I smiled to let her know it was OK; I was there to help, to talk. I sat down beside her and opened with a simple, "Hello".

The little girl acted shocked, and stammered a "Hi", after a long stare into my eyes. I smiled and she shyly smiled back. We talked until darkness fell and the park was completely empty.

I asked the girl why she was so sad.

The little girl looked at me with a sad face said, "Because, I'm different".

I immediately said, "That you are!"; and smiled.

The little girl acted even sadder and said, "I know."

"Little girl," I said, "you remind me of an angel, sweet and innocent."

She looked at me and smiled, then slowly she got to her feet and said, "Really?"

"Yes, you're like a little Guardian Angel sent to watch over all people walking by."

She nodded her head yes, and smiled. With that she opened the back of her pink dress and allowed her wings to

spread, then she said "I am. I'm your Guardian Angel," with a twinkle in her eye.

I was speechless -- sure I was seeing things.

She said, "For once you thought of someone other than yourself. My job here is done".

I got to my feet and said, "Wait, why did no one stop to help an angel?"

She looked at me, smiled, and said, "You're the only one that could see me," and then she was gone.

And with that, my life was changed dramatically. So, when you think you're all you have, remember, your angel is always watching over you.

Pass this to everyone that means anything at all to you.

Like the story says, we all need someone...And, every one of your friends is an Angel in their own way. The value of a friend is measured in the heart. I hope your Guardian Angel watches over you always .   *sent by Jane Montgomery*

The Portal

Over 20 years ago I read a fictional story about a device that would allow you to live forever. Strangely, I sit here thinking about that story now. The thought flooded my mind and interrupted what I was doing and said "write it now!"

The operation of the device was simple. It was just a portal that you walked through, and when you walked through five years were added to your life. There was no cost, at least not in terms of money. Each time you walked through and gained five years, five years were removed from your memory. The good thing was, you could choose which five-year period would be erased. As the story was told, no one ever walked through because no one could find five years that they wanted to give up. Suppose I had that opportunity? Could I choose five years to give up? All have had periods in their lives rougher than others. ...times of economic strain ...times of ailing and aching bodies. ...times of romantic loneliness, turmoil, or heartbreak. ...times of fear and uncertainty. and then ...times of prosperity and plenty. ...times exhilarating youthful energy and vitality. ...times where love conquers all. ...times where we can't wait until tomorrow. What were the worst five years of my life? Would I erase those if I could? Would you?

The tough times made me stronger, wiser, and more appreciative of the easy times. The tough times are just as much a part of who I am and why I am who I am as the easy times. I can look outside on a freezing day and appreciate warmth because as a teenager I carried newspapers at 4a.m. each morning on a bicycle. My hands and feet were nearly frozen daily. Would I give up those five years of the freezing paper route? Not hardly. Each age has its beauty and its strain, its pleasure and its pain and with any piece missing, we are not the same.

What I read 20 years ago was just a story. There is only one true way to get eternal life. That is also a portal. It does not require that you erase anything of the past, just get some things straight in the present that automatically washes away some things of the past. ***"Because straight is the gate, and narrow is the way, which leads to life, and few there be that find it."*** Matt 7:14   ~*A MountainWings Original*~#5094

Positive choices

Michael is the kind of guy you love to hate. He is always in a good mood and always has something positive to say. When someone would ask him how he was doing, he would reply, "If I were any better, I would be twins!" He was a natural motivator. If an employee was having a bad day, Michael was there telling the employee how to look on the positive side of the situation.

Seeing this style really made me curious, so one day I went up to Michael and asked him, "I don't get it! You can't be a positive person all of the time. How do you do it?"

Michael replied, "Each morning I wake up and say to myself, you have two choices today. You can choose to be in a good mood or you can choose to be in a bad mood. I choose to be in a good mood." Each time something bad happens, I can choose to be a victim or...I can choose to learn from it. I choose to learn from it. Every time someone comes to me complaining, I can choose to accept their complaining or... I can point out the positive side of life. I choose the positive side of life.

"Yeah, right, it's not that easy," I protested.

"Yes, it is," Michael said. "Life is all about choices. When you cut away all the junk, every situation is a choice. You choose how you react to situations. You choose how people affect your mood. You choose to be in a good mood or bad mood. The bottom line: It's your choice how you live your life."

I reflected on what Michael said. Soon hereafter, I left to start my own business. We lost touch, but I often thought about him when I made a choice about life instead of reacting to it. Several years later, I heard that Michael was involved in a serious accident, falling some 60 feet from a com-munications tower. After 18 hours of surgery and weeks of intensive care, Michael was released from the hospital with rods placed in his back.

I saw Michael about six months after the accident. When I asked him how he was, he replied, "If I were any better, I'd be twins. Wanna see my scars?"

I declined to see his wounds, but I did ask him what had gone through his mind as the accident took place.

"The first thing that went through my mind was the well-being of my soon-to-be born daughter," Michael replied. "Then, as I lay on the ground, I remembered that I had two choices: I could choose to live or...I could choose to die. I chose to live."

"Weren't you scared? Did you lose consciousness?" I asked.

Michael continued, "the paramedics were great. They kept telling me I was going to be fine. But when they wheeled me into the ER and I saw the expressions on the faces of the doctors and nurses, I got really scared. In their eyes, I read 'he's a dead man'. I knew I needed to take action."

"What did you do?" I asked.

"Well, there was a big burly nurse shouting questions at me," said Michael. "She asked if I was allergic to anything. 'Yes, I replied.' The doctors and nurses stopped working as they waited for my reply. I took a deep breath and yelled, 'Gravity'." Over their laughter, I told them, "I am choosing to live. Operate on me as if I am alive, not dead." Michael lived, thanks to the skill of his doctors, but also because of his amazing attitude... I learned from him that every day we have the choice to live fully. Attitude, after all, is everything. **"Therefore do not worry about tomorrow, for tomorrow will worry about itself. Each day has enough trouble of its own."** *Matthew 6:34.* After all, today is the tomorrow you worried about yesterday.

Profit, My Way
By Walt Banco

In the beginning there was nothing.
This was to be known as the void.
Now we have Christmas, Jesus, Santa and Freud.
There is a hunger that gnaws the soul
Needing to be fed so one can feel whole.
Lucky are those who know their need,
Fortunate when not influenced by greed.
Profit is the game at this time
Coin of the realm is small as a dime.
Profit is the game we do find,
A need there is for a better kind.
Now, profit from mistakes past
Good decisions will tend to last.
When we come to what's neglected,
We profit to do what's expected.
Mental wrangling is a dastardly plight'
Looking for what could be wrong, or be right?
Grey vision is 'tween the black and the white
White and right profit is such a delight!

Puppies For Sale

    A farmer had some puppies he needed to sell. He painted a sign advertising the pups and set about nailing it to a post on the edge of his yard. As he was driving the last nail into the post, he felt a tug on his overalls. He looked down into the eyes of a little boy.
    "Mister," he said, "I want to buy one of your puppies." "Well," said the farmer, as he rubbed the sweat off the back of his neck, "these puppies come from fine parents and cost a good deal of money." The boy dropped his head for a moment.

Then reaching deep into his pocket, he pulled out a handful of change and held it up to the farmer. "I've got thirty-nine cents. Is that enough to take a look?"

"Sure," said the farmer. And with that he let out a whistle, "Here, Dolly!" he called. Out from the dog house and down the ramp ran Dolly followed by four little balls of fur.

The little boy pressed his face against the chain link fence. His eyes danced with delight. As the dogs made their way to the fence, the little boy noticed something else stirring inside the doghouse.

Slowly another little ball appeared; this one noticeably smaller. Down the ramp it slid. Then in a somewhat awkward manner the little pup began hobbling toward the others, doing its best to catch up... "I want that one," the little boy said, pointing to the runt.

The farmer knelt down at the boy's side and said, "Son, you don't want that puppy. He will never be able to run and play with you like these other dogs would."

With that the little boy stepped back from the fence, reached down, and began rolling up one leg of his trousers. In doing so he revealed a steel brace running down both sides of his leg attaching itself to a specially made shoe. Looking back up at the farmer, he said, "You see sir, I don't run too well myself, and he will need someone who understands."

"The world is full of people who need someone who understands". Jesus said, **"If you are ashamed of me, I will be ashamed of you before my Father."** Not ashamed? Pass this on . . .but only if you mean it. Yes, I do Love God. He is my source of existence and Savior. He keeps me functioning each and everyday. Without Him, I will be nothing. Without him, I am nothing but with Him **I can do all things through Christ that strengthens me.** (Phil 4:13.)

(Reprint from Volume One)

The Question

I have a question for you. Have you ever been in love? Really in love... deep down in your soul?

I think, at 60, after praying for it (watch out what you wish for), I finally got it. I just don't think the good Lord heard me correctly.

I have always wanted it to be a good, forever, two-way street relationship. I discovered the pain; humbling, at best. But, I do believe I have figured it out, what it means, what it is, why ONE, only human person, on all of this earth, with all their faults, can mean the world to one person.

If you find it (love), it is the conduit to God. Human beings are not capable of that kind of love. When that connection occurs, it is the portal to God and the universe. Only with that one person do you have the opening to feel God.

For God is love.

It is devastating to not have access to the door.

That is what "I" have learned.

They say (whoever "they" are) that if you missed a lesson in Chapters 1 or 2, it will catch up with you in Chapter 28 or 29 or even at 60!   *by Barbara Valentino, MountainWings #5098*

Remember the Duck

There was a little boy visiting his grandparents on their farm. He was given a slingshot to play with out in the woods. He practiced in the woods, but he could never hit the target. Getting a little discouraged; he headed back to dinner. As he was walking back, he saw Grandma's pet duck. Just out of impulse, he let the slingshot fly, hit the duck square in the head, and killed it. He was shocked and grieved. In a panic, he hid the dead duck in the woodpile, only to see his sister watching. Sally had seen it all, but she said nothing.

After lunch the next day Grandma said, "Sally, let's wash the dishes."

But Sally said, "Grandma, Johnny told me he wanted to help in the kitchen." Then she whispered to him, "Remember the duck?" So Johnny did the dishes.

Later that day, Grandpa asked if the children wanted to go fishing and Grandma said, "I'm sorry but I need Sally to help make supper."

Sally just smiled and said, " Well that's all right because Johnny told me he wanted to help. She whispered again, "Remember the duck?" So Sally went fishing, and Johnny stayed to help.

After several days of Johnny doing both his chores and Sally's, he finally couldn't stand it any longer. He came to Grandma and confessed that he had killed the duck.

Grandma knelt down, gave him a hug, and said, "Sweetheart, I know. You see, I was standing at the window and I saw the whole thing. But because I love you, I forgave you. I was just wondering how long you would let Sally make a slave of you."

Thought for the day and every day thereafter: Whatever is in your past, whatever you have done and the devil keeps throwing it up in your face (lying, debt, fear, hatred, anger, unforgiveness, bitterness, etc.) whatever it is, you need to know that God was standing at the window and HE saw the whole thing, HE has seen your whole life. He wants you to know that He loves you and that you are forgiven. He is just wondering how long you will let the devil make a slave of you. The great thing about God is that when you ask for forgiveness, He not only forgives you, but He forgets - It is by God's Grace and Mercy that we are saved.

The Right to Sneeze

They walked in tandem, each of the ninety-three students filing into the already crowded auditorium. With rich maroon gowns flowing and the traditional caps, they looked almost as grown up as they felt. Dads swallowed hard behind broad smiles, and moms freely brushed away tears.

This class would not pray during the commencements----- not by choice but because of a recent court ruling prohibiting it. The principal and several students were careful to stay within the guidelines allowed by the ruling. They gave inspirational and challenging speeches, but no one mentioned divine guidance and no one asked for blessings on the graduates or their families. The speeches were nice, but they were routine.......until the final speech received a standing ovation.

A solitary student walked proudly to the microphone. He stood still and silent for just a moment, and then, it happened. All 92 students, every single one of them, suddenly **SNEEZED!!!!**

The student on stage simply looked at the audience and said, "GOD BLESS YOU, each and every one of you!" And he walked off stage...The audience exploded into applause. The graduating class found a unique way to invoke God's blessing on their future with or without the court's approval. Isn't this a wonderful story? Pass it on to all your friends........and GOD BLESS YOU!!!!

The Right Words
~by Susan Tier~ (MW #2120)

Lord, give me the right words to say
To broken hearts that come my way
To those who have been hurt before
That, I not hurt them any more
To those whose hearts have hardened up
To those who won't hold out their cup
That, Lord, You long to overflow
With love and mercy. Lord, let me know

That I might have the words to say
That I might plant a seed today
That glory would be given to You
Through all I say and all I do
Lord, give me the right words to say
More hearts are breaking every day
They're out there crying in the night
I long to help them see the light
But, fragile are those souls and weak
So this is why Your words I seek
And pray Thee give me words to say
That I, not one soul, turn away.

Run Through the Rain

by Bob Perks - BobPerks.com

She had been shopping with her Mom in Wal-Mart. She must have been 6 years old, this beautiful brown-haired, freckle-faced image of innocence. It was pouring outside. The kind of rain that gushes over the tops of rain gutters, so much in a hurry to hit the Earth it had no time to flow down the spout. Drains in the nearby parking lot were filled to capacity and some were blocked so that huge puddles laced around parked cars.

We all stood there under the awning and just inside the door of the Wal-Mart. We waited, some patiently, others irritated... because nature messed up their hurried day.

I am always mesmerized by rainfall. I get lost in the sound and sight of the heavens washing away the dirt and dust of the world. Memories of running, splashing so carefree as a child come pouring in as a welcome reprieve from the worries of my day.

Her voice was so sweet as it broke the hypnotic trance we were all caught in.

"Mom, let's run through the rain," she said.

"What?" Mom asked!

"Let's run through the rain!" she repeated.

"No, honey. We'll wait until it slows down a bit," Mom replied. This young child waited about another minute and repeated,

"Mom, let's run through the rain."

"We'll get soaked if we do," Mom said.

"No, we won't, Mom. That's not what you said this morning," the young girl said as she tugged at her Mom's arm.

"This morning? When did I say we could run through the rain and not get wet?"

"Don't you remember? When you were talking to Daddy about his cancer, you said, 'If God can get us through this, He can get us through anything!'"

The entire crowd stopped dead silent. I swear you couldn't hear anything but the rain. We all stood silently. No one came or left in the next few minutes. Her Mom paused and thought for a moment about what she would say. Now some would laugh it off and scold her for being silly. Some might even ignore what was said.

But this was a moment of affirmation in a young child's life. A time when innocent trust can be nurtured so that it will bloom into faith.

"Honey, you are absolutely right. Let's run through the rain. If God let's us get wet, well maybe we just needed washing,"

Then off they ran. We all stood watching, smiling and laughing as they darted past the cars and yes through the puddles. They held their shopping bags over their heads just in case.

They got soaked. But they were followed by a few who screamed and laughed like children all the way to their cars. I want to believe that somewhere down the road in life, Mom will find herself reflecting back on moments they spent together, captured like pictures in the scrapbook of her cherished memories. Maybe when she watches proudly as her daughter graduates, or as her daddy walks her down the aisle on her wedding day. She will laugh again. Her heart will beat a little faster. Her smile will tell the world they love each other. But only they... will share that precious moment, when they ran through the rain believing that God would get them through.

And Yes, I did. I ran. I got wet. I needed washing.

Circumstances or people can take away your material possessions, they can take away your money, they can take away your health. But no one can ever take away your precious memories.

So, don't forget to make time and take the opportunities... To make memories every day! I believe that friends are quiet angels who lift us to our feet when our wings have trouble remembering how to fly. **I HOPE YOU WILL TAKE THE TIME TO RUN THROUGH THE RAIN**

(Reprint from Volume One)

Sandstorms

I am sure that all of you heard about the terrible sandstorms in Iraq April 8-9, 2003 (the worst in 100 years some say) and the drenching rain that followed the next day.

Our troops were bogged down and couldn't move effectively.

The media was already wondering if the troops were in a "quagmire" and dire predictions of gloom and doom came from the left wing media.

What they didn't report was that later, after the weather had cleared, the Marine group that was mired the worst looked out at the plains they were just about to cross. What did they see? Hundreds if not thousands of antitank and antipersonnel mines had been uncovered by the wind and then washed off by the rain. If they had proceeded as planned, many lives would have undoubtedly been lost. As it were, they simply drove around them and let the demolition teams destroy them later.

Praise to His mighty name!
Thank you God, for protecting our young men!

One person once asked George Washington if he thought God was on his side. His reply is reported to be, "It is not that God should be on our side, but that we be on His."

School Shootings!
A Thought Provoking Read

In light of the recent school shootings in Santee and ElCajon, California, and all the others since Columbine; let's see, I think it all started when Madeline Murray O'Hare complained she didn't want any prayer in our schools, and we said OK.

Then someone said you better not read the Bible in school.... the Bible that says thou shalt not kill, thou shalt not steal, and love your neighbor as yourself. And we said, OK.

Dr. Benjamin Spock said we shouldn't spank our children when they misbehave because their little Personalities would be warped and we might damage their self-esteem. And we said, an expert should know what he's talking about so we said OK, we won't spank them anymore.

Then someone said teachers and principals better not discipline our children when they misbehave. And the school administrators said no faculty member in this school better touch a student when they misbehave because we don't want any bad publicity, and we surely don't want to be sued. (There's a big difference between disciplining and touching, beating, smacking, humiliating, kicking, etc.) And we accepted their reasoning.

Then some wise school board member said, since boys will be boys and they're going to do it anyway, let's give our sons all the condoms they want, so they can have all the fun they desire, and we won't have to tell their parents they got them at school. And we said, that's another great idea.

And then someone said let's print magazines with pictures of nude women and call it wholesome, down-to-earth appreciation for the beauty of the female body. And we said we have no problem with that.

And someone else took that appreciation a step further and published pictures of nude children and then stepped further still by making them available on the internet. And we said they're entitled to their free speech.

And the entertainment industry said, let's make TV shows and movies that promote profanity, violence, and illicit sex. And let's record music that encourages rape, drugs, murder, suicide, and satanic themes. And we said it's just entertainment, it has no adverse effect, and nobody takes it seriously anyway, so go right ahead.

Now we're asking ourselves why our children have no conscience, why they don't know right from wrong, and why it doesn't bother them to kill strangers, their classmates, and themselves.

Probably, if we think about it long and hard enough, we can figure it out. I think it has a great deal to do with "WE REAP WHAT WE SOW."

> Dear God, Why didn't you save the students in Santee?   Sincerely, Concerned Student
> AND THE REPLY: Dear Concerned Student
> , I am not allowed in schools.
>   Sincerely,   God.

Funny how simple it is for people to trash God and then wonder why the world's going to hell.

Funny how we believe what the newspapers say, but question what the Bible says.

Funny how everyone wants to go to heaven provided they do not have to believe, think, say, or do anything the Bible says.

Funny how someone can say "I believe in God" but still follow Satan who, by the way, also "believes" in God.

Funny how we are quick to judge but not to be judged.

Funny how you can send a thousand 'jokes' through e-mail and they spread like wildfire, but when you start sending messages regarding the Lord, people think twice about sharing.

Funny how the lewd, crude, vulgar and obscene pass freely through cyberspace . ***Are you laughing?***

Funny how when you go to forward this message, you will not send it to many on your address list because you're not sure what they believe, or what they will think of you for sending it to them.

Funny how I can be more worried about what other people think of me than what God thinks of me. If you discard this thought process, don't sit back and complain about what bad shape America is in.

Scripture Kitty
by Al Allaway

God's whispered call was getting louder. The choosing of 88 verses of Scripture for my professional photo slide show ***"And Let the Heavens Declare..."*** was certainly done with some Divine intervention.

Earlier, I had "heard" His call to do some Inspirational Praise and Worship programs, using slides of His beautiful Creation. But, as often happens with encounters with God, there was no further instruction on the how-to and where-from keys to the equation.

Another full year passed while I concentrated on reading my Bible through again from cover to cover. This time, I made 3x5 file cards of any Bible verse which might possibly apply; ending the year with over 500 index cards.

"Now, what, Lord?" I prayed.

No apparent or obvious answer! Was God asleep?

"Come on," I pleaded, "I can't do this by myself."

The cards had been loosely stacked in chronological order starting with Genesis and ending with Revelation. They made a tall tower on my mom's old wobbly-legged card table, which she had loaned to us for use in our tiny motorhome.

We had this pedigreed Siamese cat named Fiesty who allowed us to travel with her, so who should come bounding down the hall about that time? Fiesty, and the cards went flying in all directions.

"That Darn Cat never ran into a table leg before; what's wrong with her?"

And I then had to consider playing 552 card pick-up. And how to get them all back in order? But, before I strangled the cat, it dawned on me that maybe there was an easier way...

Considering that the general outline was to include seven major parts, this appeared to be as good a time as any to sort verses into seven random piles, such as: *Love*; *Creation*; *Glory*; *Nature*; *Praise*; *Strength*; and *Hope*.

"Okay, how does having seven piles of scripture cards instead of one get me any closer to an answer?" I asked myself, but really sending the thought waves up to my Father, who still appeared to be ignoring me.

"Put it away for awhile," suggested wife Del, "You're trying too hard; let it rest."

"But..."

The phone rang, it was my mother.

"How about coming over for some gin rummy?" she pleaded, "I'm lonesome, today."

Mom had been raised in a very strict Puritan Christian home where cards were an absolute "no-no". But like many people, she had rebelled and allowed the pendulum of her life to swing the exact opposite direction. In her retirement, Mom lived for her cards, for bingo, any games of chance, and dreams of breaking Las Vegas.

"Okay, Mom," I replied, "Just as soon as I solve this problem that's been buggin' me".

"What kind of problem?"

I explained about the scripture cards.

"That's simple," she continued, "Just shuffle each stack and use them however they fall."

Whoa!

Now, I've always had a good dose of Faith in God, so it didn't take long for Mom's idea to germinate into a worthwhile solution.

So I said, "Okay, Lord, how about this? We shuffle each category three times, and trust You to put the Scriptures in an acceptable order." I suggested a rule that I could by-pass any card that didn't seem to fit the pictures or the music, and put it back on the bottom of the deck. Otherwise, all cards **had to be used in whatever order** they ended up.

The amazing thing is that it worked! Pastors of churches were asking me years later how I ever had managed to create such an agreeable blend of verse. But, we know who did all the work, don't we?

God had sent an answer to my plea for help in the form of a tiny little Siamese cat named Fiesty. She had never been so clumsy as to run blindly into a table leg before or anytime afterwards, either.

And Mom could never admit that God might have used her as well.

God rest them both! *(Excerpted from* **"Snowbirds Guarding the Gold"***)*

Seven Wonders

A group of students were asked to list what they thought were the present Seven Wonders of the World. Though there was some disagreement, the following got the most votes:

1. Egypt's Great Pyramids
2. Taj Mahal
3. Grand Canyon
4. Panama Canal
5. Empire State Building
6. St. Peter's Basilica
7. China's Great Wall

While gathering the votes, the teacher noted that one quiet student who had not returned her paper. So she asked the girl if she was having trouble with her list.

The girl replied, "Yes, a little. I couldn't quite make up my mind because there were so many."

The teacher said, "Well, tell us what you have, and maybe we can help you out."

The girl hesitated, then read, "I think the Seven Wonders of the World are:

        1. To touch
        2. To taste
        3. To see
        4. To hear

She hesitated a little, and then added

        5. To feel
        6. To laugh
        7. And to love

The room was so full of silence, you could have heard a pin drop......A gentle reminder to all of you...... ***"The most precious things are before you: Your family, your faith, your love, your good health and above all, your friends."***

The Silversmith

Some time ago, a few ladies met to study Scriptures...While reading the third chapter of Malachi, they came upon a remarkable expression in the third verse: **"And He shall sit as a refiner and purifier of silver"** (Malachi 3:3)"

One lady proposed to visit a silversmith, and report to them on what he said about the subject. She went accordingly, and without telling the object of her errand, begged the silversmith to tell her about the process of refining silver... After he had fully described it to her, she asked, "But Sir, do you sit while the work of refining is going on?" "Oh, yes madam," replied the silversmith; "I must sit with my eyes steadily fixed on the furnace, for if the time necessary for refining be exceeded in the slightest degree, the silver will be injured."

The lady at once saw the beauty, and comfort too, of the expression, "He shall sit as a refiner and purifier of silver." God sees it needful to put His children into a furnace; His eye is steadily intent on the work of purifying, and His wisdom and love are both engaged in the best manner for us...Our trials do not come at random, and He will not let us be tested beyond what we can endure... Before she left, the lady asked one final question, "When do you know the process is complete?" "Why, that is quite simple," replied the silversmith.

"When I can see my own reflection image in the silver, the refining process is finished."

Slow Dance

This poem was written by a terminally ill young girl in a New York Hospital. It was sent by a medical doctor -

>Have you ever watched kids
>On a merry-go-round?
>Or listened to the rain
>Slapping on the ground?
>Ever followed a butterfly's erratic flight?
>Or gazed at the sun into the fading night?
>You better slow down.
>Don't dance so fast.
>Time is short.
>The music won't last.
>Do you run through each day
>On the fly?
>When you ask How are you?
>Do you hear the reply?

When the day is done
Do you lie in your bed
With the next hundred chores
Running through your head?
You'd better slow down
Don't dance so fast.
Time is short.
The music won't last.
Ever told your child,
We'll do it tomorrow?
And in your haste,
Not see his sorrow?
Ever lost touch,
Let a good friendship die
Cause you never had time
To call and say, "Hi"
You'd better slow down
Don't dance so fast.
Time is short.
The music won't last.
When you run so fast to get somewhere
You miss half the fun of getting there.
When you worry and hurry through your day,
It is like an unopened gift....
Thrown away.
Life is not a race.
Do take it slower
Hear the music
Before the song is over.
You'd better slow down
Don't dance so fast.
Time is short.
The music won't last.

Slow Down... Now!

Jack took a long look at his speedometer before slowing down: 73 in a 55 zone. 4th time in as many months. How could a guy get caught so often? When his car had slowed to 10 miles an hour, Jack pulled over, but only partially. Let the cop worry about the potential traffic hazard. Maybe some other car will tweak his backside with a mirror.

The cop was stepping out of his car, the big pad in hand. Bob? Bob from Church? Jack sunk farther into his trench coat. This was worse than the coming ticket. A Christian cop catching a guy from his own church. A guy who happened to be a little eager to get home after a long day at the office. A guy he was to play golf with tomorrow. Jumping out of the car, Jack approached a man he saw every Sunday, a man he'd never seen in uniform.

"Hi, Bob. Fancy meeting you like this."

"Hello, Jack." No smile.

"Guess you caught me red-handed in a rush to see my wife and kids."

"Yeah, I guess." Bob seemed uncertain. Good.

"I've seen some long days at the office lately. I'm afraid I bent the rules a bit - just this once." Jack toed at a pebble on the pavement. "Diane said something about roast beef and potatoes tonight. Know what I mean?"

"I know what you mean. I also know that you have a reputation in our precinct." Ouch. This was not going in the right direction. Time to change tactics.

"What'd you clock me at?"

"Seventy. Would you sit back in your car please?"

"Now wait a minute here, Bob. I checked as soon as I saw you. I was barely nudging 65." The lie seemed to come easier with every ticket.

"Please, Jack, in the car."

Flustered, Jack hunched himself through the still-open door. Slamming it shut, he stared at the dash board. He was in no rush to open the window. The minutes ticked by. Bob scribbled away on the pad. Why hadn't he asked for a driver's license? Whatever the reason, it would be a month of Sundays before Jack ever sat near this cop again.

A tap on the door jerked his head to the left. There was Bob, a folded paper in hand. Jack rolled down the window a mere two inches, just enough room for Bob to pass him the slip.

"Thanks." Jack could not quite keep the sneer out of his voice. Bob returned to his police car without a word. Jack watched his retreat in the mirror. Jack unfolded the sheet of paper. How much was this one going to cost? Wait a minute. What was this? Some kind of joke? Certainly not a ticket. Jack began to read:

"Dear Jack, Once upon a time I had a daughter. She was six when killed by a car. You guessed it - a speeding driver. A fine and three months in jail, and the man was free. Free to hug his daughters. All three of them. I only had one, and I'm going to have to wait until Heaven before I can ever hug her again. A thousand times I've tried to forgive that man. A thousand times I thought I had. Maybe I did, but I need to do it again. Even now. Pray for me. And be careful. My son is all I have left. --Bob"

Jack turned around in time to see Bob's car pull away and head down the road. Jack watched until it disappeared. A full 15 minutes later, he too, pulled away and drove slowly home, praying for forgiveness and hugging a surprised wife and kids when he arrived. Life is precious. Handle with care.

This is an important message, please pass it along to your friends. Drive safely and carefully. Remember, cars are not the only thing recalled by their maker. Funny how you can send a thousand 'jokes' through e-mail and they spread like wildfire, but when you start sending messages regarding the Lord, and the sanctity of life, people think twice about sharing.

Funny how you can be more worried about what other people think of you than what God thinks of you. Pass this on - you may save a life. Maybe not, but we'll never know if you don't.

The Small Tree

I hired a plumber to help me restore an old farmhouse, and after he had just finished a rough first day on the job: a flat tire made him lose an hour of work, his electric drill quit and his ancient one ton truck refused to start. While I drove him home, he sat in stony silence.

On arriving, he invited me in to meet his family. As we walked toward the front door, he paused briefly at a small tree, as if to pray, touching the tips of the branches with both hands.

When opening the door he underwent an amazing transformation. His tanned face was wreathed in smiles and he hugged his two small children and gave his wife a kiss.

Afterward he walked me to the car. We passed the tree and my curiosity got the better of me. I asked him about what I had seen him do earlier.

"Oh, that's my trouble tree," he replied. "I know I can't help having troubles on the job, but one thing's for sure, those troubles don't belong in the house with my wife and the children. So I just hang them up on the tree every night when I come home and ask God to take care of them. Then in the morning I pick them up again."

"Funny thing is," he smiled, "when I come out in the morning to pick 'em up, there aren't nearly as many as I remember hanging up the night before."

The Soldier at Valley Forge

I want you to close your eyes and picture in your mind the soldier at Valley Forge, as he holds his musket in his bloody hands.

He stands barefoot in the snow, starved from lack of food, wounded from months of battle and emotionally scarred from the eternity away from his family, surrounded by nothing but death and carnage of war.

He stands tough, with fire in his eyes and victory on his breath. He looks at us now in anger and disgust and tells us this...

"I gave you a birthright of freedom born in the Constitution and now your children graduate too illiterate to read it. I fought in the snow barefoot to give you the freedom to vote and now you stay at home because it rains. I left my family destitute to give you the freedom of speech and you remain silent on critical issues, because it might be bad for business. I orphaned my children to give you a government to serve you and it has stolen democracy from the people".

It's the soldier not the reporter who gives you the freedom of the press.

It's the soldier not the poet who gives you the freedom of speech.

It's the soldier not the campus organizer who allows you to demonstrate.

It's the soldier who salutes the flag, serves the flag, whose coffin is draped with the flag that allows the protester to burn the flag!!!

"Lord, hold our troops in your loving hands. Protect them as they protect us. Bless them and their families for the selfless acts they perform for us in our time of need. Amen."

When you read this, please stop for a moment and say a prayer for our U.S. troops in Afghanistan, Iraq and all over this world.

Of all the gifts you could give a US Soldier, Prayer is the very best one.....

Somebody Said...

Somebody said it takes about six weeks to get back to normal after you've had a baby ...somebody doesn't know that once you're a mother, "normal", is history.

Somebody said you learn how to be a mother by instinct. somebody never took a three-year-old shopping.

Somebody said being a mother is boring .somebody never rode in a car driven by a teenager with a driver's permit.

Somebody said if you're a "good" mother, your child will "turn out good"...somebody thinks a child comes with directions and a guarantee.

Somebody said "good" mothers never raise their voices ...somebody never came out the back door just in time to see her child hit a golf ball through the neighbor's kitchen window.

Somebody said you don't need an education to be a mother...somebody never helped a fourth grader with his math.

Somebody said you can't love the fifth child as much as you love the first... somebody doesn't have five children.

Somebody said a mother can find all the answers to her child-rearing questions in the books .. somebody never had a child stuff beans up his nose or in his ears.

Somebody said the hardest part of being a mother is labor and delivery...somebody never watched her "baby" get on the bus for the first day of kindergarten ... or on a plane headed for military "boot camp"

Somebody said a mother can do her job with her eyes closed and one hand tied behind her back ...somebody never organized seven giggling Brownies to sell cookies.

Somebody said a mother can stop worrying after her child gets married ..somebody doesn't know that marriage adds a new son or daughter-in-law to mother's heartstrings.

Somebody said a mother's job is done when her last child leaves home...somebody never had grandchildren. Somebody said your mother knows you love her, so you don't need to tell her ....somebody isn't a mother.

Pass this along to all the "mothers" in your life.

Son of the Master

A wealthy man and his son loved to collect rare works of art. They had everything in their collection, from Picasso to Raphael. They were known throughout the art world as "The Master and his son". They would often sit together and admire the great works of art. When the Vietnam conflict broke out, the son went to war. He was very courageous and died in battle while rescuing another soldier. The father was notified and grieved deeply for his only son.

About a month later, just before Christmas, there was a knock at the door. A young man stood at the door with a large package in his hands. He said, "Sir, you don't know me, but I am the soldier for whom your son gave his life. He saved many lives that day, and he was carrying me to safety when a bullet struck him in the heart and he died instantly. He often talked about you, and your love for art."

The young man held out this package. "I know this isn't much. I'm not really a great artist, but I think your son would have wanted you to have this." The father opened the package. It was a portrait of his son, painted by the young man. He stared in awe at the way the soldier had captured the personality of his son in the painting. The father was so drawn to the eyes that his own eyes welled up with tears. He thanked the young man and offered to pay him for the picture. "Oh, no sir, I could never repay what your son did for me. It's a gift."

The father hung the portrait over his mantle. Every time visitors came to his home he took them to see the portrait of his son before he showed them any of the other great works he had collected.

The father died a few months later. There was to be a great auction of his paintings. Many influential people gathered, excited over seeing the great paintings and having an opportunity to purchase one for their collection. On the platform sat the painting of the son. The auctioneer pounded his gavel. "We will start the bidding with this picture of the son.. Who will bid for this picture?" There was silence.

Then a voice in the back of the room shouted, "We want to see the famous paintings of the Master. Skip this one."

But the auctioneer persisted. "Will someone bid for this painting? Who will start the bidding? $100, $200?"

Another voice shouted angrily. "We didn't come to see this painting. We came to see the Van Goghs, the Rembrandts. Get on with the real bids!" But still the auctioneer continued. "The son! The son! Who'll take the son?"

Finally, a voice came from the very back of the room. It was the longtime gardener of the man and his son. "I'll give $10 for the painting." Being a poor man, it was all he could afford.

"We have $10, who will bid $20?" "Give it to him for $10. Let's see the masters." "$10 is the bid, won't someone bid $20?" The crowd was becoming angry. They didn't want the picture of the son. They wanted the more worthy investments for their collections. The auctioneer pounded the gavel. "Going once, twice, SOLD for $10!" A man sitting on the second row shouted, "Now let's get on with the collection!"

The auctioneer laid down his gavel. "I'm sorry, the auction is over."

"What about the paintings?" "I am sorry. When I was called to conduct this auction, I was told of a secret stipulation in the will. I was not allowed to reveal that stipulation until this time. Only the painting of the son would be auctioned. Whoever bought that painting would inherit the entire estate, including the all the paintings. The man who took the son gets everything!"

God gave His son 2,000 years ago to die on a cruel cross. Much like the auctioneer, His message today is: "The son, the son, who'll take the son?" Because, you see, whoever takes the Son gets everything. Please send this to ten people and back to the one who sent it to you. Do what ever you like, but remember that maybe "one" of the people you might have taken time to send this to, may be just the person who needs to hear this message. You have a choice to make. God bless!

Speed the Brick

A young and successful executive was traveling down a neighborhood street, going a bit too fast in his new Jaguar. He was watching for kids darting out from between parked cars and slowed down when he thought he saw something. As his car passed, no children appeared. Instead, a brick smashed into the Jag's side door! He slammed on the brakes and drove the Jag back to the spot where the brick had been thrown.

The angry driver then jumped out of the car, grabbed the nearest kid and pushed him up against a parked car shouting, "What was that all about and who are you? Just what the heck are you doing? That's a new car and that brick you threw is going to cost a lot of money. Why did you do it?"

The young boy was apologetic. "Please, mister... please, I'm sorry...I didn't know what else to do," he pleaded. "I threw the brick because no one else would stop..." With tears dripping down his face and off his chin, the youth pointed to a spot just around a parked car. "It's my brother," he said. "He rolled off the curb and fell out of his wheelchair and I can't lift him up."

Now sobbing, the boy asked the stunned executive, "Would you please help me get him back into his wheelchair? He's hurt and he's too heavy for me."

Moved beyond words, the driver tried to swallow the rapidly swelling lump in his throat. He hurriedly lifted the handicapped boy back into the wheelchair, then took out his fancy handkerchief and dabbed at the fresh scrapes and cuts. A quick look told him everything was going to be okay.

"Thank you and may God bless you," the grateful child told the stranger. Too shook up for words, the man simply watched the boy push his wheelchair-bound brother down the sidewalk toward their home.

It was a long, slow walk back to the Jaguar. The damage was very noticeable, but the driver never bothered to repair the dented side door. He kept the dent there to remind him of this message:

Don't go through life so fast that someone has to throw a brick at you to get your attention!

God whispers in our souls and speaks to our hearts. Sometimes when we don't have time to listen, He has to throw a brick at us. It's our choice.

Start OVER

When you've trusted God and walked his way
When you've felt his hand lead you day by day
But your steps now take you another way... **Start over.**
When you've made your plans and they've gone awry
When! you've tried your best and there's no more try
When you've failed yourself and you don't know why... **Start over.**
When you've told your friends what you plan to do
When you've trusted them and they didn't come through
And you're all alone and it's up to you... **Start over.**
When you've failed your kids and they're grown and gone
When you've done your best but it's turned out wrong
And now your grandchildren come along.. **Start over.**
When you've prayed to God so you'll know his will
When you've prayed and prayed and you don't know still
When you want to stop cause you've had your fill... **Start over.**
When you think you're finished and want to quit
When you've bottomed out in life's deepest pit
When you've tried and tried to get out of it... **Start over.**
When the year has been long and successes few
When December comes and you're feeling blue
God gives a January just for you... **Start over.**
Starting over means "Victories Won"
Starting over means "A Race Well Run"
Starting over means "God's Will Done"
Don't just sit there.............. **START OVER.**

Stevie

I try not to be biased, but I had my doubts about hiring Stevie. His placement counselor assured me that he would be a good, reliable busboy. But I had never had a mentally handicapped employee and wasn't sure I wanted one. I wasn't sure how my customers would react to Stevie. He was short, a little dumpy with the smooth facial features and thick-tongued speech of Down syndrome. I wasn't worried about most of my trucker customers because truckers don't generally care who buses tables as long as the meat loaf platter is good and the pies are homemade.

The four-wheeler drivers were the ones who concerned me; the mouthy college kids traveling to school; the yuppie snobs who secretly polish their silverware with their napkins for fear of catching some dreaded "truck stop germ"; the pairs of white shirted business men on expense accounts who think every truck stop waitress wants to be flirted with. I knew those people would be uncomfortable around Stevie so I closely watched him for the first few weeks. I shouldn't have worried. After the first week, Stevie had my staff wrapped around his stubby little finger, and within a month my truck regulars had adopted him as their official truck stop mascot.

After that, I really didn't care what the rest of the customers thought of him. He was like a 21-year-old in blue jeans and Nikes, eager to laugh and eager to please, but fierce in his attention to his duties. Every salt and pepper shaker was exactly in its place, not a bread crumb or coffee spill was visible when Stevie got done with the table. Our only problem was persuading him to wait to clean a table until after the customers were finished. He would hover in the background, shifting his weight from one foot to the other, scanning the dining room until a table was empty. Then he would scurry to the empty table and carefully bus dishes and glasses onto his cart and meticulously wipe the table up with a practiced flourish of his rag. If he thought a customer was watching, his brow would pucker with added concentration. He took pride in doing his job exactly right, and you had to love how hard he tried to please each and every person he met.

Over time, we learned that he lived with his mother, a widow who was disabled after repeated surgeries for cancer. They lived on their Social Security benefits in public housing two miles from the truck stop. The Social worker, which stopped to check on him every so often, admitted they had fallen between the cracks. Money was tight, and what I paid him was probably the difference between them being able to live together and Stevie being sent to a group home.

That's why the restaurant was a gloomy place that morning last August, the first morning in three years that Stevie missed work. He was at the Mayo Clinic in Rochester getting a new valve or something put in his heart. His social worker said that people with Down syndrome often had heart problems at an early age so this wasn't unexpected, and there was a good chance he would come through the surgery in good shape and be back at work in a few months.

A ripple of excitement ran through the staff later that morning when word came that he was out of surgery, in recovery and doing fine. Frannie, my head waitress, let out a war hoop and did a little dance in the aisle when she heard the good news. Belle Ringer, one of our regular trucker customers, stared at the sight of the 50-year-old grandmother of four doing a victory shimmy beside his table. Frannie blushed, smoothed her apron and shot Belle Ringer a withering look. He grinned. "OK, Frannie, what was that all about?" he asked.

"We just got word that Stevie is out of surgery and going to be okay."

"I was wondering where he was. I had a new joke to tell him. What was the surgery about?" Frannie quickly told Belle Ringer and the other two drivers sitting at his booth about Stevie's surgery, then sighed. "Yeah, I'm glad he is going to be OK", she said. "But I don't know how he and his Mom are going to handle all the bills. From what I hear, they're barely getting by as it is." Belle Ringer nodded thoughtfully, and Frannie hurried off to wait on the rest of her tables. Since I hadn't had time to round up a busboy to replace Steve and really didn't want to replace him, the girls were busing their own tables that day until we decided what to do.

After the morning rush, Frannie walked into my office. She had a couple of paper napkins in her hand a funny look on her face. "What's up?" I asked. "I didn't get that table where Belle Ringer and his friends were sitting cleared off after they left, and Pony Pete and Tony Tipper were sitting there when I got back to clean it off" she said. "This was folded and tucked under a coffee cup." She handed the napkin to me, and three $20 bills fell onto my desk when I opened it. On the outside, in big, bold letters, was printed "Something For Stevie."

"Pony Pete asked me what that was all about," she said, "so I told him about Stevie and his Mom and everything, and Pete looked at Tony and Tony looked at Pete, and they ended up giving me this." She handed me another paper napkin that had "Something For Stevie" scrawled on its outside. Two $50 bills were tucked within its folds. Frannie looked at me with wet, shiny eyes, shook her head and said simply, "Truckers."

That was three months ago. Today is Thanksgiving, the first day Stevie is supposed to be back to work. His placement worker said he's been counting the days until the doctor said he could work, and it didn't matter at all that it was a holiday. He called 10 times in the past week, making sure we knew he was coming, fearful that we had forgotten him or that his job was in jeopardy. I arranged to have his mother bring him to work, met them in the parking lot and invited them both to celebrate his day back. Stevie was thinner and paler, but couldn't stop grinning as he pushed through the doors and headed for the back room where his apron and busing cart were waiting.

"Hold up there, Stevie, not so fast," I said. I took him and his mother by their arms. "Work can wait for a minute. To celebrate you coming back, breakfast for you and your mother is on me." I led them toward a large corner booth at the rear of the room. I could feel and hear the rest of the staff following behind as we marched through the dining room. Glancing over my shoulder, I saw booth after booth of grinning truckers empty and join the procession. We stopped in front of the big table. Its surface was covered with coffee cups, saucers and dinner plates, all sitting slightly crooked on dozens of folded paper napkins.

"First thing you have to do, Steve, is clean up this mess," I said. I tried to sound stern. Stevie looked at me, and then at his mother, then pulled out one of the napkins. It had "Something for Stevie" printed on the outside. As he picked it up, two $10 bills fell onto the table. Stevie stared at the money, then at all the napkins peeking from beneath the tableware, each with his name printed or scrawled on it. I turned to his mother. "There's more than $10,000 in cash and checks on that table, all from truckers and trucking companies that heard about your problems. Happy Thanksgiving."

Well, it got real noisy about that time, with everybody hollering and shouting, and there were a few tears, as well. But you know what's funny? While everybody else was busy shaking hands and hugging each other, Stevie, with a big, big smile on his face, was busy clearing all the cups and dishes from the table. Best worker I ever hired. *(Reprint from Volume One)*

The Story of Carl

This is beautiful. ENJOY. Please take time to read. It will touch your heart.

Carl was a quiet man. He didn't talk much. He would always greet you with a big smile and a firm handshake.

Even after living in our neighbor-hood for over 50 years, no one could really say they knew him very well. Before his retirement, he took the bus to work each morning. The lone sight of him walking down the street often worried us. He had a slight limp from a bullet wound received in World War II. Watching him, we worried that he may not make it through our changing uptown neighborhood with its ever- increasing random violence, gangs, and drug activity.

When he saw the flyer at our local church asking for volunteers for caring for the gardens behind the pastor's residence, he responded in his characteristically unassuming manner. Without fanfare, he just signed up.

He was well into his 87th year when the very thing we had always feared finally happened. He was just finishing his watering for the day when three gang members approached him. Ignoring their attempt to intimidate him, he simply asked if they would like a drink from the hose. The tallest and toughest-looking of the three answered with a malevolent little smile. As Carl offered the hose to him, the other two grabbed Carl's arm, throwing him down. As the hose snaked crazily over the ground, dousing everything in its way, Carl's assailants stole his retirement watch and his wallet, and then fled.

Carl tried to get himself up, but he had been thrown down on his bad leg. He lay there trying to gather himself as the minister came running to help him. Although the pastor had witnessed the attack from his window, he couldn't get there fast enough to stop it.

"Carl, are you okay? Are you hurt?" he kept asking as he helped Carl to his feet. Carl just passed a hand over his brow and sighed, shaking his head. "Just some punk kids. I hope they'll wise-up someday." His wet clothes clung to his slight frame as he bent to pick up the hose. He adjusted the nozzle again and started to water. Confused and a little concerned, the pastor asked, "Carl, what are you doing?". "I've got to finish my watering. It's been very dry lately," came the calm reply. Satisfying himself that Carl really was all right, the pastor could only marvel. Carl was a man from a different time and place.

A few weeks later the three returned. Just as before their threat was unchallenged. Carl again offered them a drink from his hose. This time they didn't rob him. They wrenched the hose from his hand and drenched him head to foot in the icy water. When they had finished their humiliation of him, they sauntered off down the street, throwing catcalls and curses, falling over one another laughing at the hilarity of what they had just done. Carl just watched them. Then he turned toward the warmth giving sun, picked up his hose, and went on with his watering.

The summer was quickly fading into fall. Carl was doing some tilling when he was startled by the sudden approach of someone behind him. He stumbled and fell. As he struggled to regain his footing, he turned to see the tall leader of his summer tormentors reaching down for him. He braced himself for the expected attack.

"Don't worry old man, I'm not gonna hurt you this time." The young man spoke softly, still offering the tattooed and scarred hand to Carl. As he helped Carl get up, the man pulled a crumpled bag from his pocket and handed it to Carl. "What's this?" Carl asked.

"It's your stuff," the man explained. "It's your stuff back. Even the money in your wallet." "I don't understand," Carl said. "Why would you help me now?" The man shifted his feet, seeming embarrassed and ill at ease. "I learned something from you," he said. "I ran with that gang and hurt people like you. We picked you because you were old and we knew we could do it. But every time we came and did something to you, instead of yelling and fighting back, you tried to give us a drink. You didn't hate us for hating you. You kept showing love against our hate." He stopped for a moment. "I couldn't sleep after we stole your stuff, so here it is back. "He paused for another awkward moment, not knowing what more there was to say. " That bag's my way of saying thanks for straightening me out, I guess." And with that, he walked off down the street. Carl looked at the sack in his hands and gingerly opened it. He took out his retirement watch and put it back on his wrist. Opening his wallet, he checked for his wedding photo. He gazed for a moment at the young bride that still smiled back at him from all those years ago.

Carl died one cold day after Christmas that winter. Many people attended his funeral in spite of the weather. In particular the pastor noticed a tall young man that he didn't know sitting quietly in a distant corner of the church. The pastor spoke of

Carl's garden as a lesson in life. In a voice made thick with unshed tears, he said, "Do your best and make your garden as beautiful as you can. We will never forget Carl and his garden."

The following spring another flyer went up. It read: "Person needed to care for Carl's garden." The flyer went unnoticed by the busy parishioners until one day when a knock was heard at the pastor's office. Opening the door, he saw a pair of scarred and tattooed hands holding the flyer. "I believe this is my job, if you'll have me," the young man said. The pastor recognized him as the same young man who had returned the stolen watch and wallet to Carl. He knew that Carl's kindness had turned this man's life around, so he handed him the keys to the garden shed, and said, "Yes, go take care of Carl's garden and honor him."

The man went to work and, over the next several years, he tended the flowers and vegetables just as Carl had done. In that time, he went to college got married and became a prominent member of the community. But he never forgot his promise to Carl's memory and kept the garden as beautiful as he thought Carl would have.

One day he approached the new minister and told him that he couldn't care for the garden any longer. He explained with a shy and happy smile. "My wife just had a baby boy last night, and she's bringing him home on Saturday."

"Well, congratulations!" said the minister, "That's wonderful! What's the baby's name?" "Carl," the repented man replied.

$$\begin{array}{c} \text{The Best Mathematical Equation ever seen:} \\ 1 \text{ cross} \\ + \ 3 \text{ nails} \\ \hline = 4 \text{ given} \end{array}$$

Suburban Lawns

Imagine the conversation The Creator might have had with St. Francis about: --- *Grass!* --------- Listen in:

"Frank, you know all about gardens and nature. What in the world is going on down there in the "States"? What happened to the dandelions, violets, thistle and stuff I started eons ago? I had a perfect, no-maintenance garden plan. Those plants grow in any type of soil, withstand drought and multiply with abandon. The nectar from the long-lasting blossoms attracted butterflies, honey bees and flocks of songbirds. I expected to see a vast garden of colors by now. But all I see are these green rectangles."

"It's the tribes that settled there, Lord. The Suburbanites. They started calling your flowers 'weeds' and went to great extent to kill them and replace them with grass."

"Grass? But it's so boring. It's not colorful. It doesn't attract butterflies, birds and bees, only grubs and sod worms. It's temperamental with temperatures. Do these Suburbanites really want all that grass growing there?"

"Apparently so, Lord. They go to great pains to grow it and keep it green.. They begin each spring by fertilizing grass and poisoning any other plant that crops up in the lawn."

"The spring rains and cool weather probably make grass grow really fast.. That must make the Suburbanites happy."

"Apparently not, Lord. As soon as it grows a little, they cut it —sometimes twice a week."

"They cut it? Do they then bale it like hay?"

"Not exactly, Lord. Most of them rake it up and put it in bags."

"They bag it? Why? Is it a cash crop? Do they sell it?"

"No, sir. Just the opposite. They pay to throw it away."

"Now let me get this straight. They fertilize grass so it will grow. And when it does grow, they cut it off and pay to throw it away?"

224

"Yes, sir."

"These Suburbanites must be relieved in the summer when we cut back on the rain and turn up the heat. That surely slows the growth and saves them a lot of work."

"You aren't going believe this, Lord. When the grass stops growing so fast, they drag out hoses and pay more money to water it so they can continue to mow it and pay to get rid of it."

"What nonsense! At least they kept some of the trees. That was a sheer stroke of genius, if I do say so myself. The trees grow leaves in the spring to provide beauty and shade in the summer. In the autumn they fall to the ground and form a natural blanket to keep moisture in the soil and protect the trees and bushes. Plus, as they rot, the leaves form compost to enhance the soil. It's a natural circle of life."

"You better sit down, Lord. The Suburbanites have drawn a new circle. As soon as the leaves fall, they rake them into great piles and have them hauled away."

"No! What do they do to protect the shrub and tree roots in the winter and keep the soil moist and loose?"

"After throwing away your leaves, they go out and buy something they call mulch. They haul it home and spread it around in place of the leaves."

"And where do they get this mulch?"

"They cut down trees and grind them up."

"Enough! I don't want to think about this anymore. Saint Catherine, you're in charge of the arts. What movie have you scheduled for us tonight?"

"Dumb and Dumber, Lord. It's a real stupid movie about..."

"Never mind. I think I just heard the whole story."

Teddy's Teacher

Her name was Mrs. Thompson. As she stood in front of her 5th grade class on the very first day of school, she told the children a lie. Like most teachers, she looked at her students and said that she loved them all the same. But that was impossible, because there in the front row, slumped in his seat, was a little boy named Teddy Stoddard. Mrs. Thompson had watched Teddy the year before and noticed that he didn't play well with the other children, that his clothes were messy and that he constantly needed a bath. And Teddy could be unpleasant. It got to the point where Mrs. Thompson would actually take delight in marking his papers with a broad red pen, making bold X's and the F's on his papers.

At the school where Mrs. Thompson taught, she was required to review each child's past records and she put Teddy's off until last. However, when she reviewed his file, she was in for a surprise. Teddy's first grade teacher had written, "Teddy is a bright child with a ready laugh. He does his work neatly and has good manners...he is a joy to be around."

His second grade teacher wrote, "Teddy is an excellent student, well liked by his classmates, but he is troubled because his mother has a terminal illness and life at home must be a struggle."

His third grade teacher wrote, "His mother's death had been hard on him. He tries to do his best, but his father doesn't show much interest and his home life will soon affect him if some steps aren't taken."

Teddy's fourth grade teacher wrote, "Teddy is withdrawn and doesn't show much interest in school. He doesn't have many friends and he sometimes sleeps in class."

By now, Mrs. Thompson realized the problem and she was ashamed of herself. She felt even worse when her students brought her Christmas presents, wrapped in beautiful ribbons and bright paper, except for Teddy's. His present was clumsily wrapped in the heavy, brown paper that he got from a grocery bag. Mrs. Thompson took pains to open it in the might agree to sit in the place at the wedding that was usually reserved for the mother of the groom. Of course, Mrs. Thompson did. And guess what? She wore that bracelet, the one with several rhinestones missing. And she made sure she was wearing the perfume that Teddy remembered his mother wearing on their last Christmas together. They hugged each other, and Dr. Stoddard whispered in Mrs. Thompson's ear, "Thank you Mrs. Thompson for believing in me. Thank you so much for making me feel important and showing me that I could make a difference." Mrs. Thompson, with tears in her eyes, whispered back. She said, "Teddy, you have it all wrong. You were the one who taught me that I could make a difference. I didn't know how to teach until I met you."

Warm someone's heart today . . . pass this along. Please remember that wherever you go, and whatever you do, you will have the opportunity to touch and/or change a person's outlook. Please try to do it in a positive way. "Friends are angels who lift us to our feet when our wings have trouble remembering how to fly."

The U in JesUs

Before U were thought of, or time had begun,
God even stuck U in the name of His Son..
And each time U pray, you'll see it's true
You can't spell out JesUs and not include U..
You're a pretty big part of His wonderful name,
For U, He was born; that's why He came..
And His great love for U is the reason He died..
It even takes U to spell crUcified..
Isn't it thrilling and splendidly grand
He rose from the dead, with U in His plan..
The stones split away, the gold trUmpet blew,

and this word resUrrection is spelled with a U..
When JesUs left earth at His upward ascension,
He felt there was one thing He just had to mention..
"Go into the world and tell them it's true
That I love them all - Just like I love U"..
So many great people are spelled with a U,
Don't they have a right to know JesUs too?
It all depends now on what U will do,
He'd like them to know, but it all starts with U..
As with all good things, pass this on.....

There Are Angels Among Us...

There came a frantic knock at the doctor's office door,
A knock, more urgent than he had ever heard before.
"Come in, Come in," the impatient doctor said,
"Come in, Come in, before you wake the dead."
In walked a frightened little girl,
A child no more than nine,
It was plain for all to see,
She had troubles on her mind.
"Oh doctor, I beg you,
Please come with me,
My mother is surely dying,
She's as sick as she can be."
"I don't make house calls,
Bring your mother here,"
"But she's too sick,
So you must come or she will die I fear."
The doctor, touched by her devotion,
Decided he would go,
She said he would be blessed,
More than he could know.
She led him to her house

Where her mother lay in bed,
Her mother was so very sick
She couldn't raise her head.
But her eyes cried out for help
And help her the doctor did,
She would have died that very night
Had it not been for her kid.
The doctor got her fever down
And she lived through the night,
And morning brought the doctor signs,
That she would be all right.
The doctor said he had to leave
But would return again by two,
And later he came back to check,
Just like he said he'd do.
The mother praised the doctor
For all the things he'd done,
He told her she would have died,
Were it not for her little one.
"How proud you must be
Of your wonderful little girl,
It was her pleading that made me come,
She is really quite a pearl!
"But doctor, my daughter died
Over three years ago,
Is the picture on the wall
Of the little girl you know?"
The doctors legs went limp
For the picture on the wall,
Was the same little girl
For whom he'd made this call.
The doctor stood motionless,
For quite a little while,
And then his solemn face,
Was broken by his smile.
He was thinking of that frantic knock
Heard at his office door,

And of the beautiful little angel
That had walked across his floor.

Things God Won't Ask...

God won't ask what kind of car you drove,
but He'll ask how many people you drove who didn't have transportation.
God won't ask the square footage of your house,
but He'll ask how many people you welcomed into your home.
God won't ask about the clothes you had in your closet,
but He'll ask how many you helped to clothe.
God won't ask what your highest salary was,
but He'll ask if you compromised your character to obtain it.
God won't ask what your job title was,
but He'll ask if you performed your job to the best of your ability.
God won't ask how many friends you had,
but He'll ask how many people to whom you were a friend.
God won't ask in what neighborhood you lived,
but He'll ask how you treated your neighbors.
God won't ask about the color of your skin,
but He'll ask about the content of your character.
God won't ask why it took you so long to seek Salvation,
but He'll lovingly take you to your mansion in heaven, and not to the gates of Hell.

Three Trees

Once there were three trees on a hill in the woods. They were discussing their hopes and dreams when the first tree said, "Someday I hope to be a treasure chest. I could be filled with gold, silver and precious gems. I could be decorated with intricate carving and everyone would see the beauty."

Then the second tree said, "Someday I will be a mighty ship. I will take kings and queens across the waters and sail to the corners of the world. Everyone will feel safe in me because of the strength of my hull."

Finally the third tree said, "I want to grow to be the tallest and straightest tree in the forest. People will see me on top of the hill and look up to my branches, and think of the heavens and God and how close to them I am reaching. I will be the greatest tree of all time and people will always remember me."

After a few years of praying that their dreams would come true, a group of woodsmen came upon the trees. When one came to the first tree he said, "This looks like a strong tree, I think I should be able to sell the wood to a carpenter," and he began cutting it down. The tree was happy, because he knew that the carpenter would make him into a treasure chest.

At the second tree the woodsman said, "This looks like a strong tree, I should be able to sell it to the shipyard." The second tree was happy because he knew he was on his way to becoming a mighty ship.

When the woodsmen came upon the third tree, the tree was frightened because he knew that if they cut him down his dreams would not come true. One of the woodsmen said, "I don't need anything special from my tree, I'll take this one," and he cut it down.

When the first tree arrived at the carpenters, he was made into a feed box for animals. He was then placed in a barn and filled with hay. This was not at all what he had prayed for. The second tree was cut and made into a small fishing boat. His dreams of being a mighty ship and carrying kings had come to an end. The third tree was cut into large pieces and left alone in the dark.

The years went by, and the trees forgot about their dreams. Then one day, a man and woman came to the barn. She gave birth and they placed the baby in the hay in the feed box that was made from the first tree. The man wished that he could have made a crib for the baby, but this manger would have to do. The tree could feel the importance of this event and knew that it had held the greatest treasure of all time.

Years later, a group of men got in the fishing boat made from the second tree. One of them was tired and went to sleep. While they were out on the water, a great storm arose and the tree didn't think it was strong enough to keep the men safe. The men woke the sleeping man, and He stood and said "Peace" and the storm stopped. At this time, the tree knew that it had carried the King of Kings in its boat.

Finally, someone came and got the third tree. It was carried through the streets as the people mocked the man who was carrying it. When they came to a stop, the man was nailed to the tree and raised in the air to die at the top of a hill. When Sunday came, the tree came to realize that it was strong enough to stand at the top of the hill and be as close to God as was possible, because Jesus had been crucified on it.

The moral of this story is that when things don't seem to be going your way, always know that God has a plan for you. If you place your trust in Him, He will give you great gifts. Each of the trees got what they wanted, just not in the way they had imagined. We don't always know what God's plans are for us. We just know that His ways are not our ways, but His ways are always best.

Timing to Share
by Jean M. Olsen

"Is this Mrs. Olsen?" asked an unfamiliar voice over the phone.

"Yes," I replied.

"This is Dr. Mae Strange, just around the corner from you. Remember talking with me four years ago? I had just moved in and you had left your card on my door."

"Oh, yes. I had seen your Music Studio sign and wanted to welcome you to the neighborhood." I also remembered wondering if she might need a teacher and would ask for my help, but that hadn't happened.

"Right, " Dr. Strange continued. "I was out, but we talked later on the phone."

"Oh, yes. I remember. I mentioned teaching piano at a school for missionary kids in Kenya,"

" I kept your card. I now have a number of beginners requesting lessons, but don't have time to take them. When we talked before, you said that you like to teach beginners. Would you consider teaching for me?"

"Well, I'm not sure I'm the right person. I don't have a degree or formal college training."

"You told me you'd completed the Royal School of Music course in Kenya. That's an excellent course and that's good enough for me. You're just the person I'm looking for."

I am now teaching ten lessons a week at her Music Studio, and I love it.

The beautiful part is that, about a month before Dr. Strange's call, my husband and I bought our first home, something we'd never expected to do. We are retired missionaries in our 70s on a modest income. We'd previously rented my mother's house, but when she died it had to be sold and the assets divided.

We had to find another place or buy the house ourselves. So we took a leap of faith. The bank approved out application for a loan. Then God provided a job I love to do – right around the corner from home – just when we needed help with mortgage payments.

Perfect job! Perfect place! Perfect timing! Praise the Lord!

Timmy

Timmy was a little five year old boy that his Mom loved very much and, being a worrier, she was concerned about him walking to school when he started Kindergarten. She walked him to school the first couple of days but when he came home one day, he told his mother that he did not want her walking him to school everyday. He wanted to be like the "big boys." He protested loudly, so she had an idea of how to handle it.

She asked a neighbor, Mrs. Goodnest, if she would surreptitiously follow her son to school, at a distance behind him that he would not likely notice, but close enough to keep a watch on him. Mrs. Goodnest said that since she was up early with her toddler anyway, it would be a good way for them to get some exercise as well so she agreed.

The next school day, Mrs. Goodnest and her little girl, Marcy, set out following behind Timmy as he walked to school with another neighbor boy. She did this for the whole week. As the boys walked and chatted, kicking stones and twigs, the little friend of Timmy noticed that this same lady was following them as she seemed to do every day all week. Finally, he said to Timmy, "Have you noticed that lady following us all week? Do you know her?" Timmy nonchalantly replied, "Yea, I know who she is." The friend said, "Well who is she?"

"That's just Shirley Goodnest" Timmy said. "Shirley Goodnest? Who the heck is she and why is she following us?"

"Well," Timmy explained, "every night my Mom makes me say the 23rd Psalm with my prayers 'cuz she worries about me so much. And in it, the prayer psalm says, "Shirley Goodnest and Marcy shall follow me all the days of my life," so I guess I'll just have to get used to it.

Tommy's True Theology

Some twelve years ago, I stood watching my university students file into the classroom for our first session in the Theology of Faith. That was the first day I first saw Tommy. My eyes and my mind both blinked. He was combing his long flaxen hair, which hung six inches below his shoulders. It was the first time I had ever seen a boy with hair that long. I guess it was just coming into fashion then. I know in my mind that it isn't what's on your head but what's in it that counts; but on that day I was unprepared and my emotions flipped. I immediately filed Tommy under "S" for strange...very strange.

Tommy turned out to be the "atheist in residence" in my Theology of Faith" course. He constantly objected to, smirked at or whined about the possibility of an unconditionally loving Father/God. We lived with each other in relative peace for one semester, although I admit he was for me at times a serious pain in the back pew.

When he came up at the end of the course to turn in his final exam, he asked in a slightly cynical tone, "Do you think I'll ever find God?"

I decided instantly on a little shock therapy. "No!" I said very emphatically.

"Oh," he responded, "I thought that was the product you were pushing."

I let him get five steps from the classroom door and then called out, "Tommy! I don't think you'll ever find him, but I am absolutely certain that he will find you!"

He shrugged a little and left my class and my life. I felt slightly disappointed at the thought that he had missed my clever line, "He will find you!" At least I thought it was clever.

Later I heard that Tommy had graduated and I was duly grateful. Then a sad report. I heard that Tommy had terminal cancer. Before I could search him out, he came to see me.

When he walked into my office, his body was very badly wasted, and the long hair had all fallen out as a result of chemotherapy. But his eyes were bright and his voice was firm, for the first time, I believe.

"Tommy, I've thought about you so often. I hear you are sick.", I blurted out.

"Oh, yes, very sick. I have cancer in both lungs. It's a matter of weeks."

"Can you talk about it, Tom?" I asked.

"Sure, what would you like to know?" he replied. "What's it like to be only twenty four and dying?"

"Well, it could be worse."

"Like what?"

"Well, like being fifty and having no values or ideals, like being fifty and thinking that booze, seducing women and making money are the real 'biggies' in life."

I began to look through my mental file cabinet under "S" where I had filed Tommy as strange. (It seems as though everybody I try to reject by classification, God sends back into my life to educate me.)

"But what I really came to see you about," Tom said, "is something you said to me on the last day of class." (He remembered!) He continued, "I asked you if you thought I would ever find God and you said, 'No!, which surprise me. Then you said, 'But he will find you.' I thought about that a lot, even though my search for God was hardly intense at that time."

(My "clever" line. He thought about that a lot!)

"But when the doctors removed a lump from my groin and told me that it was malignant, then I got serious about locating God. And when the malignancy spread into my vital organs, I really began banging bloody fists against the bronze doors of heaven."

"But God did not come out. In fact, nothing happened. Did you ever try anything for a long time with great effort and with no success? You get psychologically glutted, fed up with trying. And then you quit. Well, one day I woke up, and instead of throwing a few more futile appeals over that high brick wall to a God who may be or may not be there, I just quit. I decided that I didn't really care . . . about God, about an afterlife, or anything like that. I decided to spend what time I had left doing something more profitable. I thought about you and your class and I remembered something else you had said: 'The essential sadness is to go through life without loving. But it would be almost equally sad to go through life and leave this world without ever telling those you loved that you had loved them. So, I began with the hardest one, my Dad. He was reading the newspaper when I approached him. "Dad".

"Yes, what?" he asked without lowering the newspaper.

"Dad, I would like to talk with you. I mean . . . It's really important."

The newspaper came down three slow inches. "What is it?"

"Dad, I love you. I just wanted you to know that. "

Tom smiled at me and said with obvious satisfaction, as though he felt a warm and secret joy flowing inside of him. "The newspaper fluttered to the floor. Then my father did two things I could never remember him ever doing before. He cried and he hugged me. And we talked all night, even though he had to go to work the next morning. It felt so good to be close to my father, to see his tears, to feel his hug, to hear him say that he loved me.

It was easier with my mother and little brother. They cried with me, too, and we hugged each other, and started saying real nice things to each other. We shared the things we had been keeping secret for so many years. I was only sorry about one thing: that I had waited so long.

Here I was, just beginning to open up to all the people I had actually been close to. Then, one day I turned around and God was there. He didn't come to me when I pleaded with him. I guess I was like an animal trainer holding out a hoop, 'C'mon, jump through. C'mon, I'll give you three days, three weeks.' Apparently God does things in his own way and at his own hour. But the important thing is that he was there. He found me. You were right. He found me even after I stopped looking for him."

"Tommy," I practically gasped, "I think you are saying something very important and much more universal than you realize. To me, at least, you are saying that the surest way to find God is not to make him a private possession, a problem solver, or an instant consolation in time of need, but rather by opening to love. You know, the Apostle John said that. He said: 'God is love, and anyone who lives in love is living with God and God is living in him.' Tom, could I ask you a favor? You know, when I had you in class you were a real pain. But (laughingly) you can make it all up to me now. Would you come into my present Theology of Faith course and tell them what you have just told me? If I told them the same thing it wouldn't be half as effective as if you were to tell them."

"Ooh ..... I was ready for you, but I don't know if I'm ready for your class."

"Tom, think about it. If and when you are ready, give me a call."

In a few days Tom called, said he was ready for the class, that he wanted to do that for God and for me. So we scheduled a date. However, he never made it. He had another appointment, far more important than the one with my class. Of course, his life was not really ended by his death, only changed. He made the great step from faith into vision. He found a life far more beautiful than the eye of man has ever seen or the ear of man has ever heard or the mind of man has ever imagined.

Before he died, we talked one last time. "I'm not going to make it to your class," he said.

"I know, Tom."

"Will you tell them for me? Will you . . . tell the whole world for me?"

"I will, Tom. I'll tell them. I'll do my best."

So, to all of you who have been kind enough to hear this simple statement about love, thank you for listening. And to you, Tommy, somewhere in the sunlit, verdant hills of heaven: "I told them, Tommy . . . as best I could."

-.-.*John Powell*, A professor at Loyola University in Chicago

Tonsils Needing Ice Cream
by Sally Robbins (from Guideposts)

What I remember most about the summer of 1934, when Dad got his tonsils out, is how hot it was. The middle of July in Blackwood, VA, and we hadn't seen a drop of rain or felt a cool breeze for weeks. The ground was parched, the flowers drooping. Normally, I could at least cool down with an ice-cold drink. The ice man hadn't been around though and the last block of ice in our icebox had long since melted.

Dad was recovering from his operation in the downstairs bedroom when Mom rushed out to the kitchen telephone. She reefed on the poor crank and shouted at the Operator to connect to the doctor's office.

"He's hemorrhaging badly," she said, urgency in her voice. "What can we do?" Then I heard her repeat the doctor's instructions. "Ice. Make a compress of ice and pack it around his throat."

But there was no ice for miles around. We lived ten miles from town. Dad couldn't be moved and Mom didn't dare leave him.

She tried wrapping Cad's neck with cloths drenched in cold water, but it was no use. His throat kept swelling and he was still bleeding.

Tears filled her eyes, Mom said brokenly, "Lord, you take over. I'm lost."

I was worried, so I too wailed a prayer of my own. "God, please help my Daddy. Please!"

Mom took me in her arms just as the wind began to blow. The sky grew dark as dusk, then simply opened up. The hammering noise on the roof was deafening as thunder rolled and lighting flashed. Mom kissed me on the forehead, then grabbed a pail and ran outside. Soon she was back, and in ten minutes Dad's bleeding had been stopped by large balls of ice she'd collected from the heaven-sent hailstorm.

Tonsils always need ice cream!

Too Much Change...

Several years ago a pastor friend of mine moved to Houston, Texas. Some weeks after he arrived, he had occasion to ride the bus from his home to the downtown area. When he sat down, he discovered that the driver had accidentally given him ten cents too much change..

As he considered what to do, there alternately appeared to him little angelic figures sitting on his shoulders and whispering instructions into his ears. One said, "You better give the dime back. It would be wrong to keep it."

On the other shoulder a voice said, "Oh forget it. It's just ten cents.. Who would worry about this little amount. Anyway the bus company already gets too much fare. With their millions every-day they will never miss it.. Accept it as a gift from God and keep quiet."

When his stop came he paused momentarily at the front door, and, handing the driver the dime he said, "Here. You handed me too much change." The driver replied, "Aren't you the new pastor in town? I have been thinking lately about going to church somewhere. I just wanted to see what you would do if I gave you ten cents too much change."

When my friend stepped off the bus he literally grabbed the nearest light pole, held on, and said, "O God, I almost sold your Son for ten cents."

Written by Alan Johnson, Romans, "The Freedom" WITandWISDOM(tm),

The Torn Quilt

As I faced my Maker at the last judgment, I knelt before the Lord along with all the other souls. Before each of us laid our lives like the squares of a quilt in many piles. An Angel sat before each of us sewing our quilt squares together into a tapestry that is our life. But as my angel took each piece of cloth off the pile, I noticed how ragged and empty each of my squares was. They were filled with giant holes. Each square was labeled with a part of my life that had been difficult, the challenges and temptations I was faced with in everyday life. I saw hardships that I endured, which were the largest holes of all.

I glanced around me. Few others had such squares. Other than a tiny hole here and there, the other tapestries were filled with rich color and the bright hues of worldly fortune. I gazed upon my own life and was disheartened. My angel was sewing the ragged pieces of cloth together, threadbare and empty, like binding air.

Finally the time came when each life was to be displayed, held up to the light, the scrutiny of truth. The others rose, each in turn, holding up their tapestries. So filled their lives had been. My angel looked upon me, and nodded for me to rise. My gaze dropped to the ground in shame. I hadn't had all the earthly fortunes. I had love in my life, and laughter. But there had also been trials of illness, and death, and false accusations that took from me my world as I knew it. I had to start over many times. I often struggled with the temptation to quit, only to somehow muster the strength to pick up and begin again. My life was what it was, and I had to accept it for what it was.

I rose and slowly lifted the combined squares of my life to the light. An awe-filled gasp filled the air. I gazed around at the others who stared at me with wide eyes.

Then, I looked upon the tapestry before me. Light flooded the many holes, creating an image, the face of Christ.

Then our Lord stood before me, with warmth and love in His eyes. He said, "Every time you gave over your life to Me, it became My life, My hardships, and My struggles. Each point of light in your life is when you stepped aside and let Me shine through, until there was more of Me than there was of you.

My prayer is that all our quilts be threadbare and worn, allowing Christ to shine through.

Touché

A college student challenged a senior citizen, saying it was impossible for their generation to understand his. "You grew up in a different world," the student said. "Today we have television, jet planes, space travel, nuclear energy, computers.."

Taking advantage of a pause in the student's litany, the geezer said, "You're right. We didn't have those things when we were young; so we invented them! What are you doing for the next generation??"

(I love old people! They have a lot to offer!!!)

Twas' the Night Jesus Came

Twas' the night Jesus came and all through the house, not a person was praying,
The Bible was left on the shelf without care, for no one thought Jesus would come there..

The children were dressing to crawl into bed, not once ever kneeling or bowing their head..

And Mom in the rocking chair with babe on her lap, was watching the Late Show as I took a nap..

When out of the east there rose such a clatter, I sprang to my feet to see what was the matter..

Away to the window I flew like a flash, tore open the shutters and lifted the sash..

When what to my wondering eyes should appear, but Angels proclaiming that Jesus was here..

The light of His face made me cover my head... was Jesus returning just like He'd said..

And though I possessed worldly wisdom and wealth, I cried when I saw Him in spite of myself..

In the Book of Life which he held in his hand, was written the name of every saved man..

He spoke not a word as he searched for my name, My head hung in shame.. when He said "it's not here"

The people whose names had been written with love, He gathered to take to his Father above..

With those who were ready He rose without sound, while all of the others were left standing around...

I fell to my knees but it was too late, I'd waited too long and thus sealed my fate.

I stood and I cried as they rose out of sight, Oh, if only I'd know that this was the night....

In the words of this poem the meaning is clear the coming of Jesus is now drawing near...

There's only one life and when comes the last call, We'll find out that the Bible was true after all..

Twinkle, Twinkle Little Star

When the house lights dimmed and the concert was about to begin, the mother returned to her seat and discovered that the child was missing. Suddenly, the curtains parted and spotlights focused on the impressive Steinway on stage. In horror, the mother saw her little boy sitting at the keyboard, innocently picking out "Twinkle, Twinkle Little Star."

At that moment, the great piano master made his entrance, quickly moved to the piano, and whispered in the boy's ear, "Don't quit. Keep playing."

Then, leaning over, Paderewski reached down with his left hand and began filling in a bass part. Soon his right arm reached around to the other side of the child, and he added a running obbligato. Together, the old master and the young novice transformed what could have been a frightening situation into a wonderfully creative experience.

The audience was so mesmerized that they couldn't recall what else the great master played. Only the classic, " Twinkle, Twinkle Little Star."

Perhaps that's the way it is with God. What we can accomplish on our own is hardly noteworthy. We try our best, but the results aren't always graceful flowing music. However, with the hand of the Master, our life's work can truly be beautiful.

The next time you set out to accomplish great feats, listen carefully. You may hear the voice of the Master, whispering in your ear, "Don't quit. Keep playing."

May you feel His arms around you and know that His hands are there, helping you turn your feeble attempts into true masterpieces. Remember, God doesn't seem to call the equipped, rather, He equips the 'called.' Life is more accurately measured by the lives you touch than by the things you acquire. So touch someone by passing this little message along.

May God bless you and be with you always!

Two Pots

A Water Bearer in India had two large pots, each hung on the ends of a pole which he carried across his neck. One of the pots had a crack in it, while the other pot was perfect & always delivered a full portion of water. At the end of the long walk from the stream to the house, the cracked pot arrived only half full. For a full two years this went on daily, with the bearer delivering only one and a half pots full of water to his house. Of course, the perfect pot was proud of its accomplishments, perfect for which it was made, but the poor cracked pot was ashamed of its imperfection, and miserable that it was able to accomplish only half of what it had been made to do.

After two years of what it perceived to be a bitter failure, it spoke to the Water Bearer one day by the stream. "I am ashamed of myself, and I want you to throw me away and replace me. I have been able to deliver only half my load because this crack in my side causes water to leak out all the way back to your house. Because of my flaw, you have to do all of this work, and you don't get full value from your efforts."

The bearer said to the pot, "Did you notice that there were flowers only on your side of the path, but not on the other pot's side? That's because I have always known about your flaw, and I planted flower seeds on your side of the path, and every day while we walk back, you've watered them. For two years I have been able to pick these beautiful flowers to decorate the table. Without you being just the way you are, there would not be this beauty with which to grace my house."

MORAL: Each of us has our own unique flaws. We are all cracked pots in one way or another. But, it's the cracks and flaws we each have that make our lives together so very interesting and rewarding. You've just got to take each person for who and what they are, and look for the good in them.

Blessings to all my crackpot friends.

Unfolding a Rose

A new Christian was walking with a more mature friend in a garden one day and feeling a bit insecure about God's will for his life, he inquired what he should do. His friend walked up to a rosebush, handed him a rosebud, and told him to open it without tearing off any petals..

The new Christian looked in disbelief at his friend and tried to figure out what a rosebud could possibly have to do with his wanting to know the WILL OF GOD for his life But because of his high respect for his friend proceeded to TRY to unfold the rose, while keeping every petal intact...It wasn't long before he realized how impossible it was to do so.. Noticing the younger Christian's inability to unfold the rosebud while keeping it intact, his friend began to recite the following poem....

It is only a tiny rosebud,
A flower of GOD's design;
But I cannot unfold the petals
With these clumsy hands of mine..
The secret of unfolding flowers
Is not known to such as I..
GOD opens this flower so sweetly,
When in my hands they fade and die..
If I cannot unfold a rosebud,
This flower of GOD's design,
Then how can I think I have wisdom
To unfold this life of mine?
So I'll trust in Him for His leading
Each moment of every day..
I will look to him for His guidance
Each step of the pilgrim way..
The pathway that lies before me,
Only my Heavenly Father knows..
I'll trust Him to unfold the moments,
Just as He unfolds the rose..
(Reprint from Volume One)

Use This Day Wisely

Life can be very frustrating at times. One of the biggest causes of frustration and anger is disappointment over not getting what we expect. We expect life to work out in our favor. We have this mental picture of the way it should be. We want to be loved and appreciated and all that.

But the truth is, we'll never get everything we want or we expect. No one ever does. If we can accept that fact, it will do a lot to minimize our big disappointments.

Anybody can become angry; that is easy; but to be angry with the right person, and to the right degree, and at the right time, and for the right purpose, and in the right way---- that is not within everybody's power and is not easy.

Don't be angry, just love someone today and enjoy this beautiful day that is given you. This is the beginning of a new day. God has given you this day to use as you will. You can waste it or you can use it for good. What you do today is important because you're exchanging a day of your life for it.

When tomorrow comes, this day will be gone forever, leaving something you have traded for it. You want it to be gain, not loss; good, not evil;; success, not failure; in order that you shall not regret the price you paid.

Be a blessing to someone today!
T. STEFFANSON, PORTLAND FIRE BUREAU

Visiting Day

He had been looking forward to this moment all day long, after six days of labor and it had finally arrived - Visiting Day!

The man with the keys arrived to swing open the large, heavy doors. The cold gray hall sprang to life in the warm glow of light. He could hardly control his emotions. The families began to arrive. He peers from the corner of the room longing for the first glimpse of his loved ones. He lives for these weekends. He lives for these visits. As the cars arrive, he watches intently.

Then, finally, they arrive, for whom he would do anything. They embrace, eat a light lunch and reminisce how things used to be. At one point, they break into singing, with interruptions of laughter and applause.

But all too soon it is over. A tear comes to his eyes as they depart. Then the men with the keys close the heavy doors. He hears the key turn in the lock marking the end of a special day.

There he stands, alone again. He knows that most of his visitors will not contact him again till next week. As the last car pulls away from the parking lot, *Jesus* retreats into loneliness as He waits until next Sunday – and another Visiting Day.

Warm up for Mother's Day

After 21 years of marriage, I discovered a new way of keeping alive the spark of love. A little while ago I had started to go out with another woman. It was really my wife's idea.

"I know that you love her," she said one day, taking me by surprise.

"But I love YOU," I protested.

"I know, but you also love her."

The other woman that my wife wanted me to visit was my mother, who has been a widow for 19 years, but the demands of my work and my three children had made it possible to visit her only occasionally. That night I called to invite her to go out for dinner and a movie.

"What's wrong, aren't you well?" she asked. My mother is the type of woman who suspects that a late night call or a surprise invitation is a sign of bad news.

"I thought that it would be pleasant to pass some time with you," I responded. "Just the two of us." She thought about it for a moment, then said, "I would like that very much."

That Friday after work, as I drove over to pick her up I was a bit nervous. When I arrived at her house, I noticed that she, too, seemed to be nervous about our date. She waited in the door with her coat on. She had curled her hair and was wearing the dress that she had worn to celebrate her last wedding anniversary. She smiled from a face that was as radiant as an angel's.

"I told my friends that I was going to go out with my son, and they were impressed," she said, as she got into the car. "They can't wait to hear about our meeting". We went to a restaurant that, although not elegant, was very nice and cozy. My mother took my arm as if she were the First Lady. After we sat down, I had to read the menu. Her eyes could only read large print. Half way through the entrees, I lifted my eyes and saw Mom sitting there staring at me. A nostalgic smile was on her lips.

"It was I who used to have to read the menu when you were small," she said.

"Then it's time that you relax and let me return the favor," I responded. During the dinner we had an agreeable conversation -nothing extraordinary -but catching up on recent events of each others life.

We talked so much that we missed the movie. As we arrived at her house later, she said, "I'll go out with you again, but only if you let me invite you". I agreed.

"How was your dinner date?" asked my wife when I got home.

"Very nice. Much more so than I could have imagined," I answered.

A few days later my mother died of a massive heart attack. It happened so suddenly that I didn't have a chance to do anything for her. Some time later I received an envelope with a copy of a restaurant receipt from the same place mother and I had dined. An attached note said: "I paid this bill in advance. I was almost sure that I couldn't be

there but never-the-less, I paid for two plates - one for you and the other for your wife. You will never know what that night meant for me. I love you."

At that moment I understood the importance of saying, in time: "I LOVE YOU" and to give our loved ones the time that they deserve. Nothing in life is more important than God and your family. Give them the time they deserve, because these things cannot be put off till "some other time".

sent by Sharon Jacobs

Watch This!

It's my sons' favorite words, both the two and five-year-old.

They will often holler out just before they perform some stunt, put a block in place, ride the tricycle in a circle, drive a race car on the video screen, form a letter, read a word, touch their toes, tie their shoes, eat a piece of broccoli, turn a light on, turn a light off, put a plastic liner in the trash can, put trash in the trash can, and a thousand other things.

I realized that we never stop saying, "Watch This." Children use "Watch This" to get attention or to gratify themselves that someone notices, admires, appreciates and cares about them. As we age, our methods change but the "Watch This" continues.

Far too many teenagers get in trouble not because they really seek the trouble, nor because they are afraid their parents will find out. They are counting on their parents finding out.

People have married to spite their parents. It's a Watch This. Much of our debt is because we were trying to say, Watch This. See what I've: got – done - built   See what I: drive – earn - wear See whom I: date – am friends with – am

Watch This

Many of our problems stem from self-esteem, either too much or too little. It causes us to focus too much on the "Watch This" phenomenon.

When I saw it in my sons, I tried to recognize it in me. It was there.

No one can completely get rid of "Watch This," but when you recognize it, you can handle it better.

Now whenever I do something, I ask, "Is this a 'Watch This' or do I have a pure motive?"

Children and adults use "Watch This" to get attention or to gratify themselves that someone notices, admires, appreciates and cares about them.

Remember the phrase, "Dance like nobody's watching?" Maybe we should live like nobody's watching, except from heaven. ~*A MountainWings Original*~ #2134

The Weathered Old Barn

A stranger came by the other day with an offer that set me to thinking. He wanted to buy the old barn that sits out by the highway. I told him right off that he was crazy. He was a city type, you could tell by his clothes, his car, his hands, and the way he talked. He said he was driving by and saw that beautiful barn sitting out in the tall grass and wanted to know if it was for sale. I told him he had a funny idea of beauty.

Sure, it was a handsome building in its day. But then, there's been a lot of winters pass with their snow and ice and howling wind. The summer sun's beat down on that old barn till all the paint's gone, and the wood has turned silver gray. Now the old building leans a good deal, looking kind of tired. Yet, that fellow called it beautiful.

That set me to thinking. I walked out to the field and just stood there, gazing at that old barn. The stranger said he planned to use the lumber to line the walls of his den in a new country home he's building down the road. He said you couldn't get paint that beautiful. Only years of standing in the weather, bearing the storms and scorching sun, only that can produce beautiful barn wood.

It came to me then. We're a lot like that, you and I. Only it's on the inside that the beauty grows with us. Sure we turn silver gray too ... and lean a bit more than we did when we were young and full of sap. But the Good Lord knows what He's doing. And as the years pass He's busy using the hard wealth of our lives, the dry spells and the stormy seasons, to do a job of beautifying our souls that nothing else can produce. And to think how often folks holler because they want life easy!

They took the old barn down today and hauled it away to beautify a rich man's house. And I reckon someday you and I'll be hauled off to Heaven to take on whatever chores the Good Lord has for us on the Great Sky Ranch.

And I suspect we'll be more beautiful then for the seasons we've been through here ... and just maybe even add a bit of beauty to our Father's house.

May today there be peace within you. May you trust God that you are exactly where you are meant to be.

Author Unknown

Went to a Party, Mum

I went to a party,
And remembered what you said.
You told me not to drink, Mum
So I had a Sprite instead.
I felt proud of myself,
The way you said I would,
That I didn't drink and drive,
Though some friends said I should.
I made a healthy choice,
And your advice to me was right,
The party finally ended,
And the kids drove out of sight.
I got into my car,
Sure to get home in one piece,
I never knew what was coming, Mum
Something I expected least.
Now I'm lying on the pavement,
And I hear the policeman say,
The kid that caused this wreck was drunk,
Mum, his voice seems far away.
My own blood's all around me,

As I try hard not to cry.
I can hear the paramedic say,
This girl is going to die.
I'm sure the guy had no idea,
While he was flying high,
Because he chose to drink and drive,
Now I would have to die.
So why do people do it, Mum
Knowing that it ruins lives?
And now the pain is cutting me,
Like a hundred stabbing knives.
Tell sister not to be afraid, Mum
Tell daddy to be brave,
And when I go to heaven,
Put "Daddy's Girl" on my grave.
Someone should have taught him,
That it's wrong to drink and drive.
Maybe if his parents had, I'd still be alive.
My breath is getting shorter, Mum
I'm getting really scared.
These are my final moments,
And I'm so unprepared.
I wish that you could hold me Mum,
As I lie here and die.
I wish that I could say, "I love you, Mum!"
So I love you and good-bye.

What is Heaven Like..

Seventeen-year-old Brian Moore had only a short time to write something for a class. The subject was what Heaven was like. "I wowed 'em," he later told his father, "It's a killer. It's the bomb. It's the best thing I ever wrote." It also was the last.

Brian's parents had forgotten about the essay when a cousin found it while cleaning out the teenager's locker at his high school. Brian had been dead only hours, but his parents desperately wanted every piece of his life near them, notes from classmates and teachers, his homework.

Only two months before, he had handwritten the essay about encountering Jesus in a file room full of cards detailing every moment of the teen's life. But it was only after Brian's death that his parents realized that their son had described his view of heaven.

"It makes such an impact that people want to share it. You feel like you are there." Mr. Moore said.

Brian Moore died May 27, 1997, the day after Memorial Day. He was driving home from a friend's house when his car went off the road and struck a utility pole. He emerged from the wreck unharmed but stepped on a downed power line and was electrocuted.

The Moores framed a copy of Brian's essay and hung it among the family portraits in the living room. "I think God used him to make a point. I think we were meant to find it and make something out of it," Mrs. Moore said of the essay. She and her husband want to share their son's vision of life after death. "I'm happy for Brian. I know he's in heaven. I know I'll see him."

Brian's Essay: *"The Room..."*

In that place between wakefulness and dreams, I found myself in the room. There were no distinguishing features except for the one wall covered with small index card files. They were like the ones in libraries that list titles by author or subject in alphabetical order. But these files, which stretched from floor to ceiling and seemingly endless in either direction, had very different headings.

As I drew near the wall of files, the first to catch my attention was one that read "Girls I have liked." I opened it and began flipping through the cards. I quickly shut it, shocked to realize that I recognized the names written on each one. And then without being told, I knew exactly where I was. This lifeless room with its small files was a crude catalog system for my life.

Here were written the actions of my every moment, big and small, in a detail my memory couldn't match. A sense of wonder and curiosity, coupled with horror, stirred within me as I began randomly opening files and exploring their content. Some brought joy and sweet memories; others a sense of shame and regret so intense that I would look over my shoulder to see if anyone was watching. A file named "Friends" was next to one marked "Friends I Have Betrayed." The titles ranged from the mundane to the outright weird. "Books I Have Read," "Lies I Have Told," "Comfort I Have Given," "Jokes I Have Laughed At."

 Some were almost hilarious in their exactness: "Things I've Yelled at my Brothers."

Others I couldn't laugh at: "Things I Have Done in My Anger", "Things I Have Muttered Under My Breath at My Parents." I never ceased to be surprised by the contents. Often there were many more cards than I expected. Sometimes fewer than I hoped.. I was overwhelmed by the sheer volume of the life I had lived.

Could it be possible that I had the time in my years to fill each of these thousands or even millions of cards? But each card confirmed this truth. Each was written in my own handwriting. Each signed with my signature. When I pulled out the file marked "TV Shows I Have Watched ," I realized the file drawers grew in size to contain their contents. The cards were packed tightly, and yet after two or three yards, I hadn't found the end of the file. I shut it, shamed, not so much by the quality of shows but more by the vast time I knew that file represented.

When I came to a file marked "Lustful Thoughts," I felt a chill run through my body. I pulled the file out only an inch, not willing to test its size, and drew out a card. I shuddered at its detailed content. I felt sick to think that such a moment had been recorded. An almost animal rage broke on me. One thought dominated my mind: **No one must ever see these cards!** *No one must ever see this room! I have to destroy them!* In insane frenzy I yanked the file out. Its size didn't matter now. I had to empty it and burn the cards. But as I took it at one end and began pounding it on the floor, I could not dislodge a single card. I became desperate and pulled out a card, only to find it as strong as steel when I tried to tear it. Defeated and utterly helpless, I returned the file to its slot.

Leaning my forehead against the wall, I let out a long, self-pitying sigh. And then I saw it.. The title bore "People I Have Shared the Gospel With." The handle was brighter than those around it, newer, almost unused. I pulled on its handle and a small box not more than three inches long fell into my hands. I could count the cards it contained on one hand. And then the tears came. I began to weep. Sobs so deep that they hurt. They started in my stomach and shook through me. I fell on my knees and cried. I cried out of shame, from the overwhelming shame of it all.. The rows of file shelves swirled in my tear-filled eyes. *No one must ever, ever know of this room. I must lock it up and hide the key.*

But then as I pushed away the tears, I saw Him. *No, please not Him. Not here. Oh, anyone but Jesus.* I watched helplessly as He began to open the files and read the cards. I couldn't bear to watch His response. And in the moments I could bring myself to look at His face, I saw a sorrow deeper than my own. He seemed to intuitively go to the worst boxes. *Why did He have to read every one?* Finally He turned and looked at me from across the room. He looked at me with pity in His eyes. But this was a pity that didn't anger me. I dropped my head, covered my face with my hands and began to cry again. He walked over and put His arm around me. He could have said so many things. But He didn't say a word. He just cried with me. Then He got up and walked back to the wall of files. Starting at one end of the room, He took out a file and, one by one, began to sign His name over mine on each card.

"No!" I shouted rushing to Him! . All I could find to say was "No, no," as I pulled the card from Him. His name shouldn't be on these cards. But there it was, written in red so rich, so dark, so alive. The name of Jesus covered mine. It was written with His blood. He gently took the card back. He smiled a sad smile and began to sign the cards. I don't think I'll ever understand how He did it so quickly, but the next instant it seemed I heard Him close the last file and walk back to my side.

He placed His hand on my shoulder and said, "It is finished." I stood up, and He led me out of the room. There was no lock on its door. There were still cards to be written.

"I can do all things through Christ who strengthens me."- Phil. 4:13

"For God so loved the world that He gave His only son, that whoever believes in Him shall not perish but have eternal life." If you feel the same way forward it to as many people as you can so the love of Jesus will touch their lives also. My file "People I shared the gospel with" just got bigger, how about yours?

From Jane Montgomery,

What's Great About Hugs?

There's no such thing as a bad hug; only good ones and great ones. They're not fattening and they don't cause cancer or cavities. They're all natural; no preservatives, artificial ingredients, or pesticide residue.

Hugs are cholesterol-free, naturally sweet, 100% wholesome and they're a completely renewable resource. They don't require batteries, tune-ups or x-rays. Hugs are non-taxable, full returnable and energy efficient. They are safe in all kinds of weather; in fact, they're especially good for cold and rainy days.

Hugs can treat almost all the worlds problems and are especially effective in treating bad dreams and the Monday blahs.

Moral? Never wait until tomorrow to hug someone you could hug today.

When You Thought I Wasn't Looking
(Written by a child)

(A message every adult should read, because children are watching you and doing as you do, not as you say.)

When you thought I wasn't looking, I saw you hang my first painting on the refrigerator, and I immediately wanted to paint another one.

When you thought I wasn't looking I saw you feed a stray cat, and I learned that it was good to be kind to animals.

When you thought I wasn't looking, I saw you make my favorite cake for me and I learned that the little things can be the special things in life.

When you thought I wasn't looking I heard you say a prayer, and I knew there is a God I could always talk to and I learned to trust in God.

When you thought I wasn't looking, I saw you make a meal and take it to a friend who was sick, and I learned that we all have to help take care of each other.

When you thought I wasn't looking, I saw you give of your time and money to help people who had nothing and I learned that those who have something should give to those who don't.

When you thought I wasn't looking, I saw you take care of our house and everyone in it and I learned we have to take care of what we are given.

When you thought I wasn't looking, I saw how you handled your responsibilities, even when you didn't feel good and I learned that I would have to be responsible when I grow up.

When you thought I wasn't looking, I saw tears come from your eyes and I learned that sometimes things hurt, but it's all right to cry.

When you thought I wasn't looking, I saw that you cared and I wanted to be everything that I could be.

When you thought I wasn't looking, I learned most of life's lessons that I need to know to be a good and productive person when I grow up.

When you thought I wasn't looking, I looked at you and wanted to say, "Thanks for all the things I saw when you thought I wasn't looking."

I AM SENDING THIS TO ALL OF THE PEOPLE I KNOW WHO DO SO MUCH FOR OTHERS THAT THINK NO ONE EVER SEES. LITTLE EYES SEE A LOT. Each of us (parent, grandparent, aunt, uncle, teacher or friend) influences the life of a child. How will you touch the life of someone today? Just by sending this to someone else, you will probably make them at least think about their influence on others.

When I Whine...

Today, upon a bus, I saw a lovely girl with golden hair. I envied her; she seemed so happy. When she rose to leave, I saw her hobble down the aisle. She had one leg and used a crutch. But as she passed, she smiled. Oh, God, forgive me when I whine. I have two legs. The world is mine.

I stopped to buy some candy. The lad who sold it had such charm. I talked with him. He seemed so glad. And as I left, he said to me, "I thank you. You have been so kind. It's nice to talk with folks like you. You see," he said, "I'm blind." Oh, God, forgive me when I whine. I have two eyes. The world is mine.

Later, while walking down the street, I saw a child with eyes so blue. He stood and watched the others play. I stopped a moment, then I said, "Why don't you join the others, dear?" He looked ahead without a word, and then I knew he couldn't hear. Oh, God, forgive me when I whine. I have two ears. The world is mine.

With feet to take me where I want to go, with eyes to see the sunset's glow, with ears to hear what I should know. Oh, God, forgive me when I whine. I'm blessed indeed. The world is mine.

Who's Your Daddy?

A seminary professor was vacationing with his wife in Gatlinburg, TN. One morning they were eating breakfast at a little restaurant, hoping to enjoy a quiet, family meal. While they were waiting for their food, they noticed a distinguished looking, white-haired man moving from table to table, visiting with the guests.

The professor leaned over and whispered to his wife, "I hope he doesn't come over here." but sure enough, the man did come over to their table, "Where are you folks from?" he asked in a friendly voice.

"Oklahoma," they answered.

"Great to have you here in Tennessee," the stranger said. "What do you do for a living?"

"I teach at a seminary," he replied.

"Oh, so you teach preachers how to preach, do you? Well, I've got a really great story for you." And with that, the gentleman pulled up a chair and sat down at the table with the couple.

The professor groaned and thought to himself, "Great,,,Just what I need,,,another preacher story!"

The man started, "See that mountain over there? (pointing out the restaurant window). Not far from the base of that mountain, there was a boy who suffered a lot of shame because he had been born to an unwed mother. He had a hard time growing up, because every place he went, he was always asked the same question, 'Hey boy, Who's your daddy?' Whether he was at school, in the grocery store or drug store, people would

260

ask the same question, ' Who's your daddy?'. He would hide at recess and lunchtime from other students because that question hurt him so bad.

"When a new preacher came to his church he would go in late and leave early to avoid hearing the question, 'Who's your daddy?' But one day, the new preacher said the benediction so fast he got caught and had to walk out with the crowd.

"Just about the time he got to the back door, the new preacher, not knowing anything about him, put his hand on his shoulder and asked him, 'Son, who's your daddy?' The whole church got deathly quiet. He could feel every eye in the church looking at him. Now everyone would finally know the answer to the question, 'Who's your daddy?'.

"This new preacher, though, sensed the situation around him and using discernment that only the Holy Spirit could give said the following to that scared little boy,,,"Wait a minute! he said. 'I know who you are. I see the family resemblance now. Your are a child of God.'

"With that, he patted the boy on his shoulder and said 'Boy, you've got a great inheritance. Go and claim it.' With that, the boy smiled for the first time in a long time and walked out the door a changed person. He was never the same again. Whenever anybody asked him,' Who's you daddy?' he'd just tell them, 'I'm a child of God'."

The distinguished gentleman got up from the table and said "You know, if that new preacher hadn't told me that I was one of God's children, I probably never would have amounted to anything." And he walked away.

The seminary professor and his wife were stunned. He called the waitress over and asked her, "Do you know who that man was who just left that was sitting at our table?"

The waitress grinned and said, "Of course. Everybody here knows him. That's Ben Hooper. He's the former governor of Tennessee!"

Someone in your life today needs a reminder that they're one of God's children!

"The grass withers and the flowers fall, but the word of God stands forever." ~~Isaiah

YOU'RE ONE OF GOD'S CHILDREN!!!!! HAVE A GREAT DAY. May the Lord shine upon you today and every day!

Why God Created Eve

>>10. God worried that Adam would be lost in the Garden of Eden because he wouldn't ask directions. **>>9.** God knew that someday Adam would need someone to hand him the TV remote. (Parenthetically, it has been noted that men don't want to see what's ON TV; they want to see WHAT ELSE is on.) **>>8.** God knew that Adam would never make a doctor's appointment. **>>7.** God knew that when Adam's fig leaf wore out, he would never buy a new one for himself. **>>6.** God knew that Adam would not remember to take out the garbage. **>>5.** God wanted man to be fruitful and multiply, but he knew Adam would never be able to handle labor pains and childbirth. **>>4.** As "keeper of the garden," Adam would need help in finding his tools. **>>3.** Adam needed someone to blame for the Apple Incident, and for anything else that was really his fault. **>>2.** As the Bible says: "It is not good for man to be alone." **And the No. 1 reason of all :** [Tada, drum roll, fanfare, etc.] God stepped back, looked at Adam, and declared: "I can do better than that.!

Windows?

by Pamela Barnett (from Guideposts)

I was 20, newly married and making the long drive to Camp Pendleton to visit my husband, Jimmy, who was stationed there for infantry training. As I crested a hill on the two-lane road, a car came straight at me. I later learned a drunk driver, trying to pass six cars on a blind hill, had hit me head-on, causing my car to spin around. Then I got hit again, and the gas tank exploded in a ball of fire.

I awoke in the hospital with both legs and an arm broken, third-degree burns over 20 percent of my body and a severe head injury. My left ear had been burned away and one hand was so badly mangled that it might have to be removed. Doctors had little hope for my survival. My family came from all around the country, expecting a funeral. When my condition stabilized, one by one they had to return to their homes and jobs.

About a month after the accident, Jimmy, who had been by my side every day, also had to leave. I was still in extensive care, in traction, and the damage to my eyes meant I could only see shadow and light. Recovery would be a long and painful process, especially without Jimmy there.

"This is too much to bear," I cried out to God one day. "Please let me know that you are here. I have never felt so alone in my life."

Almost instantly I noticed a bright sunbeam sweeping across the sheets next to my face. It seemed to quiver with energy and radiate peace and reassurance. The light remained with me all day. It was a simple thing, a light from a window, but it gave me comfort.

After I was released from the hospital, I told Jimmy the story of how that ray of sunlight had consoled me during the time he couldn't be with me.

When I finished, he had a puzzled look on his face. "Pam, you were in intensive care," he said quietly. "There are no windows."

Winfrey Interviews Graham

Last year I watched Billy Graham being interviewed by Oprah Winfrey on television. Oprah told him that in her childhood home, she use to watch him preach on a little black and white TV while sitting on a linoleum floor.

She went on to the tell viewers that in his lifetime Billy has preached to twenty-million people around the world, not to mention the countless numbers who have heard him whenever his crusades are broadcast. When she asked if he got nervous before facing a crowd, Billy replied humbly, "No, don't get nervous before crowds, but I did today before I was going to meet with you."

Oprah's show is broadcast to twenty-million people every day. She is comfortable with famous stars and celebrities but seemed in awe of Dr. Billy Graham.

When the interview ended, she told the audience, "You don't often see this on my show, but we're going to pray." Then she asked Billy to close in prayer. The camera panned the studio audience as they bowed their heads and closed their eyes just like in one of his crusades.

Oprah sang the first line from the song that is his hallmark "Just as I am, without a plea," misreading the line and singing off-key, but her voice was full of emotion and almost cracked.

When Billy stood up after the show, instead of hugging her guest, Oprah's usual custom, she went over and just nestled against him. Billy wrapped his arm around her and pulled her under his shoulder. She stood in his fatherly embrace with a look of sheer contentment.

I once read the book "Nestle, Don't Wrestle" by Corrie Ten Boom. The power of nestling was evident on the TV screen that day. Billy Graham was not the least bit condemning, distant, or hesitant to embrace a public personality who may not fit the evangelistic mold. His grace and courage are sometimes stunning.

In an interview with Hugh Downs, on the 20/20 program, the subject turned to homosexuality. Hugh looked directly at Billy and said, "If you had a homosexual child, would you love him?"

Billy didn't miss a beat. He replied with sincerity and gentleness, "Why, I would love that one even more."

The title of Billy's autobiography, "Just As I Am," says it all. His life goes before him speaking as eloquently as that charming southern drawl for which he is known.

If, when I am eighty years old, my autobiography were to be titled "Just As I Am," I wonder how I would live now? Do I have the courage to be me? I'll never be a Billy Graham, the elegant man who draws people to the Lord through a simple one-point message, but I hope to be a person who is real and compassionate and who might draw people to nestle within God's embrace.

Do you make it a point to speak to a visitor or person who shows up alone at church, buy a hamburger for a homeless man, call your mother on Sunday afternoons, pick daisies with a little girl, or take a fatherless boy to a baseball game?

Did anyone ever tell you how beautiful you look when you're looking for what's beautiful in someone else?

Billy complimented Oprah when asked what he was most thankful for; he said, "Salvation given to us in Jesus Christ" then added, "and the way you have made people all over this country aware of the power of being grateful."

When asked his secret of love, being married fifty-four years to the same person, he said, "Ruth and I are happily incompatible."

How unexpected. We would all live more comfortably with everybody around us if we would find the strength in being grateful and happily incompatible

Let's take the things that set us apart, that make us different, that cause us to disagree, and make them an occasion to compliment each other and be thankful for each other. Let us be big enough to be smaller than our neighbor, spouse, friends, and strangers. ***Every day, may we to Nestle, not Wrestle!***

Winter Morning Guest
By John Edmund Haggai

One winter morning in 1931, I came down to breakfast - and found the table empty. It was cold outside. The worst blizzard on record had paralyzed the city. No cars were out. The snow had drifted up two stories high against our house, blackening the windows.

"Daddy, what's happening?" I asked. I was six years old. Gently Dad told me our fuel and food supplies were exhausted. He'd just put the last piece of coal on the fire. Mother had eight ounces of milk left for my baby brother Tom. After that - nothing.

"So what are we going to eat?" I asked.

"We'll have our devotions first, John Edmund," he said, in a voice that told me I should not ask questions. My father was a pastor. As a Christian he'd been chased out of his Syrian homeland. He arrived as a teenager in the United States with no money and barely a word of English - nothing but his vocation to preach. He knew hardship of a kind few see today. Yet my parents consistently gave away at least 10 percent of their income, and no one but God ever knew when we were in financial need.

That morning, Dad read the scriptures as usual, and afterwards we knelt for prayer. He prayed earnestly for the family, for our relatives and friends, for those he called the "missionaries of the cross" and those in the city who'd endured the blizzard without adequate shelter. Then he prayed something like this: "Lord, Thou knowest we have no more coal to burn. If it can please Thee, send us some fuel. If not, Thy will be done - we thank Thee for warm clothes and bed covers, which will keep us comfortable, even without the fire. Also, Thou knowest we have no food except milk for Baby Thomas. If it can please Thee..."

For someone facing bitter cold and hunger, he was remarkably calm. Nothing deflected him from completing the family devotions - not even the clamor we now heard beyond the muffling wall of snow.

Finally someone pounded on the door. The visitor had cleared the snow off the windowpane, and we saw his face peering in.

"Your door's iced up," he yelled. "I can't open it." The devotions over, Dad jumped up. He pulled; the man pushed. When the door suddenly gave, an avalanche of snow fell into the entrance hall. I didn't recognize the man, and I don't think Dad did either because he said politely, "Can I help you?"

The man explained he was a farmer who'd heard Dad preach in Allegany three years earlier. "I awakened at four o'clock this morning," he said, "and I couldn't get you out of my mind. The truck was stuck in the garage, so I harnessed the horses to the sleigh and came over."

"Well, please come in," my father said. On any other occasion, he'd have added, "And have some breakfast with us." But, of course, today there was no breakfast.

The man thanked him. And then - to our astonishment - he plucked a large box off the sleigh. More than sixty years later, I can see that box as clear as yesterday. It contained milk, eggs, butter, pork chops, grain, homemade bread and a host of other things. When the farmer had delivered the box, he went back out and got a cord of wood. Finally, after a very hearty breakfast, he insisted Dad take a ten-dollar bill.

Almost every day Dad reminded us that "God is the Provider." And my experience throughout adult life has confirmed it. **"I have never seen the righteous forsaken nor their children begging bread."** (Psalm 37:25) The Bible said it. But Dad and Mom showed me it was true.

Words Over Coffee
By Bonnie Fulkerson

Hi Sally, how are you today?"

"Oh, all right I guess," Sally answered.

"What's the matter? You look a little blue." Ruth was concerned because the last time they had gotten together Sally had been radiant.

"Oh, you know, things are not going well at work and the kids are driving me crazy, the usual stuff," Sally replied.

"That's not the real problem, all that stuff was happening before and you were still radiant. You said after accepting the Lord into your life you looked at everything differently and life was wonderful." Ruth took her friends hand and waited.

"Well," Sally hesitated, "it's just that I don't feel it anymore. I just can't get with it. When I pray it's just hurried bursts and it's so hard to get up Sunday mornings to be on time for church, I just don't feel like going." Sally sighed, then went on, "I just don't feel God's presence in my life anymore. You know, that feeling you get when everyone is worshipping and singing together. Sometimes I wonder if I an even a real Christian anymore."

"Everyone feels that way sometimes, Sally. You can't rely on your feelings to know that you belong to God. That feeling of being close to the Lord is wonderful, it is what we are talking about when we sing things about being 'hungry for the Lord' but it has nothing to do with our salvation."

After ordering coffee they sat back and chatted some more. "You mean that everyone goes through these times?" Sally asked.

"Of course, did you think you were the only one? Even the Apostle Paul had his ups and downs in the Spirit. He taught, *'Be constant in season and out of season.'* Ruth got up and hugged her friend.

Sally looked relieved. "So if that feeling is not what Christianity is all about, what else is there?" Sally asked.

"Well first off let's deal with how you know you are a Christian. The first thing of course, is belief. Someone you don't believe in can't save you. You believe in God and his son Jesus, don't you?" Ruth smiled across the table at her friend.

"You know I do, you've heard me say it enough," Sally laughed.

"That brings us to the second part, which is confession. Sally, do you believe that Jesus is the Christ, the Son of the living God?" Ruth waited for her friend to respond.

"Didn't we just cover that? Yes, I believe that Jesus is the Christ and the Son of God. Thee, is that what you wanted to hear? Sally was getting a little exasperated.

Ruth smiled joyfully as she answered, "There is another part of belief that few people learn about right off. Most people think that believing that Jesus IS, is all there is, but there is another facet to belief. Sally, do you believe Jesus?"

"What do you mean, 'Believe Jesus?' I already said I believe in Jesus."

"Did you catch what you just said? There is a big difference between 'believing in' and 'believing' Jesus." Ruth waited while Sally thought it over. "Remember, even Satan believes 'IN' Jesus. We must take it a step further; we must believe Jesus when He tells us, *'Whoever confesses me before men, him I will also confess before my Father who is in heaven.'*

"What this means is, that the moment you said, 'I believe that Jesus is the Christ, the Son of the living God,' He turned to His Father and said, 'Father, that is my friend Sally,' and God turned to His scribes and said, 'That is Sally, enter her name in the Book' and it was done. So now your name is in the Lamb's book of life and nothing can ever take it out again."

Worth your time.

It had been some time since Jack had seen the old man. College, girls, career, and life itself got in the way. In fact, Jack moved clear across the country in pursuit of his dreams.

There, in the rush of his busy life, Jack had little time to think about the past and often no time to spend with his wife and son. He was working on his future, and nothing could stop him. Over the phone, his mother told him, "Mr. Belser died last night"

. Memories flashed through his mind like an old newsreel as he sat quietly remembering his childhood days. "Jack, did you hear me?"

"Oh, sorry, Mom. Yes, I heard you. It's been so long since I thought of him. I'm sorry, but I honestly thought he died years ago," Jack said.

"Well, he didn't forget you. Every time I saw him he'd ask how you were doing. He'd reminisce about the many days you spent over 'his side of the fence' as he put it," Mom told him.

"I loved that old house he lived in," Jack said.

"You know, Jack, after your father died, Mr. Belser stepped in to make sure you had a man's influence in your life," she said.

"He's the one who taught me carpentry," he said. "I wouldn't be in this business if it weren't for him. He spent a lot of time teaching me things he thought were important . . .

Mom, I'll be there for the funeral, "Jack said.

As busy as he was, he kept his word. Jack caught the next flight to his hometown. Belser's funeral was small and uneventful. He had no children of his own, and most of his relatives had passed away.

The night before he had to return home, Jack and his Mom stopped by to see the old house next door one more time. Standing in the doorway, Jack paused for a moment. It was like crossing over into another dimension, a leap through space and time. The house was exactly as he remembered. Every step held memories. Every picture, every piece of furniture. Jack stopped suddenly.

"What's wrong, Jack?" his Mom asked.

"The box is gone," he said.

"What box?" Mom asked.

"There was a small gold box that he kept locked on top of his desk. I must have asked him a thousand times what was inside. All he'd ever tell me was 'the thing I value most,'" Jack said. It was gone. Everything about the house was exactly how Jack remembered it, except for the box. He figured someone from the Belser family had taken it.

"Now I'll never know what was so valuable to him," Jack said. "I better get some sleep. I have an early flight home, Mom."

It had been about two weeks since Mr. Belser died. Returning home from work one day Jack discovered a note in his mailbox. "Signature required on a package. No one at home. Please stop by the main post office within the next three days," the note read.

Early the next day Jack retrieved the package. The small box was old and looked like it had been mailed a hundred years ago. The handwriting was difficult to read, but the return address caught his attention. "Mr. Harold Belser" it read.

Jack took the box out to his car and ripped open the package. There inside was the gold box and an envelope. Jack's hands shook as he read the note inside. "Upon my death, please forward this box and its contents to Jack Bennett. It's the thing I valued most in my life." A small key was taped to the letter. His heart racing and tears filling his eyes, Jack carefully unlocked the box

There inside he found a beautiful gold pocket watch. Running his fingers slowly over the finely etched casing, he unlatched the cover.

Inside he found these words engraved: "Jack, Thanks for your time! Harold Belser."

"The thing he valued most . . . was . . . my time."

Jack held the watch for a few minutes, then called his office and cleared his appointments for the next two days.

"Why?" Janet, his assistant asked.

"I need some time to spend with my son," he said. "Oh, by the way, Janet . . . thanks for your time!"

"Life is not measured by the number of breaths we take but by the moments that take our breath away." - *Unknown*

Have a great day. Oh, and thank you for your time. :)

Wrinkles
By Patricia Clark

This is about the wrinkles,
Pesky little crinkles.
They grow into lines.
Deep inverted ridges
Distinguish the men,
Extinguish the youth in women.
There's work they can do
Since without solicitation they appeared.
Work them into smiles.
Make a laugh
Don't let them rest
And steal the best years of your life.
Keep them working, stretching, molding
Into a smiling laughing face
Every chance you get.

Wrong Number; Caller ID

Isn't it amazing how God works in our lives! On a Saturday night several weeks ago, a pastor was working late, and decided to call his wife before he left for home. It was about 10:00 PM, but his wife didn't answer the phone.

The pastor let the phone ring many times. He thought it was odd that she didn't answer, but decided to wrap up a few things and try again in a few minutes. When he tried again she answered right away. He asked her why she hadn't answered before, and she said that it hadn't rung at their house. They brushed it off as a fluke and went on their merry ways.

The following Monday, the pastor received a call at the church office, which was the phone that he'd used that Saturday night. The man that he spoke with wanted to know why he'd called on Saturday night.

The pastor couldn't figure out what the man was talking about. Then the man said, "It rang and rang, but I didn't answer." The pastor remembered the mishap and apologized for disturbing him, explaining that he'd intended to call his wife.

The man said, "That's, OK. Let me tell you my story. You see, I was planning to commit suicide on Saturday night, but before I did, I prayed, 'God if you're there, and you don't want me to do this, give me a sign now.' At that point my phone started to ring. I looked at the caller ID, and it said, 'Almighty God.' I was afraid to answer!"

The reason why it showed on the man's caller ID that the call came from "Almighty God" is because the church that the pastor attends is called Almighty God Tabernacle!!

WWJD Is For Photographers Too
by Al Allaway

Fog was creeping over the city on gray silent feet, like the padded paws of a stealthy cat. It was only late afternoon, but the fog was getting thicker by the minute in a head-to-head race with rush hour traffic. Combining slick, wet streets and short winter days would make the day into a recipe for traffic disasters, injuries and death.

Photographer Rod Seiber had dreamed about winning the Pulitzer Prize for twenty-five years, ever since being hired long ago by the **San Francisco Herald.** He knew that many prize news-photos resulted from a simple matter of luck, the photographer being in the right place at the right time. A scenario he never seemed able to achieve.

When the really big news stories broke, he was always on assignment somewhere else, doing some dang beauty pageant or some weird awards at the local garden club.

The last airplane disaster in the Bay Area happened when he was in Brazil, doing a story on coffee beans. And when the earth shook in San Francisco, killing dozens, he was on vacation with his family at Disneyland.

And even Disneyland had been a disaster. Work was Rod's god, and 'vacations' were only a family obligation, which had to be tolerated. He was obsessed with getting that once-in-a-lifetime, award-winning news photo. He'd rather be working, anyway!

Rod was pushy. He believed that the only way to succeed was to push, and push hard, and when push came to shove, Rod was an expert in having his own way. His City Editor recognized him as a top-notch photographer, great with composition and technical matters, but he never had the courage to tell Rod about his faults; like his pushy attitudes. His lack of diplomacy and self-centered attitudes would stand in the way of any further promotions.

Rod had often been told that he would get further with people if he would treat them kindly. "Always remember, W.W.J.D", his kindly mother had taught him; "What Would Jesus Do?" It was a kind and thoughtful way to treat everyone. Rod ignored his mother's advice.

Streetlights were feebly trying to pierce the ever-thickening fog when Rod gathered up his equipment in preparation for his long commute home to Marin County. But, just as he started out, a series of alarm tones began to cycle from the fire scanner radio.

Pausing, he was torn between staying to listen and keeping his promise to his wife, Katie. She had earlier scolded (threatened, was more like it) him for being such a work-aholic and ignoring his family. Today was son Timmy's tenth birthday and she had made him promise faithfully that he would be home on time for his dinner and party.

"Calling phantom box two-one-two-three", blurted the fire radio, "Structure fire in the St. Francis Hotel, ninth floor, Market and Geary". After a long list of engine, squad and truck companies being dispatched, the sequence ended with the time, "Sixteen forty-five hours", said the dispatcher.

Rod had already made up his mind which course of action he would follow. "Quarter to five", he said to no one in particular, "I'll still have time to swing by the fire on my way home."

"Hey, Mac, you can't park there," hollered the sweating policeman. Rod had pulled his car up on the sidewalk next to a fire hydrant.

"Stuff it, cop," he yelled back, "I'm the Press, and I can park anywhere I damn well please!" He grabbed his photo gear and was gone through the fog before the policeman had a chance to reply.

The fire in the St. Francis Hotel that night was a nasty one, extracting a "fourth alarm" from the city's resources. But, it was not a spectacular fire, at least from a visible point of view. Everything was shrouded in the fog; with only a fuzzy orange glow visible to those confined to the street. And no matter how rude or aggressively Rod pushed; he could not gain access into the building. He did manage to bump into and effectively hinder firefighters and disrupt the command post.

"Damned idiots," he mumbled as he searched for his car. Rod was in a foul mood funk, depressed because he had failed to get any news-photos.

His gray funk turned to pink anger, and then rose to crimson rage. He stood at the curb, sputtering and dumbfounded. A big canvas 3 Inch fire hose had been hooked up to the hydrant by which he had parked. It was throbbing and swollen under 70 pounds per square inch of water pressure and the only direction it could go was in one window and out the other side of his car. It was funny, but he was furious. The cop had not ticketed him, but was probably laughing his sox off after a late arriving fire engine had hooked up to this hydrant and laid the supply line down to the next block.

Exactly two hours later, Rod, still fuming, crossed the Golden Gate Bridge and exited the 101 Freeway onto the Sausalito Parkway. Home at last, but was he going to catch it from Katie. Rehearsing his fog excuse, he opted to leave out the part about the fire hose. Besides, the fog was still as thick as ever, so would be a believable reason for being late.

Ahead, softened by the fog, a tight cluster of red and blue flashing lights began to appear. Hazy at first, Rod began to realize that here at last might be the elusive photo-op. A large truck was jack-knifed on the curb, on top of a mangled bicycle.

Through the swirling fog, Rod could see what was left of the body of a small boy. Paramedics were bending over the lad and one put an oxygen mask over the victim's face.

"Press, here," hollered Rod, "Out of my way; I'm from the *Herald*!" Bright flashes of light were being emitted from his strobe, as photo after photoflash blinded everybody at the scene and left latent images of dancing white footballs under every eyelid. Rod was crazy with an adrenaline rush, but couldn't see any better than the others he had blinded.

He went too far when he removed the oxygen mask in order to photograph the boys mangled face and then a cop wrestled him to the ground, breaking his glasses.

"Outa here, now!" growled the police officer, "Or I'll arrest you for obstruction."

..oOo..

Timmy waited expectantly for his dad to come home from work. Timmy loved his dad and cried often because dad was always busy and had too little time to spend with his son. But, he had promised that morning that "nothing" could happen in the news-world that could cause him to miss Timmy's birthday.

Time passed slowly, until finally mom fed him a nearly cold supper.

Observing one sad and lonely little boy, Katie decided she would let Timmy open his present without waiting for Rod. It was a brand new ten-speed, which Timmy had been dreaming about.

"This ought to cheer him up", thought Katie.

And it did! "It was your father's idea", offered Katie, always trying to patch up failing relationships.

Timmy, beaming from ear to ear, asked, "Can I try it out, please, huh, mommy, huh?"

"Not a good idea", Mom replied, "It's dark and foggy out there."

"But, mom!"

"Well, okay, but stay in the neighborhood".

"I'll just go up to the Parkway exit, and watch for dad!"

..oOo..

Back in his darkroom at the *Herald*, Rod was in a rush to develop his film and get some prints up to the city desk in time for the early edition.

"Does anybody have a name yet, on that dead kid in Sausalito?" he had queried while dashing through the newsroom, "I think I've got some swell pictures!" He had stopped at a payphone before leaving Sausalito to call Katie. The phone call had been a series of repeating interruptions:

"Sorry, I'm late, but…"

"Listen to me, Timmy's not come home…"

"Never mind that…"

"Rod, listen for once in your life…"

"Not now, I've gotta work; they're holding the presses. I finally got a decent scoop. See 'ya later." He clicked off the phone and headed back south across the Golden Gate to downtown.

Now, in his darkroom, he was positioning a wet negative into the enlarger, when he was interrupted, by a loud knocking.

"Hey, Rod," came the voice muffled by the door, "Your wife's on the phone with an emergency. Something about your kid missing."

"Not now," screamed Rod, "Tell her I'll call her back in about ten minutes."

Focusing the negative on the enlarger platen, Rod could begin to see the outline of features, like the jack-knifed truck and trailer and crumpled bicycle. He made his exposure and slipped the printing paper into the developer, lit only by a dim red light. The paper was pure white until a slightly graying image began to form, darker and darker... revealing a familiar face, the face of a ten year old boy, who was....

Blood rushed to Rod's head, almost making him pass out.

"Oh, God, forgive me!" wept Rod. It was the image he had "stolen" under the oxygen mask; it was a full-face picture of Timothy Seiber, his own son!

Learn today the peace of the phrase "WWJD*", before it's too late.

(* "What Would Jesus Do?")

Three Yellow Roses

I walked into the grocery store not particularly interested in buying groceries. I wasn't hungry. The pain of losing my husband was still too raw. And this grocery store held so many sweet memories. He often came with me and then he'd pretend to go off and look for something special. I knew what he was up to. I'd always spot him walking down the aisle with the three yellow roses in his hands.

He knew I loved yellow roses. With a heart filled with grief, I only wanted to buy my few items and leave, but even grocery shopping was different since he had passed on.

Shopping for one took time, a little more thought than it had for two. Standing by the meat, I searched for the perfect small steak and remembered how he had loved his steak.

Suddenly a woman came beside me. She was lovely in a soft green pantsuit I watched as she picked up a large package of T-bones, dropped them in her basket, hesitated, and then put them back. She turned to go and once again reached for the pack of steaks. She saw me watching her and she smiled. "My husband loves T-bones, but honestly, at these prices, I don't know."

I swallowed the emotion down my throat and met her pale blue eyes. "My husband passed away eight days ago," I told her. Glancing at the package in her hands, I fought to control the tremble in my voice. "Buy him the steaks and cherish every moment you have together."

She shook her head and I saw the emotion in her eyes as she placed the package in her basket and wheeled away.

I turned and pushed my cart across the length of the store to the dairy products. There, I stood trying to decide which size milk I should buy. A Quart, I finally decided and moved on to the ice cream. If nothing else, I could always fix myself an ice cream cone.

I placed the ice cream in my cart and looked down the aisle toward the front. I saw first the green suit, then recognized the pretty lady coming towards me. In her arms she carried a package. On her face was the brightest smile I had ever seen. I would swear a soft halo encircled her blonde hair as she kept walking toward me, her eyes holding mine. As she came closer, I saw what she held and tears began misting in my eyes.

"These are for you," she said and placed three beautiful long stemmed yellow roses in my arms. "When you go through the line, they will know these are paid for." She leaned over and placed a gentle kiss on my cheek, then smiled again. I wanted to tell her what she'd done, what the roses meant, but still unable to speak, I watched as she walked away as tears clouded my vision.

I looked down at the beautiful roses nestled in the green tissue wrapping and found it almost unreal. How did she know? Suddenly the answer seemed so clear. I wasn't alone.

Oh, you haven't forgotten me, have you? I whispered, with tears in my eyes. He was still with me, and she was his angel. Every day be thankful for what you have and who you are.

Please read all of this and if you appreciate life, send this to your friends.

- Even though I clutch my blanket and growl when the alarm rings. Thank you, Lord, that I can hear. There are many who are deaf.
- Even though I keep my eyes closed against the morning light as long as possible. Thank you, Lord, that I can see. Many are blind.
- Even though I huddle in my bed and put off rising. Thank you, Lord, that I have the strength to rise. There are many who are bedridden.
- Even though the first hour of my day is hectic, when socks are lost, toast is burned, tempers are short, and my children are so loud. Thank you, Lord, for my family. There are many who are lonely.
- Even though our breakfast table never looks like the pictures in magazines and the menu is at times unbalanced. Thank you, Lord, for the food we have. There are many who are hungry.
- Even though the routine of my job often is monotonous. Thank you, Lord, for the opportunity to work. There are many who have no job.
- Even though I grumble and bemoan my fate from day to day and wish my circumstances were not so modest.
- Thank you, Lord, for life.

Pass this on to the friends you know. It might help a bit to make this world a better place to live, right? A friend is someone we turn to when our spirits need a lift. A friend is someone to treasure.

For friendship is a gift. A friend is someone who fills our lives with Beauty, Joy and Grace and makes the world we live in a better and happier place.   YOU ARE MY FRIEND!

God bless you and yours!!! *from Alisha Niebuhr*

The Yellow Shirt

The baggy yellow shirt had long sleeves, four extra-large pockets trimmed in black thread and snaps up the front. It was faded from years of wear, but still in decent shape. I found it in 1963 when I was home from college on Christmas break, rummaging through bags of clothes Mom intended to give away. "You're not taking that old thing, are you?" Mom said when she saw me packing the yellow shirt. "I wore that when I was pregnant with your brother in 1954!"

"It's just the thing to wear over my clothes during art class, Mom. Thanks!" I slipped it into my suitcase before she could object. The yellow shirt became a part of my college wardrobe. I loved it. After graduation, I wore the shirt the day I moved into my new apartment and on Saturday mornings when I cleaned.

The next year, I married. When I became pregnant, I wore the yellow shirt during big-belly days. I missed Mom and the rest of my family, since we were in Colorado and they were in Illinois. But that shirt helped. I smiled, remembering that Mother had worn it when she was pregnant, 15 years earlier. That Christmas, mindful of the warm feelings the shirt had given me, I patched one elbow, wrapped it in holiday paper and sent it to Mom. When Mom wrote to thank me for her "real" gifts, she said the yellow shirt was lovely. She never mentioned it again.

The next year, my husband, daughter and I stopped at Mom and Dad's to pick up some furniture. Days later, when we uncrated the kitchen table, I noticed something yellow taped to its bottom. The shirt!

And so the pattern was set.

On our next visit home, I secretly placed the shirt under Mom and Dad's mattress. I don't know how long it took for her to find it, but almost two years passed before I discovered it under the base of our living-room floor lamp. The yellow shirt was just what I needed now while refinishing furniture. The walnut stains added character.

In 1975 my husband and I divorced. With my three children, prepared to move back to Illinois. As I packed, a deep depression overtook me. I wondered if I could make it on my own. I wondered if I would find a job. I paged through the Bible, looking for comfort. In Ephesians, I read, *"So use every piece of God's armor to resist the enemy whenever he attacks, and when it is all over, you will be standing up."*

I tried to picture myself wearing God's armor, but all I saw was the stained yellow shirt. Slowly, it dawned on me. Wasn't my mother's love a piece of God's armor? My courage was renewed.

Unpacking in our new home, I knew I had to get the shirt back to Mother. The next time I visited her, I tucked it in her bottom dresser drawer.

Meanwhile, I found a good job at a radio station. A year later I discovered the yellow shirt hidden in a rag bag in my cleaning closet. Something new had been added. Embroidered in bright green across the breast pocket were the words "I BELONG TO PAT."

Not to be outdone, I got out my own embroidery materials and added an apostrophe and seven more letters. Now the shirt proudly proclaimed, "I BELONG TO PAT'S MOTHER." But I didn't stop there. I zig-zagged all the frayed seams, then had a friend mail the shirt in a fancy box to Mom from Arlington, VA. We enclosed an official looking letter from "The Institute for the Destitute," announcing that she was the recipient of an award for good deeds. I would have given anything to see Mom's face when she opened the box. But, of course, she never mentioned it.

Two years later, in 1978, I remarried. The day of our wedding, Harold and I put our car in a friend's garage to avoid practical jokers. After the wedding, while my husband drove us to our honeymoon suite, I reached for a pillow in the car to rest my head. It felt lumpy. I unzipped the case and found, wrapped in wedding paper, the yellow shirt. Inside a pocket was a note: "Read John 14:27-29. I love you both, Mother."

That night I paged through the Bible in a hotel room and found the verses: *"I am leaving you with a gift: peace of mind and heart. And the peace I give isn't fragile like the peace the world gives. So don't be troubled or afraid. Remember what I told you: I am going away, but I will come back to you again. If you really love me, you will be very happy for me, for now I can go to the Father, who is greater than I am. I have told you these things before they happen so that when they do, you will believe in me."*

The shirt was Mother's final gift. She had known for three months that she had terminal Lou Gehrig's disease. Mother died the following year at age 57.

I was tempted to send the yellow shirt with her to her grave. But I'm glad I didn't, because it is a vivid reminder of the love-filled game she and I played for 16 years. Besides, my older daughter is in college now, majoring in art. And every art student needs a baggy yellow shirt with big pockets.

You'll Find Jesus, There..

The surgeon sat beside the boy's bed; the boy's parents sat across from him. "Tomorrow morning," the surgeon began, "I'll open up your heart..."

"You'll find Jesus there," the boy interrupted. The surgeon looked up, annoyed.

"I'll cut your heart open," he continued, "To see how much damage has been done..."

"But when you open up my heart, you'll find Jesus in there."

The surgeon looked to the parents, who sat quietly. "When I see how much damage has been done, I'll sew your heart and chest back up and I'll plan what to do next."

"But you'll find Jesus in my heart. The Bible says He lives there. The hymns all say He lives there. You'll find Him in my heart."

The surgeon had had enough. "I'll tell you what I'll find in your heart. I'll find damaged muscle, low blood supply, and weakened vessels. And I'll find out if I can make you well."

"You'll find Jesus there too. He lives there." The surgeon left.

The surgeon sat in his office, recording his notes from the surgery. "...damaged aorta, damaged pulmonary vein, widespread muscle degeneration. No hope for transplant, no hope for cure. Therapy: painkillers and bed rest. Prognosis:," here he paused, "death within one year." He stopped the recorder, but there was more to be said. "Why?" he asked aloud. "Why did You do this? You've put him here; You've put him in this pain; and You've cursed him to an early death. why?"

The Lord answered and said, *"The boy, My lamb, was not meant for your flock for long, for he is a part of My flock, and will forever be. Here, in My flock, he will feel no pain, and will be comforted as you cannot imagine. His parents will one day join him here, and they will know peace, and My flock will continue to grow."*

The surgeon's tears were hot, but his anger was hotter. "You created that boy, and You created that heart. He'll be dead in months. Why?"

The Lord answered, *"The boy, My lamb, shall return to My flock, for he has done his duty: I did not put My lamb with your flock to lose him, but to retrieve another lost lamb."* The surgeon wept.

The surgeon sat beside the boy's bed; the boy's parents sat across from him. The boy awoke and whispered, "Did you cut open my heart?" "Yes," said the surgeon.

"What did you find?" asked the boy.

"I found Jesus there," said the surgeon.

INDEX of Authors, Contributors & Quotable Sources

ADAMS, John	116
ALLAWAY, Al	23, 127, 195, 259
ALLAWAY, Jacky	154
And Let the Heavens Declare	195
BACKHOUSE, Kelly	76
BANKO, Walter	94, 186
BARNETT, Pamela	249
CAMPFIELD, Jerral	134
CHURCHILL, Sir Winston	177
CLARK, Patricia	61, 98, 257
CLAYSON, Jane	105
COOLIDGE, Calvin	117
CURRIER, Kathy	44, 71
DOWNS, Hugh	251
FLEMING, Sir Alexander	177
Forty Days of Purpose	4
FUDD, Gomer	47
FULKERSON, Bonnie	95, 254
GERLACH, Adrianne	108
GIBBS, Nancy	21
GLENN, Lloyd	30
GRAHAM, Billy	105, 250
GRAHAM, Anne	105
Guideposts Magazine	228, 249
HAGGAI, John	252
HENRY, Patrick	117
HOPE, Bob	14
JACOBS, Sharon	238
JEFFERSON, Thomas	116
JOHNSON, Alan	230
KAYE, Mitchell	36
KELLY, Dr. Howard	97
KENNEDY, John F.	41
LANDERS, Ann	175
LINCOLN, Abraham	117

MADISON, James	117
MARGRET, Ann	14
MARR, Jerry	151
McGUFFEY, William H.	117
McLOUD, Jody	88
MILHOUS, Frances	162
MONTGOMERY, Jane	183, 245
MOON, Debbie	36
MOORE, Brian	240
MOORE, Catherine	171
MountainWings	12, 87, 94, 109, 119, 124, 171, 184, 188, 190
NIEBUHR, Alicia	265
OLSEN, Jean	223
PERKS, Bob	191
POWELL, John	228
Purpose Driven Life	4
ROBBINS, Sally	228
ROOSEVELT, Theodore	87
ROSER, Stan & Dottie	179
SCOTT, Darrell & Rachel	71
Snowbirds Guarding the Gold	197
STEFFANSON, Therald	103, 236
STRANGE, Mae	223
TEN BOOM, Corrie	251
THOMAS, George	85
THOMAS, Mike S.	157
THOMPSON, Samuel	147
TIER, Susan	190
VALENTINO, Barbara	188
WARD, William A.	87
WARREN, Rick	4
WINFREY, Oprah	250
WRIGHT, Joe	127
Yakima Herald Republic	23

Books by Al Allaway

"Snowbirds Guarding the Gold" R*V Life & House-Sitting Adventures* in Yuma, AZ and Yakima, WA 1ˢᵗ Books Library, 2002, List $9.50. ("A Rib-Tickling Expose' ...of sorts" ...*The Yakima Herald-Republic*) 156pp

"All-Ways the Rebel" Some serious and some funny letters written home about both World Wars and life in prison, by Al's dad. (Publish America, expect release end of 2007)

"Mystery of the Lmuma Mine" A novella for and about young adults (ages 12 and up) based on writer's true-life teenage experiences contrasted between a strict disciplinary Catholic boarding school and a hard-rock Nevada gold mine. (December 2004 at Publish America, List $14.95). Large print edition available 2007 at Lulu.com

"Jonathan of Scots" A full-length historical novel centered in 1640 Scotland, England and America. Jonathan has many adventures associated with the Stuart kings of England, whose religious beliefs were being challenged by Oliver Cromwell during the 2ⁿᵈ English Civil War. A must read for all Scots. Released December, 2006. List $19.95.

Treasure in the Park" Exciting novella about a 75 year old volunteer (named Marty) who works in the local state park and starts finding $100 bills while raking leaves. This opening leads to a terrorism plot, a murder, some gang wars, and a missing 8-year old kid. Marty knows the money (now $50,000) must relate to other events, but has a moral challenge he must solve if he's going to report it.. Available 2007 Lulu.com

www.ingramcontent.com/pod-product-compliance
Lightning Source LLC
Chambersburg PA
CBHW020746160426

43192CB00006B/256